Practical Next.js for E-Commerce

Create E-Commerce Sites with the Next.js Framework

Alex Libby

Apress®

Practical Next.js for E-Commerce: Create E-Commerce Sites with the Next.js Framework

Alex Libby
BELPER, UK

ISBN-13 (pbk): 978-1-4842-9611-0   ISBN-13 (electronic): 978-1-4842-9612-7
https://doi.org/10.1007/978-1-4842-9612-7

Managing Director, Apress Media LLC: Welmoed Spahr
Acquisitions Editor: James Robinson-Prior
Development Editor: James Markham
Coordinating Editor: Gryffin Winkler

Cover designed by eStudioCalamar

Cover image by vector_corp on freepik (www.freepik.com)

Distributed to the book trade worldwide by Apress Media, LLC, 1 New York Plaza, New York, NY 10004, U.S.A. Phone 1-800-SPRINGER, fax (201) 348-4505, e-mail orders-ny@springer-sbm.com, or visit www.springeronline.com. Apress Media, LLC is a California LLC and the sole member (owner) is Springer Science + Business Media Finance Inc (SSBM Finance Inc). SSBM Finance Inc is a **Delaware** corporation.

For information on translations, please e-mail booktranslations@springernature.com; for reprint, paperback, or audio rights, please e-mail bookpermissions@springernature.com.

Apress titles may be purchased in bulk for academic, corporate, or promotional use. eBook versions and licenses are also available for most titles. For more information, reference our Print and eBook Bulk Sales web page at http://www.apress.com/bulk-sales.

Any source code or other supplementary material referenced by the author in this book is available to readers on GitHub (https://github.com/Apress). For more detailed information, please visit https://www.apress.com/gp/services/source-code.

Paper in this product is recyclable

This is dedicated to my family, with thanks for their love and support while writing this book.

Table of Contents

About the Author

Alex Libby is a front-end web developer and seasoned computer book author from England. His passion for all things open source dates back to the days of his degree studies when he first came across web development and he has been hooked ever since. When he isn't busy developing new features or fixing website bugs for his day job, Alex enjoys tinkering with different open source libraries to see how they work. He has spent a stint maintaining the jQuery Tools library and enjoys writing about open source technologies, principally for front-end UI development.

About the Technical Reviewer

 **Massimo Nardone** has more than 25 years of experience in security, web and mobile development, cloud, and IT architecture. His true IT passions are security and Android. He has been programming and teaching how to program with Android, Perl, PHP, Java, VB, Python, C/C++, and MySQL for more than 20 years. He holds a Master of Science degree in Computing Science from the University of Salerno, Italy.

He has worked as a CISO, CSO, security executive, IoT executive, project manager, software engineer, research engineer, chief security architect, PCI/SCADA auditor, and senior lead IT security/cloud/SCADA architect for many years. His technical skills include security, Android, cloud, Java, MySQL, Drupal, Cobol, Perl, web and mobile development, MongoDB, D3, Joomla, Couchbase, C/C++, WebGL, Python, Pro Rails, Django CMS, Jekyll, Scratch, and more.

He worked as visiting lecturer and supervisor for exercises at the Networking Laboratory of the Helsinki University of Technology (Aalto University). He holds four international patents (PKI, SIP, SAML, and Proxy areas). He is currently working for Cognizant as head of cyber security and CISO to help both internally and externally with clients in areas of information and cyber security, like strategy, planning, processes, policies, procedures, governance, awareness, and so forth. In June 2017, he became a permanent member of the ISACA Finland Board.

Massimo has reviewed more than 45 IT books for different publishing companies and is the co-author of *Pro Spring Security: Securing Spring Framework 5 and Boot 2-based Java Applications* (Apress, 2019), *Beginning EJB in Java EE 8* (Apress, 2018), *Pro JPA 2 in Java EE 8* (Apress, 2018), and *Pro Android Games* (Apress, 2015).

Acknowledgments

Writing a book can be a long but rewarding process; it is not possible to complete it without the help of other people. I would like to offer a huge vote of thanks to my editors – in particular, Gryffin Winkler, Nirmal Selvaraj, and James Robinson-Prior; my thanks also to Massimo Nardone as my technical reviewer, James Markham for his help during the process, and others at Apress for getting this book into print. All have made writing this book a painless and enjoyable process, even with the edits!

My thanks also to my family for being understanding and supporting me while writing. I frequently spend a lot of late nights writing alone, or pass up times when I should be with them, so their words of encouragement and support have been a real help in getting past those bumps in the road and producing the finished book that you now hold in your hands.

Lastly, it is particularly poignant that the book was written at a time where the world has emerged from events of an unprecedented nature, and is still finding the new norm. It was too easy to think about those who lost the greatest thing we as humans could ever have; life hasn't been easy for anyone. Having a project to work on, no matter how simple or complex it might be, has helped me get through those tough times and with the hope that we face a new, improved, and better future.

Introduction

Practical Next.js for E-Commerce is for people who want to learn how to quickly create e-commerce sites that are efficient and fast using the Next.js framework and associated tools.

This project-oriented book simplifies the setting up of a Next.js-based e-commerce site as a basis for developing an offer that we can customize to our needs, for any future project. It will equip you with a starting toolset that you can use to create future e-commerce offerings and incorporate the processes into your workflow, and that will allow you to take your sites to the next level.

Throughout this book, I'll take you on a journey through creating the base skeleton of our site, before adding products, a checkout and payment process, and styling the site. We will also touch on subjects such as adapting the offer for mobile devices, testing elements of the site, and deploying into production – showing you how easy it is to develop a starting website that we can augment later quickly. With the minimum of fuss and plenty of practical exercises, we'll focus on topics such as building the functionality, styling, testing in a self-contained environment, and more – right through to producing the final result viewable from any browser!

Practical Next.js for E-Commerce uses nothing more than standard JavaScript (upon which React/Next.js is based), CSS and HTML, three of the most powerful tools available for developers: you can enhance, extend, and configure any part of your website as requirements dictate. With Next.js, the art of possible is only limited by the extent of your imagination and the power of JavaScript tools available in any browser!

PART I

In the Beginning

CHAPTER 1

Getting Started

I'm not a betting man – indeed, I can't remember the last time I placed any form of bet, even if it was in a game! But – I will bet you one thing: over the previous few years (say five, for argument's sake), you purchase more online than in a brick-and-mortar outfit, right?

Chances are that I've probably lost that bet (I did say I'm not a betting man). Still, the reality is that we live in an age where e-commerce is big business and that not having any form of e-commerce website offer means you lose business daily. The need for an online site has become particularly acute over the last two to three years, with the horrific events of the pandemic – businesses of all sizes have had to adapt to a new world of selling online.

But what does this have to do with a book about Next.js and e-commerce, I hear you ask? Simple – today's customers are time-poor and expect sites to be fast, reliable, and, above all, simple to use. It's a tall order, right?

It's not as large as you might think: welcome to the world of SPAs, or single-page applications. As a concept, it's not clear when these came into being, but there are reports that it could have been as far back as 2003, so not a new concept. However, it's taken off over the last few years in frameworks or libraries such as React, Angular, Vue, and of course, Next.js!

Over these following few pages, I'll take you through what makes single-page applications a perfect fit for e-commerce websites and why this benefits customers and companies. We'll also look at how Next.js makes an excellent basis for what will become our project for this book.

Why Should We Use Next.js for E-Commerce Sites?

When it comes to creating SPA-driven e-commerce websites, we could choose any one of dozens of different frameworks to create the offer – each has its advantages. The one of interest to us is Next.js; why is it such a perfect fit for use in an e-commerce environment?

© Alex Libby 2023
A. Libby, *Practical Next.js for E-Commerce*, https://doi.org/10.1007/978-1-4842-9612-7_1

There are lots of reasons from both a developer and business perspective – we'll look at the business side in a moment, but let's first take a look at some of the advantages for us developers:

- We can reduce load times through the use of concepts such as lazy loading and automatic code splitting – this helps maintain excellent performance, a great user experience, and faster time to market.

- Next.js offers lots of support for developers – it was written by Guillermo Rauch, CEO of Vercel, one of the biggest hosting companies available worldwide.

- Search engine optimization (SEO) support is top-notch, owing to rendering content both client and server-side.

- Next.js compiles to a static site when compiled, so there are no links to any databases or sources – this reduces the risk of hacking and makes for a faster site as we already have the data available. In our case, data will be stored using Next.js' context feature; we will talk to Stripe's API when required.

I know there are some downsides, though, from a developer's perspective. Some people find Next.js too opinionated as a framework, although its abstraction of many features to simplify the development process means it has to decide a few things for us!

Some people are also not keen on the routing it uses; it is page-based, which makes it very easy (and removes the need for dedicated routing code), although it does dictate how you need to set up the routing!

Okay – that all aside, let's move on. As a developer, you've chosen to use Next.js (and, therefore, this book) as you like the look of what you see. However, one important subject we need to cover is how we sell the benefits of Next.js to those who control the purse strings. There are several reasons to choose Next.js, so let's take a moment to look at these in more detail.

Selling the Benefits of Using Next.js

As developers, we want to focus on the exciting stuff – setting up Next.js and building our site – but we need to know how we can sell the benefits of using Next.js to those in control of budgets.

Yes, this is probably the most important part: there is no sense in trying out new technology if we don't have buy-in from the business! Fortunately, this is one of those occasions where we shouldn't have a problem with selling the benefits of Next.js – there are some great reasons why we (as the business) should make the transition to using this framework:

- Adaptability and responsiveness are critical to a great user experience; we can serve different screen sizes and devices from the same codebase.

- Data security – As with most frameworks that follow the Jamstack principles, websites created with NextJS are static. It means there is no direct connection to the database, dependencies, user data, or other sensitive information, which helps keep the site secure.

- Faster time to market – NextJS is perfect for creating a minimum viable product (MVP) as fast as possible, thanks to many premade components. This way of building allows you to get feedback quickly and improve your product accordingly without wasting time and money.

- Fully omnichannel – Websites and apps created with NextJS are accessible from any device so that you can market and sell your products and services through multiple channels.

- Short page load time – Static websites are fast by nature, so visitors and customers will be content with the performance of NextJS websites and web apps.

- Support on demand – The number of React developers available is growing, as are those who know NextJS. It makes it easy to find an agency or freelancer to make some changes if needed or premade components available for use.

- SEO support is top-notch when using Next.js – Conversion rates and sales will increase, which makes it ideal for your marketing team.

- Next.js makes it much easier to scale from a business perspective – Maintenance costs are lower, and performance is better. Although Next.js is based on React, anecdotal evidence suggests that Next.js is faster and easier to work with than React!

Right – let's crack on with the project! The next stage is to set the scene – I'm sure you'll want to know what we're building and how, right? As with many of my sites, it will center around items I love, and yes... it does include food.

Setting the Scene

Okay – enough selling methinks: let's get on with the technical detail!

As a project, Next.js is already well served by excellent documentation. We will take a different spin for this book and put some of this into practice by developing a simple e-commerce SPA. I'll bet you're wondering what we're going to create, right? Well, wonder no more, my friends – let me reveal all:

As I am sure, someone once said, the way to a man's heart is frequently food – as a developer, I know it's usually cakes; people all too often wander into my office with some form of food. Partaking in a few cakes may be nice, but it does nothing for my waistline!

Leaving aside the perils of eating too many sugary foods, we're going to build a simple e-commerce SPA to sell one of my favorite foods, macarons. We'll go through the steps required to set up our starting website and turn it into an e-commerce progressive web app (PWA) using Next.js and Stripe; this will use principles you can apply across any e-commerce SPA in your future projects. As with any project, we need to start somewhere, so let's first get into the technical detail of the tools we will use to create our site and set up our development environment.

Preparing the Environment

So, for our project, what tools do we need? Top of the list will, of course, be Next.js, but that's not all – there are a few other tools we need to use over and above our usual text editor.

I'm a keen fan of keeping things simple where possible (yes, I believe in the KISS principle, for those who know it) – why write ten lines of code if we only need five?

That all aside, let's take a look at the complete list of tools we will need in more detail:

- As text editors go, there is plenty we could use – My preference is Visual Studio Code, but please feel free to use yours if you have one installed that works for you.

- For data, we'll use Sanity – A headless CMS system with an API similar to GraphQL, which works well with Stripe/Next.js.

- Next.js is written for Node.js, so we must install it and NPM using a version suitable for your platform. To create the site itself, we'll use the create-next-app (`https://create-next-app.js.org/`), which will get the basic setup in place.

- To host the site, we'll use Netlify – My preference is to link to it from a GitHub site rather than use an option like dragging and dropping the code directly into Netlify. Either way, we will need free accounts for both services.

- The key tool we need is Stripe – This will host all of our products and deal with the checkout and order submission. However, there are some limitations, such as being unable to manage stock levels; I will come to this later in the book.

- As part of hosting, I will attach a custom domain name to the site to give it a little extra realism – this isn't obligatory, but will provide you with an idea of how it will work as an end-to-end solution.

- Last but by no means least, we will need some photos of cakes for our store – these we will source from `https://unsplash.com/s/photos/cupcakes`.

All of the demos in this book were written for Windows, as this is the author's development platform. Please adapt if you are using macOS or Linux on your PC.

In addition, there are a couple of assumptions I've made for this project:

- I've elected not to use TypeScript to make it simpler; please feel free to adapt the code if you prefer to have type-checking in place.

- For this book, I will assume our project folder is called `macaronmagic` and is located at the root of the `C:` drive. This is purely for convenience; if you want to rename or store it somewhere else, please adapt the code as appropriate.

- Throughout this book, I will focus on keeping things simple and focus on the core parts of building a Next.js e-commerce site: it does mean sacrificing a few features, such as stock control. It won't be an issue for our site; focusing on simplicity means we can assess how Next. js is working and use this as a basis for expanding or upgrading in the future.

Right – enough with the technical architecting: it's time to get our hands dirty and build our site! As mentioned just now, we'll use the create-next-app to set up the initial placeholder, ready for building on from the next chapter. Let's dive in and look at the steps required in more detail.

Creating the Base Site

Our first task is simple but probably the most important – we need something we can use to build our site! Fortunately, Next.js makes this very easy to complete; the first step is to get the framework installed before using a template to create our starter site. We'll then come back and explore the proposed architecture for our site and add any remaining tools we need to complete the development of our project.

INSTALLING NEXT.JS AND CREATING THE SITE

To set up the initial site, follow these steps:

1. First, fire up a Node.js terminal session, then navigate to the root of your C: drive.

2. At the prompt, enter npx create-next-app macaronmagic, then press Enter.

3. When prompted, choose the options as shown in this list:

```
Need to install the following packages:
  create-next-app
Ok to proceed? (y) y
√ Would you like to use TypeScript with this project? ... No
√ Would you like to use ESLint with this project? ... Yes
√ Would you like to use `src/` directory with this project? ... Yes
```

√ Would you like to use experimental `app/` directory with this
  project? ... No
√ What import alias would you like configured? ... @/*

Creating a new Next.js app in C:\macaronmagic.

Note   We've run through the process step by step, so you can see how it works. However, you can equally enter this command instead, which will perform the same task: `npx create-next-app --js --eslint --src-dir`.

---

4. Node will continue with installing the new site but will confirm when complete with a `Success...!` message.

5. In preparation for stages later in the book, we also need to install a selection of dependencies – for this, crack open the `package.json` file from within the project folder in your editor, then amend your `"dependencies":...` section like this:

```
"dependencies": {
  "@sanity/client": "^3.4.1",
  "@sanity/image-url": "^1.0.1",
  "@stripe/stripe-js": "^1.25.0",
  "canvas-confetti": "^1.5.1",
  "next": "13.2.4",
  "next-sanity-image": "^3.2.1",
  "react": "18.2.0",
  "react-dom": "18.2.0",
  "react-hot-toast": "^2.2.0",
  "react-icons": "^4.7.1",
  "react-tabs": "^4.2.1",
  "stripe": "^8.209.0"
}
```

6. We have several devDependencies that we need to set up – this includes moving two of the original `eslint` dependencies (`eslint` and `eslint-config-next`) that were already present in the dependencies section into devDependencies. Make sure your devDependencies block looks like this:

```
"devDependencies": {
  "eslint": "^8.36.0",
  "eslint-config-airbnb": "^19.0.4",
```

```
"eslint-config-next": "^13.2.4",
"eslint-plugin-import": "^2.25.4",
"eslint-plugin-jsx-a11y": "^6.5.1",
"eslint-plugin-react": "^7.29.3",
"eslint-plugin-react-hooks": "^4.3.0",
"sass": "^1.57.0"
}
```

We usually would install these packages manually, but this could present an issue – I will touch on this shortly when we go through the changes in more detail.

7. Save and close the file. Revert to your terminal session, then at the prompt, enter npm `install` and press Enter.

8. Node will install the packages we've added to package.json; when completed, enter npm `run dev` and press Enter to launch the development server.

9. Node will start the development server and display this message when it's ready, along with confirmation that it has compiled the site:

```
ready - started server on 0.0.0.0:3000, url: http://localhost:3000
event - compiled client and server successfully in 490 ms (166
modules)
```

Note   The compilation time of 490 ms will likely be different for you: this will depend on your hardware and what might be running in the background. Keep an eye on the timings; they should stay broadly similar until we make changes later. If they increase significantly and suddenly for no apparent reason, this could indicate a problem that needs investigation!

10. At this point, go ahead and browse to http://localhost:3000 – if all is well, we should see our new starter site running, as shown in Figure 1-1.

Figure 1-1. *The starter site running in a browser*

Great – we've got our base site in place, ready for us to develop! The developers of the Next.js create-next-app have made it a cinch to set up a base site; we've extended it to add a few more packages that we will use later in the book. Before we get into the details of setting up our development environment, let's quickly cover the changes we just made in more detail.

Understanding the Changes Made

So, what did we achieve in the last demo?

As always, we had to start somewhere, and there is no better place than to get the basic site in place! We could have created it manually from scratch, but there is no point when you have a great app like `create-next-app`, which can do most of the heavy lifting for us.

To get started, we ran the `create-next-app` tool in a Node.js terminal session, which we used to create a site called `macaronmagic`. As part of this, we ran through three questions: the first was to confirm it was OK to install `create-next-app`. Using `npx` allows us to search through any existing packages already installed; if it doesn't find it, it will download it before installing it.

We then had to answer two questions about the project configuration – the first was to confirm if we wanted to use TypeScript support, and the second was to use ESLint within the project. We answered no to the first (for simplicity) and yes to the second; Node.js then created the new application with preconfigured entries.

Once it completed the process, we updated the dependencies in package.json; these are all packages we will use later in the book. We also updated the `devDependencies` section, as some of the existing values in the dependencies block would be better served by moving to this section.

Once done and we had saved the file, we ran the install process – to round things off, we fired up the Next.js development server before previewing the results in our browser.

Okay – let's move on: now that we have our initial site in place, we do need to explore what other tools we will use, but for now, let's pause for a moment to review the initial makeup of our site in more detail.

Exploring the Site

Go ahead and open up the `macaronmagic` folder stored on your PC. It might at first glance look like we have a lot of content – don't worry, all of it is needed; there are some key areas we will use (and which will likely be familiar to those who may have already used React before).

A quick peek at the contents of the `macaronmagic` folder will display a list of files similar to that shown in Figure 1-2.

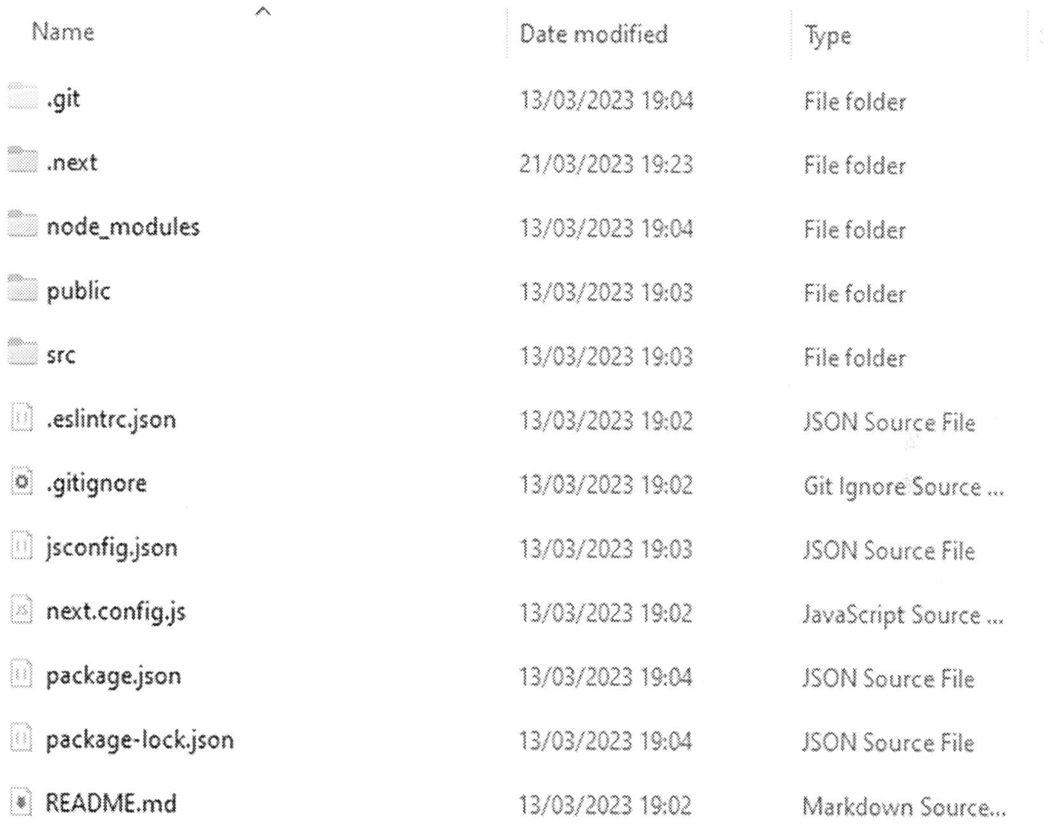

Name ^	Date modified	Type
.git	13/03/2023 19:04	File folder
.next	21/03/2023 19:23	File folder
node_modules	13/03/2023 19:04	File folder
public	13/03/2023 19:03	File folder
src	13/03/2023 19:03	File folder
.eslintrc.json	13/03/2023 19:02	JSON Source File
.gitignore	13/03/2023 19:02	Git Ignore Source ...
jsconfig.json	13/03/2023 19:03	JSON Source File
next.config.js	13/03/2023 19:02	JavaScript Source ...
package.json	13/03/2023 19:04	JSON Source File
package-lock.json	13/03/2023 19:04	JSON Source File
README.md	13/03/2023 19:02	Markdown Source...

Figure 1-2. *A standard file structure for a create-next-app site*

Some of these entries will be familiar, such as node_modules or .gitignore (and, of course, package.json). But what about the likes of the .next folder or perhaps the .eslintrc.json file? What do all of these folders and files do? Most we won't need to worry about, such as the READ.md (standard for create-next-app sites), but there are some of interest to us – these are listed in Table 1-1.

Table 1-1. *Files in a create-next-app site*

Name of file or folder	Purpose
.git	Standard Git directory containing details about the project, such as commits and location of the repository, etc.
.next	Cache folder for the site – updates when we run the site locally and manages certain features within the site.
pages	Folder to contain pages for our site, such as contact us, about, and privacy. Note: we'll use a different means to reference product pages.
src	Folder to contain any components, stylesheets, or components for the site; treat this as the source for your site.
.eslintrc.json	This is the configuration file for ESLint, which we specified when creating the original site.
.gitignore	A standard Git configuration file used to exclude files for committal.
next.config.js	This is the main configuration file for our Next.js site.
package.json & package-lock.json	Standard files for any NPM site.

Although we have a good handful of files and folders on our site, only a few are essential – the pages, public, styles folders, and the next.config.js file. Let's dig a little deeper into the pages folder, stored within the \src folder; inside this one, we have three files and an api folder, as shown in Figure 1-3.

Figure 1-3. *Contents of the pages folder in our site*

Inside this folder, we have the api folder and three files: _app.js, _document.js, and index.js. We don't need the _document.js file, but the others are important – the first (_app.js) takes care of page initialization (and, in this case, overrides the default, which is necessary for our site).

The index.js file is where most of the magic happens – this hosts the content for our homepage and represents what you saw in Figure 1-1. The remaining folder, api, treats anything within as an endpoint for our site; we'll use this to call data from Stripe later in the book.

We will add more files and folders in later exercises throughout this book.

Okay, let's move on: it's time we got together all the tools we need to complete our project. Next.js is the obvious one, but there are a few others – let's look at the list in more detail.

Understanding What Tools We Need

Although it's possible to create lots of different features for an e-commerce site, I've elected to keep things simple for this book; this gives us plenty of scope to explore new avenues later.

With this in mind, we need only three services for now – we will use other tools later for hosting but will come to those in due course. Let's look at what we need in more detail as part of the next walkthrough demo.

SIGNING UP FOR SERVICES

We have a few tools we will use throughout this book – we've already referenced a few of them when we set up the initial site; let's work through the remaining ones:

1. The first account we need is ironically not one of the tools we will use, but a valid email address! Make sure you have one you're happy to use to sign up with, as we have to create a few accounts for this project.

2. Next, let's deal with the most important one: Stripe. For this, head over to `https://dashboard.stripe.com/register`, and enter valid details for the Email, Full Name, Country, and Password fields. Leave the "Email me about..." field empty unless you want to subscribe to their mailing list. When done, hit Create account, then follow any instructions given onscreen.

A heads up – you will notice that I've included the Country field as Stripe expects you to choose your country of origin. It means that while prices you see later may be in USD, the values in Stripe's dashboard for your site may show in a different currency. We'll revisit this later to see what this means when configuring Stripe for our site.

---

3. The next account we need is for the back-end CMS, Sanity. Head over to `www.sanity.io/login/sign-up`, then select one of the options to sign up for an account. To keep things simple, I recommend email or the Google account/login option; ensure you keep details of which login option you use.

These three services are all we need for now – we will use GitHub and Netlify to host our site, but we will cover setting up accounts and logins later in the book.

Great – we are signed up for the services we need (at least for now); we're ready to start building our site! Although we've covered some routine steps in this first exercise, they highlight one crucial trend that is becoming increasingly popular with developers worldwide.

It should come as no surprise, but more and more developers are using Jamstack principles when creating websites – this means using third-party services and APIs to surface data through to the customer.

In this exercise, we've set up two accounts: one for storing our back-end content in a CMS and the other for taking payments from our site. At the same time, we also made sure we had a valid email address. We will add more services and features later in the book, but these are enough to get something created as a starting point for our site.

Summary

Creating a website can be seen as a journey, irrespective of size or complexity – where there will always be highs and lows, successes, and challenges, as we develop what will become our final solution. Over these last few pages, we've detailed some of the background theory to our project, so we have the critical elements in place – let's take a moment to review what we have learned before beginning the actual development of our site.

We began by exploring what makes SPA a perfect fit for e-commerce sites and why Next.js works so well for e-commerce. At the same time, we also explored some of the benefits of using Next.js, which will appeal to businesses, particularly those in control of the purse strings.

We then set the scene, describing what we will build and preparing the environment before creating the initial site for our project. Once we had created the site, we began to familiarize ourselves with the folder and file structure, ready for developing code later in the book. We then rounded out with a look at the remaining tools we will need to get development off the ground and ready for us to work.

A nice short chapter, I hope you agree – enough for us to get things ready so we can get stuck into developing our site. The next part of this adventure is where the fun starts: it's time to get pages set up, add in navigation, and so on… in a nutshell, there's plenty to do, so let's move on and get started with fleshing out our macaron shop website in the next chapter.

PART II

Building Our Shop

CHAPTER 2

Laying the Foundations

We've got our tools in place and worked out what we're going to build – so it's time to build our shop!

As I am sure anyone will say, laying good foundations is essential; throughout this chapter, we will set up our initial site and add critical elements such as page structure, header, images, and navigation. We have a lot of work to do, so let's crack on first with a quick overview of the site architecture, so you can see how the pages will come together to form our site.

Displaying the Site Architecture

Although it may seem like we'll be working on a lot of code over this chapter, our site isn't that big.

At its heart are six pages, plus the main index.js page – this will give us enough to create something that is hopefully realistic for a small site and one we can expand on for future projects. There is one crucial point – we will stock a good handful of products in this demo, so why don't we have pages for each product? There is a good reason for this, so let me explain.

Creating product pages for all six products is technically feasible but not a sensible idea. We can use this if we will only sell two to three products, but this makes life more complicated when making changes to the page. We may have to change all two to three pages and ensure that each page has the same changes. Have you got time to edit all X pages? I don't think so!

Instead, we will use a template file (represented here by the `[slug].js` file from within the `product` folder); React allows us to create the page dynamically, using information sourced from Sanity. It avoids the need to develop hard-coded pages for each product and means that if we need to implement a change, it will apply to all products simultaneously.

© Alex Libby 2023
A. Libby, *Practical Next.js for E-Commerce*, https://doi.org/10.1007/978-1-4842-9612-7_2

With this in mind, we can see the critical elements in a schematic of our site in Figure 2-1.

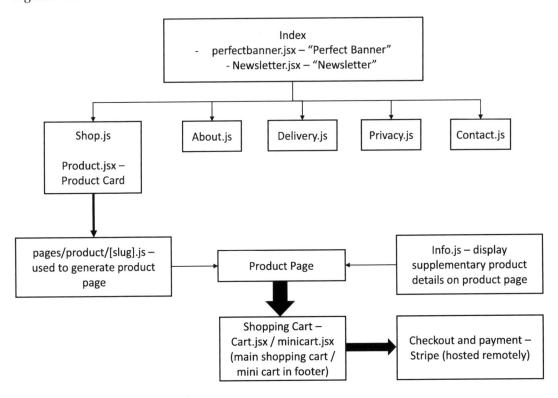

Figure 2-1. *A schematic of our site*

Although we've covered most of the important pages in this schematic, one isn't displayed but deserves special mention. We will create a template called Layout. js, which we will use to control the position of content on the page on our site. This component will have references to the NavBar, DemoBanner, and Footer components; the latter will contain the minicart, payment icons, social media icons, and links to various pages on our site.

You may find it easier to view the PDF of the site architecture in the code download accompanying this book.

What does this mean for us in terms of updating content? While we won't have to create any product pages from scratch, we will still have to create the ancillary pages, such as delivery.js, contact.js, and about.js. In total, we will have seven to eight pages which might seem a lot for a small site, but some are not critical to the core purchasing process. I've added them to give a more rounded feel to the site – these noncore pages will have some dummy text, which we can update later. You can see a sneak preview of what the site will look like when we've completed it in Figure 2-2.

Figure 2-2. *A preview of how the site will look when completed*

Now that we've explored how we will put the site together, let's start coding it. We could start anywhere on the site, but for convenience, I'm going to begin with the main index page, from which we can start to add pages as we build out our site.

The code will be available in the code download if you have any problems copying or editing your version of the site code.

Updating the Main Index Page

For the first task, we need to replace the code in the main index page that sits under the \src\pages folder – this will give us the beginnings of our site. We have a lot to cover, so without further ado, let's dive in and get started on the next exercise.

UPDATING THE MAIN INDEX PAGE

The first page to update is our main index page – to do this, follow these steps:

1. First, crack open the `index.js` file stored in the `\src\pages` folder, then delete everything within the file.

2. Next, go ahead and add this code – we have a few lines to add, starting with the requisite imports:

```
import React from "react";
import Link from "next/link";
// import { client } from "../lib/client";
import PerfectBanner from "../components/PerfectBanner";
import Newsletter from "../components/Newsletter";
```

3. Next, leave a blank line, then add this:

```
const Home = () => (
  <div>
    <div className="frontlogo">
      <div className="banner">
        <span className="tagline">Luxury macarons made by hand</span>
        <span>
          <Link className="shop-now" href="/shop">
            Shop Now
          </Link>
        </span>
      </div>
    </div>
```

4. Leave a line blank after the first half of our Home component, then add this code – it takes care of the main text and calls two additional components:

```
<div className="intro">
  <p>
    Welcome to Macaron Magic - the home of great-tasting,
    luxurious macarons, made by hand here in our workshop in the
    Peak District.
  </p>
```

```
    <p>
      We have carefully chosen a select range of flavors for your
      delight, ready for you to enjoy - just imagine...biting into
      each one, where it
      practically melts in your mouth...yum!
    </p>
    <p>
      To start, browse over to our shop where you will see the full
      range available - we'll be adding more over time. If you have
      any questions, please do let us know - our contact details are
      at the bottom of this page.
    </p>
  </div>

  <PerfectBanner />
  <Newsletter />
  </div>
);

/* ADD SERVERSIDE PROPS HERE */

export default Home;
```

5. Save and close the file: you will see that we've called two components (PerfectBanner and Newsletter.) Let's add those in now – to do this, go ahead and add a new folder called \components at the root of the src folder.

6. In a new file, add the following code – we'll begin with the imports for our first component, which is Newsletter:

```
import React from "react";
import Image from "next/image";
import newsletter from "../../public/images/newsletter.jpg";
```

7. Leave a line blank, then add the first half of our component:

```
const Newsletter = () => (
  <div className="newsletter">
    <form action="/send-data-here" method="post"
    className="email-signup">
      <span>Join our Newsletter</span>
```

```
<input type="text" id="first" name="first" placeholder="First
name" />
<input type="text" id="last" name="last" placeholder="Last
name" />
<input type="email" id="email" name="email" placeholder="Email
address" />
```

8. Immediately after, leave a line blank, then let's add the second half of our component:

```
    <button type="submit">Submit</button>
  </form>

  <span className="newsletter-image">
    <Image src={newsletter} alt="newsletter" width={500}
    height={500} />
  </span>
 </div>
);
```

9. We need to finish off with a typical export, so skip a line and add this:

```
export default Newsletter;
```

10. Save the file as Newsletter.jsx in the components folder you created in step 4. Now, open a new file, then add this code for our next component – let's first add the imports:

```
import React from "react";
import Image from "next/image";
import perfect from "../../public/images/perfect.jpg";
```

11. Next, miss a line, then add the first half of this component:

```
const PerfectBanner = () => (
  <div className="perfect-occasions">
    <div>
      <Image src={perfect} alt="perfect occasion" width="442"
      height="532" />
    </div>
```

```
<div className="perfect-message">
  <p>Perfect for </p>
  <p>special occasions</p>
```

12. As we've done before, miss the next line, then add this code:

```
<p>
  Share the love and give every guest a little explosion of
  sweetness with our show-stopping macaron towers. Perfect for
  weddings, anniversaries and parties. You could even add a
  touch of luxury to party bags and wedding favors with these
  perfect bite-sized treats.
</p>
    </div>
  </div>
);

export default PerfectBanner;
```

13. Go ahead and save the file as `PerfectBanner.jsx`, then close it.

14. There is one last step to do before we can test this demo – we need two images for our components. Go ahead and extract `perfect.jpg` and `newsletter.jpg` from the code download, then put both into a new folder called `images` under `\public`.

15. Switch to a Node.js terminal, then at the prompt, change the working folder to our project area.

16. Enter `npm run dev` and press Enter to fire up the Next.js development server. If all is well, we should see the site as shown in the extract in Figure 2-3 when browsing to `http://localhost:3000`.

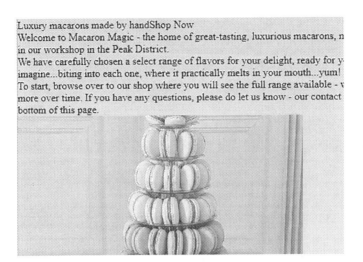

Luxury macarons made by handShop Now
Welcome to Macaron Magic - the home of great-tasting, luxurious macarons, n
in our workshop in the Peak District.
We have carefully chosen a select range of flavors for your delight, ready for y
imagine...biting into each one, where it practically melts in your mouth...yum!
To start, browse over to our shop where you will see the full range available - v
more over time. If you have any questions, please do let us know - our contact
bottom of this page.

Figure 2-3.   *The updated index page*

Okay, I know it doesn't look pretty – indeed, it's almost reminiscent of something from the early web days! Remember that – gray pages, bad formatting, and not much else? Yes, they were the days...

But I digress: we've completed some essential changes in this demo and now have the beginnings of a site. To understand what we've done, let's take a moment to review the rather lengthy exercise we've just completed in more detail to see how it fits into the bigger picture.

Understanding What Happened

So – what did we achieve in the first demo for this chapter? We began with some significant updates to the main index.js file stored in the pages folder; it pretty much replaced all of the original code.

We added some imports for React, Next/Link, and two components – PerfectBanner and Newsletter, which we will develop later in this chapter. Next up, we created the core part of the component called Home; this we consume inside a Layout component that we will create shortly. Inside the Home component, we add links for the front image (of macarons), a tagline, and a link to point to the Shop page, coming later in this book.

To finish off the Home component, we then add the introductory text, followed by calls to two components: PerfectBanner and Newsletter. With the calls in place, we now need to create these two components; we started with Newsletter and added the code for this component. It's worth noting that the form inside of Newsletter is nonfunctional; this doesn't matter as we are only creating a demo. Making the form work is something we should look to rectify if we develop the site into something ready for production.

We have one last step, which is to create the PerfectBanner component – in much the same way as we did with Newsletter, we added the relevant text and images into a new component, saving it as PerfectBanner.jsx. The last step was to source and add two images called in the components to the site so that the Home component won't throw an error due to missing media. We then previewed the result in our browser to ensure we at least had a page working, even if it's not looking its best yet!

There is one crucial point I want to highlight throughout this, though – you will notice that we have various instances of commented code. Don't worry; they are placeholders for features we will develop throughout the book. For now, we have to comment out calls or code to make sure the site still works – they will come back at the appropriate point!

Okay – let's crack on: we've updated the index.js or main homepage component, so it now starts to display content for our site. To make this work, though, we need to make some changes to the site's layout; this will help with implementing Stripe later in the book. We will do this in a two-part exercise, where we have to implement code changes to _app.jsx and create an updated layout component – let's dive in and take a look at what we need to do in more detail.

Altering the Site Layout

To update the _app.jsx file, we need to make a few changes, but nothing quite as detailed as for the previous demo!

This next demo will be in two parts, as although we have to update _app.jsx, we also have to alter the main layout file, which is layout.jsx. Let's begin first with modifying _app.jsx.

DEMO – REWORKING THE LAYOUT PAGE

To update _app.jsx, follow these steps:

1. Crack open _app.jsx in your editor, then add a couple of blank lines before the import for global.css.

2. In those blank lines, add the following imports, so you should end up with something like this:

```
import React from "react";
import { Toaster } from "react-hot-toast";
import { Layout } from "../components";

import "../styles/globals.css";
```

3. Next, leave a line blank, then add this import – it's not one we will use now, but we will do so once we plumb in Stripe:

```
// import { StateContext } from "../../context/StateContext";
```

4. We now need to alter the main component – we already have an exported default initialization for MyApp, so alter it to look like this:

```
function MyApp({ Component, pageProps }) {
  return (
    // <StateContext>
      <Layout>
        <Toaster />
        <Component {...pageProps} />;
      </Layout>
    // </StateContext>
  );
}

export default MyApp;
```

5. We have one more file to add, an index file – create a new file called index.js and save it to the root of the \src\components folder.

6. Inside that file, add this code, then save, and close it:

```
export { default as Layout } from "./Layout";
```

7. Save the file and close it.

Let's turn our attention to the second component for this exercise:

1. For this next part, please open a new file, saving it as Layout.jsx in the \src\components folder.

2. Inside that file, go ahead and add this code – we'll do it in blocks, as there is a lot to get through, starting with the two imports:

```
import React from "react";
import Head from "next/head";
```

3. Next comes the opening initialization, <Head> and <title> tags:

```
const Layout = ({ children }) => {
  return (
    <>
      <Head>
        <title>Macaron Magic | great tasting home-made
        macarons</title>
```

4. This next part might seem a little complex, but it's a standard block for adding a favicon to any site. Go ahead and add this code – I will touch on this more shortly:

```
        <link rel="apple-touch-icon" sizes="180x180"
href="/favicon/apple-touch-icon.png" />
        <link rel="icon" type="image/png" sizes="32x32"
        href="/favicon/favicon-32x32.png" />
        <link rel="icon" type="image/png" sizes="16x16"
href="/favicon/favicon-16x16.png" />
        <link rel="manifest" href="/site.webmanifest" />
        <link rel="mask-icon" href="/favicon/safari-pinned-tab.svg"
        color="#5bbad5" />
        <meta name="msapplication-TileColor" content="#da532c" />
        <meta name="theme-color" content="#ffffff" />
```

5. We need to close the component, which we will do with this code:

```
    </Head>
    <header>
      <NavBar />
      <DemoBanner />
    </header>
    <div className="layout">
      <main className="main-container">
        {children}
      </main>
      <footer>
        {/* <Footer /> */}
      </footer>
    </div>
  </>
  );
};

export default Layout;
```

6. At this point, go ahead and save, then close the file. Switch to a Node.js terminal, then at the prompt, change the working folder to our project area.

7. Enter npm run dev and press Enter to fire up the Next.js development server.

8. When browsing the site at http://localhost:3000, we won't see any changes. Don't worry, this is expected – instead, take a look at your browser console – you should see changes at this point, where we've introduced a <main>...</main> container (Figure 2-4).

```
▼<div id="__next" data-reactroot> == $0
  ▶<header>...</header>
  ▼<div class="layout">
    ▶<main class="main-container">...</main>
  </div>
  <footer></footer>
</div>
```

Figure 2-4. *The site, after updating the layout*

9. If you look further up in the <head> block, you will also see the favicon entries now appearing (Figure 2-5).

```
<title>Macaron Magic | great tasting home-made macarons</title> == $0
<link rel="apple-touch-icon" sizes="180x180" href="/favicon/apple-touch-icon.png">
<link rel="icon" type="image/png" sizes="32x32" href="/favicon/favicon-32x32.png">
<link rel="icon" type="image/png" sizes="16x16" href="/favicon/favicon-16x16.png">
<link rel="manifest" href="/site.webmanifest">
<link rel="mask-icon" href="/favicon/safari-pinned-tab.svg" color="#5bbad5">
<meta name="msapplication-TileColor" content="#da532c">
<meta name="theme-color" content="#ffffff">
```

Figure 2-5. *The new favicon entries*

Phew – we've completed two lengthy demos on the trot! It might have seemed like a lot of work, but it's worth it, so well done if you manage to get to this point without too much trouble. We've covered some important changes in this last demo, so let's pause for a moment to review them in more detail.

Breaking Apart the Code Changes

This last demo was essential, but if you ran up the site, you'd be forgiven for thinking that there wasn't any change! This apparent lack of change was to be expected, though – most of the change is behind the scenes, with only the favicon being the noticeable visual change.

To achieve this, we first updated _app.jsx, which acts as a container for Next.js sites, and everything we see is rendered from within this file. We added the requisite imports and a link to a stylesheet, followed by an import for a StateContext component coming later when we add Stripe.

It's interesting to note that although we call Component and pass into it pageProps, this component doesn't exist! It's a special component from Next.js; consider it a placeholder reference for the active page on display in our browser. We use the pageProps prop value to pass into it any values required for the page we display, and these are updated each time we route to a new page.

Moving on, we modified the Layout.jsx component next – for this, we had to replace the imports and rework the layout to match our needs. Most of the code is a set of links for the favicon; I used the favicon code generator at https://realfavicongenerator. net/ to create the code for this block of links. We wrapped it inside a set of <div> elements, which contain the site's <head> and <title> tags (the former using Next's <Head> component). There is also a second set of head tags, <head> – you might ask why we have two? Let me explain:

Next.js' <Head> component does not display any content – we use this to insert anything that should go into our page's <head> section. The <header> tag is effectively the start of where our content is rendered – for now, it contains the two components that we will have created by the end of this chapter, NavBar and DemoBanner. We also have a slot for any child components, such as individual pages (which go into the {children} slot), followed by the footer component, which we will construct later.

Phew – it seems a lot, but this is a crucial stage; apart from the work we will have to do around Stripe (in Chapter 4), this will make our lives easier when it comes to adding more content to our site. With the changes completed, we ran up the site to check that it had consumed the layout component in the markup (Figure 2-4) and that the links for the favicon appeared as expected in our browser (Figure 2-5).

Adding a Navigation Menu

Now that we have the skeleton of our main homepage in place, it's crucial to set up navigation, so we can navigate around the site without manually entering each page's address. After all, we might know how to get to a particular page, but our customers won't without some form of link!

Fortunately, Next.js makes it very easy to add a basic navigation – for this, we need to use the Link component from next/link, which we will do in the next exercise.

ADDING NAVIGATION

For our next component, we're going to create a basic navigation bar – to do so, follow these steps:

1. Crack open a new file, saving it as NavBar.js within the \src\ components folder.

2. Go ahead and add this code – as before, we'll break it into sections, starting with the imports:

```
import React from "react";
import Link from "next/link";
import { AiOutlineShopping } from "react-icons/ai";
import { Cart } from "./";

// import { useStateContext } from "../../context/StateContext";
```

3. Next, leave a line blank, then add the first half of our NavBar component:

```
const NavBar = () => {
  // const { showCart, setShowCart, totalQuantities } =
  useStateContext();

  return (
    <div className="navbar-container">
      <div className="company-name">
        <Link href="/">Mangez Macaron</Link>
```

```
<div className="navbar" logo="true">
  <Link href="/">Home</Link>
  <Link href="/about">About</Link>
  <Link href="/shop">Shop</Link>
  <Link href="/contact">Contact</Link>
```

4. Immediately below, let's complete the component with this block of code:

```
{/* <button
    type="button"
    className="cart-icon"
    onClick={() => setShowCart(true)}
  >
    <AiOutlineShopping />
    <span className="cart-item-qty">{totalQuantities}</span>
  </button>

  {showCart && <Cart />} */}
      </div>
    </div>
  </div>
);
};

export default NavBar;
```

5. Save the file as NavBar.jsx in the \src\components folder, then close it.

6. We need to make a couple more changes – open index.jsx from the \src\ components folder, then add this line of code at the bottom:

```
export { default as NavBar } from "./NavBar";
```

7. We also need to import the component into the Layout.jsx file, so crack that file open and add this import before the line starting const Layout = ({children})...:

```
import NavBar from "./NavBar";
```

8. Switch to your Node.js terminal, then change the working folder if it is not already set to our project area.

9. At the prompt, enter `npm run dev`, and wait for the development server to fire up.

10. When ready, browse to http://localhost:3000 – if all is well, we should see the text of our navigation shown in Figure 2-6, highlighted in red.

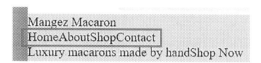

Figure 2-6. *The newly added navigation*

Great – we can now navigate around our site! Although the view may not look pretty in its unstyled state, it's nevertheless a big step forward in developing our site. We'll fix the issues around styling later in Chapter 5, but let's first review the changes we made before continuing with the next stage of development.

Exploring the Code in Detail

This last demo covered adding an essential feature to our site – we cannot expect customers to navigate around it without some form of link between each page, right? Not having any would be an immediate turnoff, but I digress…

To add the navigation bar, we used the Next/Link component from Next.js – this forms the basis of our NavBar component. As before, we started with the requisite imports before opening the component. We had set the `useStateContext` state inside the component but commented it out for now, as this won't come in until later in the book. We then added our markup – most of it uses the `Link` component, into which we pass the `href` value that represents either the homepage or a specific page such as About.

Toward the bottom is where things get a little more interesting – we added a button that, when we click it, sets `showCart` to true. If we have set this to true, it displays our cart and the number of items in the basket. At the moment, I've commented out this block as we haven't built the cart yet; we will enable it later in Chapter 4.

To finish off the component, we then updated the component index file to import the NavBar component before adding a reference to this in Layout.jsx so that we can see the navigation entries in the browser.

Updating the Header

With the navigation now in place, you might think that's all we need to do – unfortunately, that's not the case! We have one more item to add, albeit specific to this project.

We should set up a banner to tell people that this is a demo site and not to expect any orders to be delivered (or payments to be honored, for that matter). It's a simple change, so let's dive in and quickly add the component that will serve this notice to our site.

CREATING THE DEMO BANNER

To set up the DemoBanner component, follow these steps:

1. First, open a new file in your editor, then save it as DemoBanner.js in the \src\components folder.

2. Next, go ahead and add this code:

```
import React from "react";

const DemoBanner = () => {
  return (
    <div className="demo-banner-container">
      <span>
        This is a demo store - no orders will be accepted or delivered
      </span>
    </div>
  );
};

export default DemoBanner;
```

3. Save the file and close it. Crack open `Layout.jsx`, then add this import immediately below the import for NavBar:

```
import DemoBanner from "./DemoBanner";
```

4. A little further down, uncomment the call to `<DemoBanner />`, which is inside the `<header>` tag.

5. Save this file and close it. Switch to your Node.js terminal, then change the working folder if it is not already set to our project area.

6. At the prompt, enter `npm run dev`, and wait for the development server to fire up.

7. When ready, browse to http://localhost:3000 – if all is well, we should see the view shown in Figure 2-7.

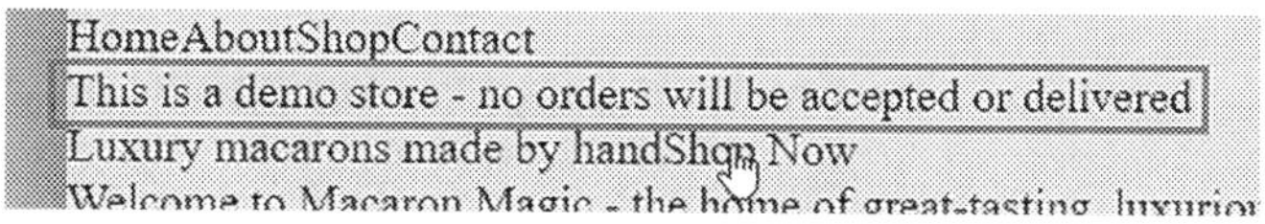

Figure 2-7. *The newly added demo banner*

I know this was something specific for our site and not something we would typically put out into production, but needs must! After all, we don't want people trying to purchase from a site available in the wild, which is (for now) nothing more than a demo version!

The good thing, though, is that it's a perfect basis for developing a more detailed banner. I'm thinking of something we would need to use to deal with cookie privacy; it fits in well with the site, and it should be easy enough to add a click handler that closes the banner once we acknowledge cookies are in use on the site.

Okay – that aside, I want to review a couple of things in more detail: let's take a quick look at the code and some of the improvements we might want to make later when developing the site.

Dissecting the Code

Although this section was labeled as "Updating the Header," the reality is that most of this won't happen until we style our content later in the book.

Instead, we focused on adding a missing element, necessary as our site is non-production: a demo banner. The banner was to advise customers that we're running a test site and not to expect any orders to be fulfilled. You never know – someone might think or expect otherwise!

Leaving aside the perils of not reading notices, let's focus on what we did – we created a new component called DemoBanner.js that contained an <span> element with a simple message. We then imported this into the Layout component so we could render it – a quick check by running the development server indeed showed our new message on display in the browser.

As an aside, we should consider splitting some of the changes we made in Layout.jsx into a separate component. We'll be creating a Footer component later, but so far haven't created an equivalent for Header. In some respects, this might be overkill given what is coming, but it feels nicer to have a consistent <Header> and <Footer> component approach!

Creating the Remaining Pages

We're making significant progress toward completing the skeleton of our site – we have the base site running and the main index page in place. It's time to flesh it out with additional pages we might find when browsing e-commerce sites.

I'm talking, of course, about pages such as About, Contact, Terms, and Privacy. As we're building a simple demo, we don't need to focus too much on what's in them, but it's equally important to know that we should update these with production-ready copy before releasing to the wild. For now, let's focus on creating the base pages, ready for use within our demo.

ADDING ANCILLARY PAGES

To add the remaining ancillary pages for our site, follow these steps:

1. First, crack open a new file, and save it as about.js in the \src\ pages folder.

2. Next, go ahead and add this code – there's a good chunk to add, so we'll do it in two halves, beginning with this block first:

```
const About = () => (
  <div className="about-us">
    <p>About Macaron Magic</p>

    <p>
      Lorem ipsum dolor sit amet, consectetur adipiscing elit. Mauris
      vulputate
      justo ac tellus egestas dictum. Aenean vestibulum diam eu
      risus cursus
      mollis. Nulla dapibus ante in felis vulputate mattis. Mauris
      sed lacus
      eget sapien rutrum interdum. Proin a semper magna. Aliquam
      eget purus
      fringilla, rutrum augue at, porta sem.
    </p>
```

3. Next, miss a line, then add the second half of the code for this page:

```
    <p>
      Aenean aliquam lectus tellus, sed venenatis nulla pretium ac.
      Vivamus cursus purus quam, eu placerat est rutrum quis. Nunc sit
      amet urna sed libero auctor imperdiet nec consequat sem. Quisque
      mauris est, fermentum in tristique quis, tincidunt a odio. Fusce
      porttitor eu est interdum consectetur. Ut aliquam semper dui,
      vulputate hendrerit sapien interdum sit amet. Nam vitae nulla et
      lorem ornare auctor. Nulla facilisi. Nam sed sollicitudin leo.
    </p>
  </div>
);

export default About;
```

4. Save the file and close it.

5. There are three other files that are very similar, so let's get these from the code download that accompanies this book. Go ahead and extract copies of `delivery.js`, `privacy.js`, and `terms.js`, then save all three to the `\src\pages` folder on the website.

6. We have one more file to add to this demo – `contact.js`. For this, crack open a new file, then add this code, which (as before) we'll do bit by bit, starting with the opening tags, title, and introduction:

```
const Contact = () => (
  <div className="contact-us">
    <p>Contact Us</p>
    <p>
      If you have an enquiry about any of our products, we'd love to
      hear from
      you.
    </p>
```

7. This block takes care of the first part of the contact form:

```
<form action="/send-data-here" method="post" className=
"contact-us-form">
  <p>Fields marked with a * are required</p>
  <label htmlFor="fullname">Your full name:</label>
  <div className="contact-field">
    <input type="text"
     id="fullname"
     name="fullname"
     placeholder="Your full name"
     required
    />
    <span>*</span>
  </div>
```

8. Miss a line, then add the second part of the form code:

```
<label htmlFor="email">Your email address:</label>
<div className="contact-field">
  <input type="email"
   id="email"
   name="email"
   placeholder="Email address"
   required
  />
  <span>*</span>
</div>
```

9. Miss a line again, then add the third and final part of the code:

```
        <label htmlFor="enquiry">Your enquiry:</label>
        <div className="contact-field">
          <textarea rows="5"
           cols="60"
           name="enquiry"
           placeholder="Your enquiry..."
          >
          </textarea>
        </div>
        <button type="submit" className="contact-submit">
          Submit
        </button>
      </form>
    </div>
  );

export default Contact;
```

10. Switch to your Node.js terminal, then change the working folder if it is not already set to our project area.

11. At the prompt, enter npm run dev, and wait for the development server to fire up.

12. When ready, browse to http://localhost:3000 – if all is well, we first click the About link in the navigation (Figure 2-8).

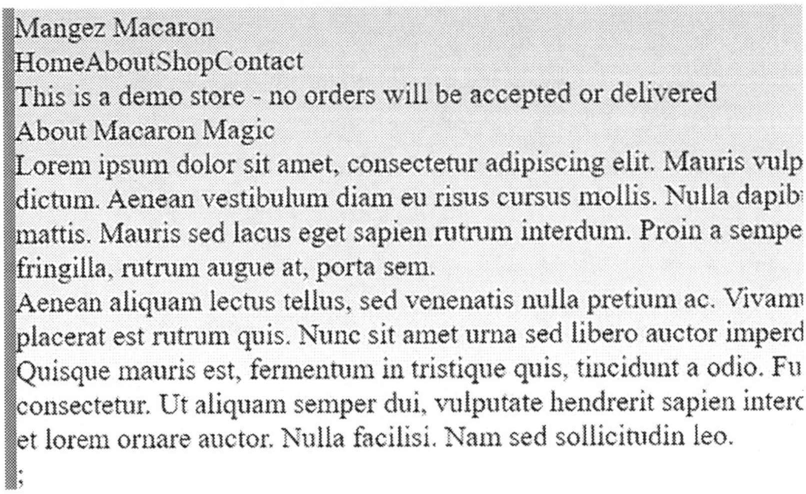

Mangez Macaron
HomeAboutShopContact
This is a demo store - no orders will be accepted or delivered
About Macaron Magic
Lorem ipsum dolor sit amet, consectetur adipiscing elit. Mauris vulp
dictum. Aenean vestibulum diam eu risus cursus mollis. Nulla dapib
mattis. Mauris sed lacus eget sapien rutrum interdum. Proin a sempe
fringilla, rutrum augue at, porta sem.
Aenean aliquam lectus tellus, sed venenatis nulla pretium ac. Vivam
placerat est rutrum quis. Nunc sit amet urna sed libero auctor imperd
Quisque mauris est, fermentum in tristique quis, tincidunt a odio. Fu
consectetur. Ut aliquam semper dui, vulputate hendrerit sapien interc
et lorem ornare auctor. Nulla facilisi. Nam sed sollicitudin leo.
;

Figure 2-8. *Some of the remaining pages – about.js...*

13. Try clicking the Contact link – we should see the screen shown in Figure 2-9.

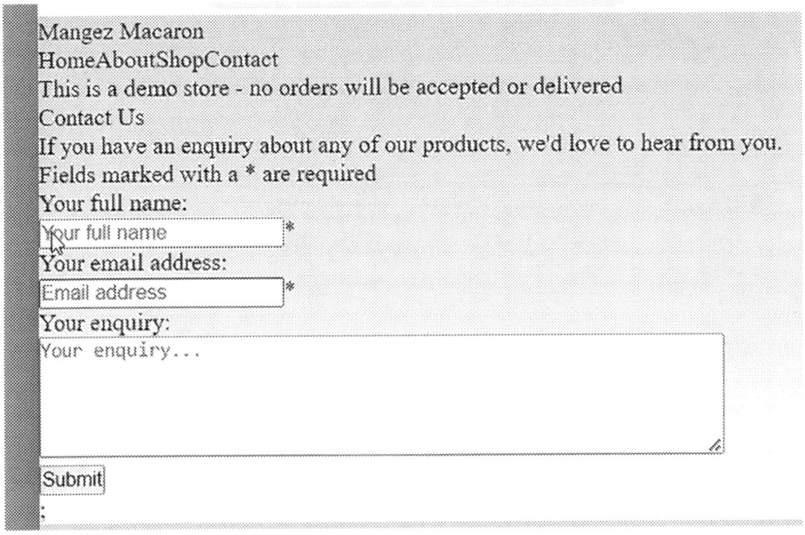

Mangez Macaron
HomeAboutShopContact
This is a demo store - no orders will be accepted or delivered
Contact Us
If you have an enquiry about any of our products, we'd love to hear from you.
Fields marked with a * are required
Your full name:
Your full name   *
Your email address:
Email address   *
Your enquiry:
Your enquiry...

Submit
;

Figure 2-9. *...and contact.js*

We're coming ever closer to having the basic skeleton in place – indeed, there is only one more element we need to add: the footer. We'll come to that in a moment, but let's quickly review the changes we made in the last demo in more detail.

Breaking Apart the Code Changes

Although the pages we added in the last demo are not core to running the site, I still like to add them to give a more realistic feel for the project and to show that it's still possible to have static and dynamic pages at the same time.

In this case, we created the about page from scratch, using the Lorem Ipsum generator to provide us with some dummy text. We put the text inside a placeholder `<div>` element with a class name of `"about-us"` – nothing complicated! As the remaining static pages were very similar (except for `contact.js`), we pulled these from the code download to save time. The exception to this was the `contact.js` page – this one is different as it has a (albeit nonfunctioning) form on it; this contains a standard HTML form with some suitably named fields as a mocked-up contact form.

To finish off the site, we previewed the results in a browser – first, we checked the About page before clicking through to the Contact page to confirm both displayed as expected in the browser. I know the designs aren't pretty, but I promise we will sort that out later in the book!

Adding a Footer

We have almost completed the construction of the skeleton for our site, but there is one more component we need to add – a footer. We've already referenced this in the Layout component but commented it out to allow the site to build for now – let's fix that by adding that component as part of the next demo.

BUILDING THE FOOTER

To create the footer component, follow these steps:

1. First, open a new file, saving it as `Footer.js` in the `\src\components` folder.

2. We have a fair bit of code to add, so we'll do it in blocks – start with adding the imports:

```
import React from "react";
import Link from "next/link";
import PaymentIcons from "../PaymentIcons";
// import MiniCart from "../MiniCart";
```

```
// import { useStateContext } from "../../../context/StateContext";

import { AiFillInstagram, AiOutlineTwitter } from "react-icons/ai";
```

3. Next, leave a blank line, then add the first part of the component:

```
const Footer = () => {
  // const { showCart } = useStateContext();

  return (
    <>
      <div className="footer-container">
        <div className="footer-content">
          <div>
            <Link href="/delivery">Delivery</Link>
            <Link href="/privacy">Privacy</Link>
            <Link href="/terms">Terms and Conditions of Sale</Link>
            <Link href="/contact">Contact Us</Link>
          </div>
          <div>Contact: hello@macaronmagic.com</div>
          {/* <MiniCart /> */}
        </div>
```

4. Go ahead and add the second part of the code to complete our Footer
    component:

```
        <div className="icon-container">
          <PaymentIcons />
          <div className="icons">
            <AiFillInstagram />
            <AiOutlineTwitter />
          </div>
        </div>
      </div>
      <p className="copyright">2022 Macaron Magic All rights
      reserved</p>
    </>
  );
};

export default Footer;
```

5. Save and close the file. We need to add another import, so crack open `Layout.jsx` and add this line below the last import at the top of the file:

```
import DemoBanner from "./DemoBanner";
```

6. Save and close `Layout.jsx`. We have one more to get, which is the Payment icons component – for this, go ahead and download a copy of `PaymentIcons.jsx` from the code download that accompanies this book. Save the file into the `\src\components` folder, along with the other components.

7. Revert to your Node.js terminal, then change the working folder if it is not already set to our project area.

8. At the prompt, enter `npm run dev`, and wait for the development server to fire up. When ready, browse to http://localhost:3000 – if all is well, we first click the About link in the navigation (Figure 2-10).

Figure 2-10. *The newly added footer for our site*

47

Excellent – we now have our skeleton in place! Granted, it won't look particularly pretty, but this chapter (and the next) is about getting the bare bones operational and adding data.

We've done the first part, so pat yourself on the back if you managed to get this far – we still have plenty to do, though! Before we get data into our site, we should take a quick look at the changes we made in the last demo in more detail.

Exploring the Code Changes Made

We began by creating a new component called Footer – into this, we added the requisite imports for React, Next/Link, and the PaymentIcons component we will build later in the demo. At the same time, we added an import for the StateContext component, although it's commented out until we create the file.

For the component itself, we created a container using a `<div>` element, inside of which we added a set of links that point to various pages on our site. We also put references to a fake email address and an instance of the MiniCart component, which we will create in Chapter 4 (but comment out for now).

To finish off the component, we added an instance of the PaymentIcons component, which contains the credit card logos for our site, along with two icons for social media and a copyright statement.

To make sure it all works, though, we needed to extract a copy of the PaymentIcons component from the code download for this book – this contains a set of SVG icons that represent each card type our site would "accept" if it were a real site. We then previewed the result in a browser to confirm all was displaying as it should before styling it later in the book.

Summary

When building a site, we should always consider it a journey and not just a series of tasks; it's a journey that will evolve over time. To show you what I mean, we began that journey back in Chapter 1, where we explored the basic concept behind the site we're developing throughout this book. In this chapter, we started to turn this into a reality. We've covered a lot of code in this chapter, so let's take a moment to review what we have learned.

We began by running through the technical architecture for our site based on what we discussed in Chapter 1. This run-through allowed us to explore the site's architecture in a more practical manner.

Next up, we moved on to updating the main homepage before refactoring the layout used for the site; this included adding site navigation at the same time. We then tweaked the header before beginning to create the additional pages and components required for the site and finishing with adding our footer component.

Phew! We've covered a lot of code – we've already seen that it doesn't look pretty when we run it. We'll fix this in Chapter 4, where we turn this ugly duckling into something more akin to a graceful swan! For now, though, we need to focus on setting up our back-end data source and hooking it into the site – this is where things will start to develop, so stay with me and I will reveal it all in the next chapter.

CHAPTER 3

Adding Products

At this stage, we have a primary site in place, but one key element is missing: data!

Yes, a shop isn't any good without products (i.e., data), so throughout this chapter, we will work through what is required to set up our data and hook it into our shop. We'll look at our options when implementing the checkout and payment process to ensure our data needs are satisfied from the outset.

Before we get into the throes of creating our data store, we must first understand how our data needs to be structured. Let's first take a peek at what fields we need to create in our shop and how they link to what will be in the Stripe checkout that we build in the next chapter.

Architecting the Data

Let's think back to Chapter 1 for a moment, where I said we would be using Sanity for our back-end data – we could have chosen any one of several different options, but I fancied doing something different!

In many cases like this, I suspect people probably choose a back-end system like GraphQL, SWR, or even React–Redux (is that even compatible with Next?). There's nothing wrong with choosing something you know: you're used to working with it while developing your projects and don't always have time to learn something new. But, as we're building a demo and it's more about the *process* and not specifics, GraphQL seems a little overkill.

Instead, I elected to go with a hosted CMS solution so that all we need to do is install a connection to it and provide the data. Sanity fits this bill very well – it works well with Next.js, has an API similar to GraphQL, and doesn't need a full-on configuration to host a little data!

This point brings the subject perfectly into data – what should ours look like? If we think ahead, Stripe only needs three bits of information as a minimum – name, description, and price. These are fields already set available by default in Stripe and look something like this (Figure 3-1) – I've already added some detail.

© Alex Libby 2023
A. Libby, *Practical Next.js for E-Commerce*, https://doi.org/10.1007/978-1-4842-9612-7_3

Details

Name	Spiced Pumpkin	Image	No image
Description	Enjoy the taste of our indulgent Chocolate Orange Macarons. Bursting with 100% natural flavours, our perfectly proportioned treats are handcrafted in our kitchen and beautifully packaged for your enjoyment.		
Created	27 Dec 2022		
Statement descriptor	None		
Feature list	None		

Figure 3-1. *A partial screenshot of data from Stripe*

Okay – so I don't have a picture in there yet, but that can change! Leaving aside the lack of media, it would make sense to replicate the same fields into our Sanity setup and add a few more we will need for our shop. With that in mind, let's look at what this means, with the list shown in Table 3-1.

Table 3-1. *List of fields required for data in Sanity*

Property	Name	Type
Name	Name	string
Image	image	string
Slug	slug	name – maxLength 90
Price	price	number
Details	details	string
SKU	sku	string
Ingredients	ingredients	string
Weight	weight	string
Delivery	delivery	string

The field types look pretty standard – we've got string values for those where we would expect to use alphanumeric characters, with number for the price field. The only oddity is Slug, but this uses the value in the name field and limits it to no more than 90 characters.

We would expect to create these fields manually using the appropriate query, right? In this case, the answer is no – this is where I will flip things on their head! What makes

Sanity so attractive for me is that you can create all of these fields in one go using a JavaScript-based schema file! Intrigued? I will reveal all very shortly, but first – let's pause for a moment to explore an essential point about security when it comes to using an external service to host our data.

Dealing with Security and Authentication Concerns

Over the last few pages, we've discussed using external services, particularly Sanity, for hosting data. The use of these services is coupled with the knowledge that Next.js compiles down to static HTML, and you may recognize some of the key elements of what has now become the Jamstack paradigm!

One of the principles of the Jamstack architectural approach is to decouple the web experience layer from the back-end; this means we can use any provider for the business logic without affecting the overall setup.

Although this makes it easier to swap in and out services, it can make it more complex – we have to bear in mind security and authentication concerns, especially if we're using external services! Exploring this is a whole subject in its own right, but for now, there are a few examples that we should be aware of:

- The data for both products, payment and checkout, will be split between two systems – any financial details are taken by Stripe and not by the project; the only data stored in Sanity is product data, which does not include any personally identifiable information (or PII) relating to specific customers.

- The main concern (if this is as such) is that we will need to use an environment file to host keys for both Sanity and Stripe (which we will cover in the next chapter). While this will store the actual key away from the plain site, there is no real way to secure them in a browser without some additional work. We could use code splitting to break up APIs and keys, then reassemble them during the build process. However, this might be overkill – using environment files is a standard practice, but one where it's not possible to completely hide all traces of environment variables. Alternatively, you might want to consider a package such as secure-env (`www.npmjs.com/package/secure-env`) – this will require a few more lines of code, but this would be an acceptable trade-off.

A word of caution – secure-env has not had any updates in three years, so it is not likely to have kept up with current security standards or be actively maintained. I've included it here as an example of what we could use, but I strongly recommend checking out other options first!

- Sanity.io is hosted on the Google Cloud Platform, which uses some of the best security practices in the industry, so data is very secure.

- You will remember that we could use either email, Google, or GitHub logins – the latter two are not transmitted to Sanity; instead, Sanity gets a token to confirm if access is authorized.

- Any data transmitted to Sanity is done via TLS; all other formats, such as SSLv2 or v3, are disabled by default.

- It's important to note that we always add data for the site locally (in our case, via a laptop or PC), but it could be on an internal server. Any data about our account, such as bandwidth usage or logins, are hosted by Sanity, so they don't get to see the data. Data will be compiled into static HTML files on build, meaning that database connections are removed, making data even more secure.

While security is always something to be mindful of in a Jamstack environment (such as ours), we can see that providers take precautions to ensure that data is protected, and so making use of external services less of a risk.

We should also not forget that sensitive data needs to be secured too – Next makes this straightforward to implement, using any one of several different plug-ins. I'll cover more on authentication in Chapter 12, once we have our site running and can begin to secure the right areas of our site.

Now that we understand the risks of using an external service to host our data, it's time for us to create that data store and add our products! Sanity is written for Node/NPM, so it is pretty straightforward to use. There are a few parts to setting up Sanity, so let's dive in and take a look, beginning with installing the CMS locally.

Getting Started with Sanity

So – where do we start?

Installing and setting up Sanity is a multistep process; there are a few things we have to do. We'll cover all of these step by step, but at a high level, here is a list of what needs to happen:

- Install Sanity.

- Log in and authenticate with Sanity.

- Create a data store (i.e., database) for storing our products.

- Configure the database.

- Add products to the database, ready for use.

Although I will take you through the installation process, we will only be able to touch briefly on how Sanity works; you might do well to look at the documentation on the main website if you want to learn more about the product at a later date!

The main documentation for Sanity is hosted at `www.sanity.io/docs`, or you can access it from the command line (see later in this chapter).

Before we get started, there are a couple of assumptions we need to be aware of which will affect the installation process:

- We'll be working out of a folder called sanity, stored at the root of our project folder.

- You have a working email address you want to use for logging into Sanity. (There are other ways to log into Sanity, but this is probably the easiest.)

There is one crucial point I also need to cover: although we are installing Sanity, this is **only to host data**. Administering our account/Sanity setup is done remotely via the dashboard in our account on the Sanity website. Keep this thought in mind as we install Sanity as part of the next exercise.

Installing Sanity

Installing Sanity is very easy – it's written for Node/NPM, so it will use a reasonably familiar process, at least for those who use Node.js. Everything is done via the command line, so you will need to have installed Node.js and NPM first; assuming you have done so (or already had it installed), let's continue with the setup process.

SETTING UP SANITY AND LOGGING IN

To install Sanity and log in, follow these steps:

1. First, navigate to the project folder, then create a new folder called `sanity` at the project's root.

2. Fire up a Node.js terminal session, then change the working folder to the sanity folder you created in step 1.

3. At the prompt, enter this command, then press Enter:

   ```
   npm i -g @sanity/cli
   ```

4. Once it completes, enter `sanity init` at the prompt and press Enter.

5. You will see a browser window with a prompt to log in or create an account – select the Email/password option, and fill in any details as requested.

You can use a Google email login or a GitHub login as alternatives, depending on what you have available. Any of them are fine – it's not critical which you use, but make sure you remember for future logins!

---

6. Once you have entered the details, press Enter, and you will see it display a message in the browser, saying Login successful.

At this point, **don't** close the window – we will continue shortly.

Perfect – we now have Sanity installed and (almost) ready for us to enter product details! To get to this stage, we followed a straightforward installation process typical to most apps written for NPM; we used the standard npm i (or npm install) command. Once installed, we ran sanity init to create an account and log into the application, which was ready for us to use in the next exercise.

At this point, I asked you to use an email account to log in – I'm guessing you may have seen the other options, such as GitHub or using Google. Any works fine, but I suspect it's more likely you will have a working email address. We haven't set up a GitHub repository for this project (which will come later in the book). If you decide to work with Sanity for future projects, you might want to look at some of the features offered with the Business options that might work better for your needs, such as single sign-on (SSO) logins to your account in Sanity.

Creating Our Data Store

Okay – so we have successfully installed Sanity and logged into our instance; the next step is to create our database and set up the schema. There are a few steps involved, so let's dive in and take a look as part of the next demo.

SETTING UP THE DATABASE

To set up the database for our site, follow these steps:

1. Switch back to the Node.js terminal – you will see Login successful and a prompt to enter Project name. Enter macaron and press Enter.

2. When prompted, if you want to use the Default dataset configuration, enter y or select yes.

3. Sanity will create a dataset – press Enter when you see Project output path (to accept the default entry, which is the current selected folder).

4. Next, use your cursor keys to select Clean project with no predefined schemas, then press Enter.

At this point, you might get prompted for more details – I was prompted for the following, although it might be different for your setup:

1. If you are prompted to choose `Typescript`, then select no. It's not essential for this project; we can add it later.

2. Sanity might ask which package manager you want to use for installing dependencies – go ahead and select npm.

3. At this point, Node will install and resolve any necessary dependencies; you will see a prompt when this is complete.

Once any additional dependencies have been installed (as required), then follow these last two steps to finish the process:

1. Switch to your editor, then open `.gitignore` at the root of your project.

2. Remove the leading slash (or /) from before the word node_modules – we don't want to upload a folder that contains thousands of extra files! Save and close the file.

3. Revert to your terminal session, then at the prompt, enter `sanity manage` and press Enter.

4. If all is well, we should see the following show in your browser window, similar to the one illustrated in Figure 3-2 – this is the Sanity admin dashboard for your site, where I've blocked out the references to my version of the site.

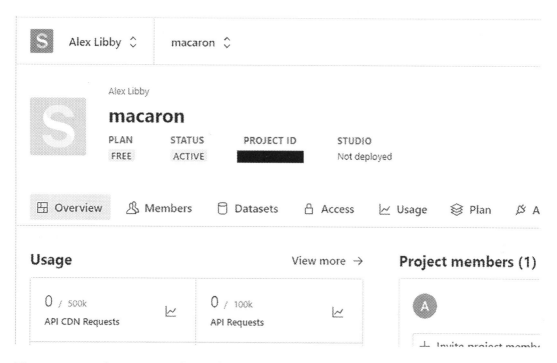

Figure 3-2. *The Sanity admin dashboard*

At this point, take a quick peek at your project folder – you will see a host of files in the sanity folder we created earlier, as shown in Figure 3-3.

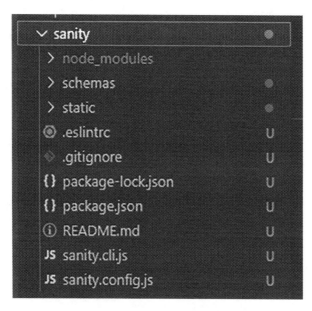

Figure 3-3. *The Sanity installation from our project folder*

We will use this application to enter your site's data in the next exercise. At this point, you can close down the Sanity admin dashboard, as we don't need it for the next demo – keep the Node.js terminal open, though!

If you want to learn more about the various commands and features available in Sanity, enter `sanity docs` at the prompt to display the Sanity documentation.

The database is starting to take shape, although we still have work to do to enter our products! It's at this point that I would point out that we might typically have had to create each field type manually, but this wasn't the case here – setting up Sanity has highlighted a few essential points, so let's review the changes we made in the last demo in more detail.

Exploring the Changes in Detail

We started where we left off from the previous exercise, with Sanity confirming that we had successfully logged into our account and set up.

We then worked our way through a series of steps – the first was entering a project name, then choosing to use the default dataset configuration. We could have decided to go custom at this point, but given this is only a demo, using the default setup is perfectly fine for this project.

Next up, we had a crucial decision to make – the type of project we were creating. Sanity gives a series of options, such as creating an e-commerce site using Shopify. While creating one, we're not using Shopify; we would also miss out on choosing what settings to use, as Sanity would do this for us automatically. This method isn't necessarily always a good thing – it might install extra settings we don't need or make choices that don't work for us. Instead, I elected to go with Clean project with no predefined schemas, so we get a blank project which we tailor to our needs.

Once selected, we were prompted for a few more settings, some of which may differ for you. I had to choose if I wanted TypeScript support or which package manager to use. I decided not to use TypeScript, as there is no real benefit for this project; I also went with npm for the package manager, as this is what we're already using in the demo. With these chosen, Node installed the remaining dependencies for our project before confirming the process was complete.

We then moved on to make one last change before firing up Sanity – depending on the editor you use, you may or may not have noticed that we had made over 10,000 file changes! This isn't true: it's due to the `.gitignore` file not excluding node_modules. We quickly removed the leading slash from the entry in our `.gitignore` file to reduce the file count to more sensible levels. To round off the project, we finished by running sanity manage; this fired up the admin dashboard for our site so we could confirm that the database had been set up correctly for our project.

Okay – let's crack on: we have a database shell set up in Sanity, so we need to configure it with a schema so it knows what types of fields it should have. We mentioned earlier that we might typically have to do this using queries, but in this case, we need to use a different method to achieve the same result.

Configuring the Data Store

For those of you familiar with setting up databases, you (quite rightly) might expect to have to use a CRUD-type query to add fields. Not so with Sanity – instead, we use a JavaScript file to create what resembles a JSON object (except it's in JavaScript code) to create our schema. Let's dive into the following exercise to see how to do this and what it means for us in practice.

CONFIGURING SANITY

To configure Sanity for first-time use, follow these steps:

1. First, fire up a Node.js terminal, then enter sanity dev at prompt and press Enter to start its dev server; if all is well, you should see something akin to this:

   ```
   ✓ Checking configuration files...
   Sanity Studio using vite@4.0.4 ready in 1900ms and running at http://
   localhost:3333/
   ```

2. Go ahead and browse to http://localhost:3333 in your browser – you should see an option to log in, as shown in Figure 3-4.

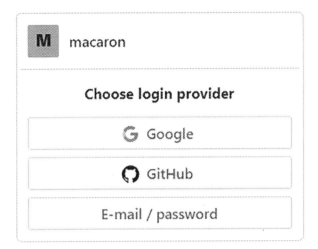

Figure 3-4. *The login window for Sanity Studio*

3. Log in with the details you used from the start of the demo – once you have logged in, you will see a window similar to the one shown in Figure 3-5.

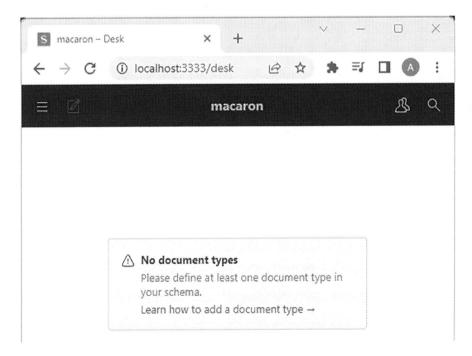

Figure 3-5. *The initial window for Sanity Studio*

Note   I've reduced the window size to make it fit better for print; you might see more options appear if you resize your window for larger resolutions, such as desktop monitors.

4. To fix this issue, we need to make two changes. First, extract a copy of `product.js` from the code download, and drop it into the `\sanity\ schemas` folder.

5. Next, crack open `sanity.config.js` in your editor, then add this line of code below the import for `schemaTypes`:

```
import product from './schemas/product'
```

6. Scroll down until you see the schema entry, then change it as shown (the changes are in bold text):

```
schema: {
  types: schemaTypes.concat([product]),
},
```

7. Save and close this file.

8. If you monitor your terminal session from step 2, you will see the development server reload. If all is well, we should see the Sanity Studio window change to show the initial Content/Product entries, as indicated in Figure 3-6.

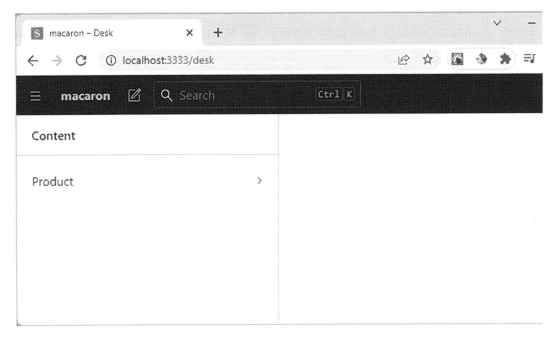

Figure 3-6. *Sanity Studio, with the updated schema changes*

Keep the window open – we're now ready to start adding products to our data source, which we will do in the next exercise.

Yes – we're getting ever closer to having a fully working database! We've not added any products yet (but don't worry, that will come shortly); we do at least have a working schema in place. We've covered some important points about creating databases in Sanity, so let's pause for a moment to review the changes we've just made, in greater detail.

Breaking Apart the Code Changes

We began with starting up the development server for Sanity – note that this is not the same as the one we use for front-end development, hence the different port address being used. Once we browsed to the URL, we were invited to log in – this had to be with the same details we used in the earlier demo.

Once logged in, it confirmed that no document types existed, and we needed to create a schema. To do this, we extracted a copy of the `product.js` file from within the code download – this creates the schema within Sanity, once we restarted the server.

To tie the schema in and get our site to recognize it, we made two changes to the `sanity.config.js` file – one to import the schema file and the other to change the `schemaTypes` entry to include the schema. As the final step, we rebooted the Sanity server and confirmed that it now showed an empty database, ready for us to enter products for our site.

Adding Products to the Store

Perfect – we've set up Sanity, so now have a database ready for adding products!

Unfortunately this is one of those tedious jobs that has to be done – in our case, it's one we have to do as we're building what is effectively a proof of concept (or demo, depending on how you would want to call it). We only need to add a handful of products, so it won't take too long; if we were working with lots of products, then we would need to investigate better ways of importing them in, depending on how they are sourced.

That all aside, Sanity makes it easy enough to add the products – I've kept some of the text the same throughout, so you can copy and paste entries, or even duplicate existing records and amend for new products. Let's take a look at how to do this in more detail, as part of the next exercise.

ADDING PRODUCTS

To add products to our data store, follow these steps:

1. First, go ahead and fire up a Node.js terminal (or switch to it if you already have one open).

2. Change the working directory to the sanity folder, then at the prompt, type `npm run dev` and press Enter.

3. Sanity will fire up the database editor server; when prompted, browse to http://localhost:3333 to start editing. If all is well, you should be presented with the screen shown in Figure 3-7, which shows the editor ready for use, and the Product database selected.

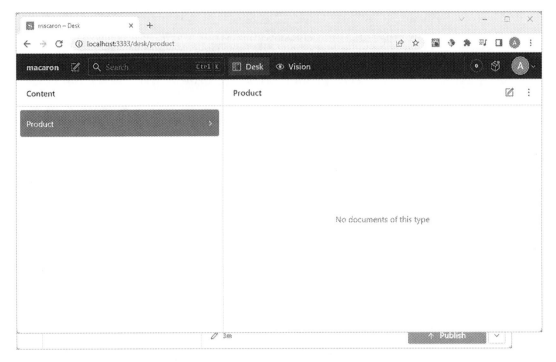

Figure 3-7. *The Sanity database editor, ready for adding new products*

4. To start adding products, click the Edit symbol to the right (it's an icon of a white square with pen on it).

5. This will display a prompt to add a new product – go ahead and add the details in Table 3-2.

Table 3-2. *Values for the first product*

Label	Value
Image	*All images are available in the code download.*
Name	Quince Cobnut – per box of 12
Slug	*Hit the Generate button to auto-generate the slug based on the Name field.*
Price	18.5
Details	Enjoy the taste of our indulgent Chocolate Orange Macarons. Bursting with 100% natural flavors, our perfectly proportioned treats are handcrafted in our kitchen and beautifully packaged for your enjoyment.
SKU	MACM001
Weight	300g
Delivery	We carefully package our macarons and use Royal Mail to post them to you under first-class postage. We do not ship to international addresses outside of the United Kingdom.

6. In addition, you will see an Ingredients field present – for this, use the text in the `ingredients.txt` file in the accompanying code download for this book.

7. Once you've added the entries, hit Publish at the bottom – Sanity automatically saves entries as you type, so this just makes each entry available for display.

8. A toast notification "The document was published" will appear and disappear – this confirms that the entry is no longer a draft and has been published.

9. Repeat steps 4 to 8 for the remaining five products, using the product spreadsheet available in the code download.

10. Once done, you can close the Sanity database editor window.

Hopefully that wasn't too painful an exercise – it's one of those jobs that has to be done, but depending on your team's size, it might not be you doing it!

In terms of the steps we took, there probably isn't anything of real note, except to say that entries are saved automatically, so that all we need to do is to publish each one once we have added the details.

You will likely have noticed a British slant in terms of some of the details, such as posting or ingredients; this is purely because I come from the United Kingdom, so it's what I know! Please feel free to amend for your country: the exact wording isn't critical as this is a demo, but it does need to comply with the field types that we set up earlier in this chapter.

Hooking Sanity into Our Project

Perfect – we now have our data sources in place, one for products and the other... well, for products! Okay, when I mean products, I'm really referring to what we need in Stripe to identify products in orders, but hey, I digress.

We've now reached a key stage, where we have to hook the Sanity data source into our project – this is so we can display products directly from our database. This is something we will do over the next few exercises – in a nutshell, the first part will be to connect Sanity into our site, then part two will cover the code and steps required to display products in our shop.

Let's make a start with hooking the Sanity database into our project, so the shop is aware of its existence.

HOOK SANITY INTO PROJECT

To hook Sanity into our project, follow these steps:

1. First, we need to create a new folder at the root of our project – call this folder `lib`.

2. Inside of this folder, create a new file called `client.js`, and add this code:

```js
import sanityClient from "@sanity/client";
import imageUrlBuilder from "@sanity/image-url";

export const client = sanityClient({
  projectId: <ENTER PROJECTID HERE>
  dataset: <ENTER DATASET VALUE HERE>,
  apiVersion: "2022-11-27",
  useCdn: true,
  token: process.env.NEXT_PUBLIC_SANITY_TOKEN,
});

const builder = imageUrlBuilder(client);

export const urlFor = (source) => builder.image(source);
```

3. You will see in the code from the previous step that we need to add an ID and dataset value. To do this, first fire up Sanity Manager, by switching to a Node.js terminal, then changing the working folder to the sanity one. At the prompt, enter sanity manage and press Enter.

4. When the Sanity Manager window is displayed, look on the Overview tab for Project ID.

5. Switch to the Datasets tab – the name of our dataset is in the column marked Title (there will only be one name, and it's likely to be called production!).

6. Now we have this information, we need to update the `client.js` file we created earlier – go ahead and open this, then replace the placeholders with your own values, and save then close the file.

7. Next, we need to generate a token so that our site can talk to the Sanity database. For this, click the API tab, then Tokens.

8. Click Add API Token on the right, then in the Name field, enter BookProject.

9. Choose Editor as access, then hit Save.

This next step is important – on the next screen you will see a copy of the token. You must save it somewhere safe, as you will **not** get to see this again. If you lose it, you will need to re-create it!

We have one more step, which is to add this new token into our site. To do this:

10. Fire up your editor, then create a new file called .env at the root of your project folder.

11. In the file, enter this line, where <XXXXX> is the token you created in steps 7-9:

```
NEXT_PUBLIC_SANITY_TOKEN = <XXXXX>
```

Save and close the file.

12. Next, go to the index.js file in the \pages folder, and uncomment the // from the `import {client} from "../lib/client"` statement.

13. Save all files open and close them.

We've now reached as far as we can go for the moment – we will test this connection in the next exercise, when we start to look at generating queries from our data store in Sanity.

In the meantime, we've covered some useful steps in the last demo that you will likely need to reuse if you create more database-driven sources using this app; let's take a moment to consider in more detail the changes we made as part of the previous exercise.

Exploring the Code Changes

One of the great things about Next.js is that it is perfectly happy to accept data from different sources; this might be anything from markdown files through to full-on WordPress databases! In our case, we've used a third-party provider to host our data, which aligns perfectly with Jamstack principles. We've separated data and the presentation layers, so if (heaven forbid) Sanity should be unavailable, it will not completely bring down our site.

To achieve this, we first added a client.js file to our setup – this creates a connection from our site to the Sanity database. This contains details of our project ID and the dataset to use, along with the `apiVersion` and project token. At the same time, we tell Sanity to use the `imageUrlBuilder` function, so it can generate the correct links for our site.

Next up, we then collected a couple of bits of information, to replace the placeholder values left in step two. This included the `projectID`, name of the dataset, as well as generating the token for our site. We then updated the `client.js` file, so that it would connect correctly. To round things off, we created an `.env` file to house the token generated from the Sanity database, before saving and closing any files left open at the end of the demo.

Creating Pages with Dynamic Data

Ladies and gentlemen...it is time...

I can't lay claim to knowing who uttered that phrase, but the sentiment is true – it is time for us to start making our site more dynamic!

So far, we've focused on creating what effectively are static pages – granted, they don't look pretty, but that's something we'll change later in this book. We should start by fetching data from our newly installed back-end CMS source and displaying it on the page.

To do this, we need to start getting familiar with Sanity's query language, GROQ, which stands for Graph-Relational Object Queries. It's relatively easy to pick up as query languages go; before we get stuck into using it on our site, let's run through a quick crash course on how to use it.

Getting Familiar with Sanity API

GROQ. What the heck is GROQ, I hear you ask?

No – it's not some alcoholic drink that dates back from the seafaring days of the early 16th century (`https://en.wikipedia.org/wiki/Grog`, to see what I mean), but Sanity's language for querying its database system.

At first, it might look a little weird or even unnatural, but it is easier to understand than it might seem! Let's take one of the examples we will be using later in this book:

```
const query = '*[_type == "product"]';
const products = await client.fetch(query);
```

The key to all of this is the star symbol at the start – this means, "go get me everything – I don't care what it is!" Okay, I might have been a little blunt about phrasing that, but yes, the star signifies everything.

However, if we didn't want everything, we would use a qualifier which we encapsulate in square brackets. In our example, we're saying, "get everything in the database, but only if it has a property of `_title` that says 'product'." We could easily have said something like this:

```
'*[_type == "product" && name != "Quince Cobnut - per box of 12"]'
```

In this instance, we've asked Sanity to return everything as before, but this time only if it has a `_type` of `product` and does **not** have a name of `"Quince Cobnut - per box of 12"`. We'd get back five products out of our original six in the database.

We could take this a lot further, as GROQ is a powerful language – for now, though, our site will focus on retrieving entries from the database for display in our shop. There are lots more we could do, such as retrieving the amount of available stock, updating it to reflect when items customers have bought, and so on. I'll return to this later in the book when we look at a few ideas for developing our shop.

If you would like to see more examples of the types of queries that GROQ can use, look at the Sanity cheat sheet at `www.sanity.io/docs/query-cheat-sheet`.

For now, though, let's turn our attention to using GROQ to get products from the database and show them in our store.

Displaying Product Listing in the Shop

Okay – we have the database in place, along with our products. The next stage is to make our site dynamic; we need to fetch those products from Sanity and display them in the site pages.

This is a four-part process, which we will do over two exercises; we first need to build the starting shop page, before creating the component that will display the products. Creating the initial product listing page is relatively straightforward, but things turn a little more complex when it comes to displaying individual products! We'll come to this shortly, but let's first begin with displaying the main shop page.

BUILDING THE SHOP PAGE

To create the shop page for our site, follow these steps:

1. First, crack open your text editor, and create a new file – save this as shop.js in the \src\pages folder.

2. Go ahead and add the following code – we'll do this in sections, starting with the three imports:

```
import React from "react";
import { client } from "../../lib/client";

import { Product } from "../components";
```

3. Next, leave a line blank, then add this block – it's the opening half of our Shop page component:

```
const Shop = ({ products }) => (
  <div>
    <div className="products-heading">
```

```
    <h2>Shop</h2>
    <p>Browse for products</p>
  </div>
```

4. Immediately below that code, add the following lines – this will complete the first part of our component:

```
  <div className="products-container">
    {products?.map((product) => (
      <Product key={product._id} product={product} />
    ))}
  </div>
  </div>
  );
```

5. For the component to work as expected, the next block is where the magic happens – this is the query we need to retrieve the products from our database. Skip a line, then add this block:

```
export const getServerSideProps = async ({ req, res }) => {
  const query = '*[_type == "product"]';
  const products = await client.fetch(query);

  res.setHeader(
    "Cache-Control",
    "public, s-maxage=10, stale-while-revalidate=59"
  );

  return {
    props: { products },
  };
};

export default Shop;
```

6. Save the file and close it.

I would normally ask you to try displaying the updated page in a browser, but as you will notice from the code, it will fail: we're missing at least component, for this to work properly! To fix that, we'll put together the code in the next demo, but for now, let's take a moment to review the code so we can understand how it all hangs together in more detail.

Breaking Apart the Code

Our shop won't be complete without a shop window – in the last demo, we started the process of constructing it, by creating a component to display our products. Ordinarily I'd work through the changes we made from top to bottom, but let's skip ahead and explore the getServerSideProps command first. There's a reason why, which I will come to shortly:

This particular command does as it says on the tin – it runs server-side (and never client) – and will return any data that must be fetched at request time. While we could get that data when we first run the site, it wouldn't make sense: we only use the data on the shop page, and we might not visit the shop in that session! Using the getServerSideProps command at this point will return the data in JSON format automatically, as long as we define the function, it's up to us to handle how the data is rendered onscreen.

The interesting part though comes when we explore the query we used inside of getServerSideProps. I've redrawn it here for convenience – Figure 3-8 shows an expanded format, with annotations to show what each part does in the query.

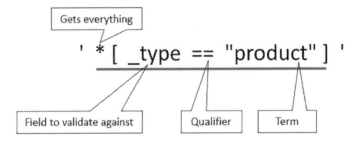

Figure 3-8. *An expanded version of the GROQ query*

At first glance, this might look like Double Dutch to some, but if we break it apart, I promise it will make sense! The critical point to note is that we made the call to getServerSideProps asynchronous to suspend execution until we have the data back from Sanity and can assign it to the query variable.

Take a closer look at the query – notice how it starts with a * symbol? Here, we are asking Sanity to "get everything"; we add a qualifier in square brackets to say "...where type (a system tag) equals "product" or the name of our database grouping". If you cast your mind back to when we added products – you will see that the word Product is highlighted in Figure 3-8; we're targeting everything in this group. The irony is that we could have just used * and not added the qualifier, as we're getting everything in the database anyway!

If we had another grouping, such as Banner, we'd need this qualifier, and we would write queries targeting that other group using something like this: `*[_type=="banner"]`.

Once we had retrieved the products using `client.fetch` (from the client.js file we added earlier), and we assigned them to a `products` variable, which we return in the props property, so they are available for use throughout the site.

With the query in place, we can add the markup to display our products. The first half of the markup contained a title and an introductory phrase at the head of the page. We then used a standard React map function to iterate through the products array returned from the query before displaying each onscreen through the Product component.

You will notice at this point that we've not yet created that Product component – don't worry, that comes next! It is also why I've not asked you to run the development server, as it will throw an error – this will be due to the missing Product component. Adding it is easy enough to do, so let's move on and create the component that will display each product on that page.

In the main, this will be pretty straightforward – most of it is just markup, with some formatting for displaying text correctly on the page. However, we should be aware of one key element – we need to use a slug. No, I'm not talking about some gross, slimy-encrusted creature, but a placeholder for each product we want to display. Let me explain what I mean – you'll soon see why this is beneficial!

Creating the Individual Product Page

Imagine a shop with half-a-dozen products, each with its product description page. If we have to make a change, it's a bit of a pain in the neck – we have to potentially do it six times, depending on the nature of the change. I'm sure you'll agree this isn't the best use of our time!

Here's where slug pages come in – for the uninitiated, we create a template that renders all of the information for that product as if it were its own hard-coded page instead of using individual pages.

That's the important part – we're not creating individual pages but one page to cover all products. It means that if we have to make any changes, we only make them once; it applies to all affected products simultaneously. Creating this page does require more work, but this is a small price to pay – let me show you what I mean as part of the next exercise.

CREATING THE PRODUCT COMPONENT

To create our product component, follow these steps:

1. First, open a new text file, saving it as `Product.jsx` in the `\src\` `components` folder.

2. We have a few lines of code to add, so as usual, we'll do it in blocks – go ahead and add the first, which takes care of some imports for our component:

```
import React from "react";
import Link from "next/link";

import { urlFor } from "../../lib/client";
```

3. Next, leave a line blank, then add the opening half of our component:

```
const Product = ({ product: { image, name, slug, price } }) => {
  return (
    <div>
      <Link href={`/product/${slug.current}`}>
        <div className="product-card">
          <img
            src={urlFor(image && image[0])}
            width={250}
            height={250}
            className="product-image"
          />
```

4. Immediately below the closing tag from the previous step, add the closing half of the component:

```
            <p className="product-name">{name}</p>
            <p className="product-price">
              $
              {price.toLocaleString("en-US", {
                maximumFractionDigits: 2,
                minimumFractionDigits: 2,
```

```
            })}
          </p>
        </div>
      </Link>
    </div>
  );
};
```

```
export default Product;
```

5. Save and close the file.

6. We need to make one last change, which is to add an export to the component index – go ahead and open the `index.js` file in the `\components` folder, and add this line at the bottom:

```
export { default as Product } from "./Product";
```

7. We should be able to preview the results – for this, switch to a Node.js terminal, then make sure the working folder is the project folder.

8. At the prompt, enter `npm run dev` and press Enter to start the Next.js development server.

9. Browse to http://localhost:3000/shop – if all is well, we should see the products listed, as shown in Figure 3-9.

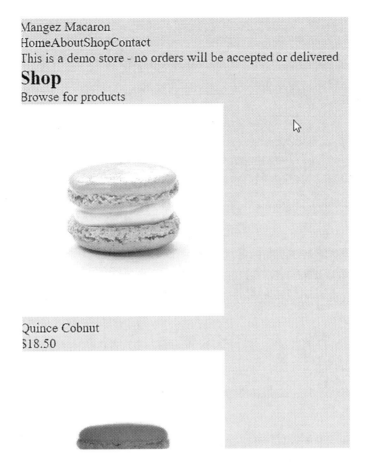

Figure 3-9. Extract of products on display in the shop

Excellent – we now have the basis for our shop! Granted, if we were to click individual products, it would result in an error: we'll fix that very shortly. The critical point here is that we can now display products from the back-end database in our shop. Before we get onto creating the template for displaying individual products, let's pause for a moment to review the code changes we've just made in more detail.

Understanding What Has Changed

One of the more useful features of Next.js is its ability to create slug, or template, pages, which we can reuse as many times as we want – in our case, to produce product pages. It is a multistage process though; we covered the first part in the previous demo, where we set up the query to get our products, before calling the Product component for each one in a loop.

In this demo we've just created, we used that information to display the product image, its name, slug, and price as a component. Most of the code in this component is fairly self-explanatory, where we display an image and associated text using placeholders, before wrapping all of it in one of Next's Link components that uses the slug value to create a link to what will be the product's individual product page.

There is however one useful feature I want to call out – if you look at the line starting const Product =.... you might be wondering what we're doing here. This is Next's way of destructuring properties passed into it as part of calling the component. So, in this instance, we extract image, name, slug, and price from the product object. As with React, this only works if we call each property with the same name – if we wanted to use different names, we'd have to do it a different way!

Okay – let's crack on: we've set up the main shop and can display a product card with appropriate details. We've mentioned that this is the interim step before we display the product's information page – it's time we set up that last step. Although we'll need more code to achieve this, you will see some similarities between it and the code we've just created. To see what I mean, let's dive in and take a look at how we can display product details effectively, using a product page template.

As I mentioned earlier, we won't go down the route of creating pages for each component, but instead use a special feature from Next.js – dynamic routing. This allows us to create a single template, but wrap the file name in square brackets, so we get something like [slug].js. Yes, I know it looks a little unnatural, but it works!

It means we can build something I've nicknamed the slug page, as we use the slug created at the beginning of the chapter for each product to identify, retrieve, and display that product's details on the page. Sounds complicated? There is a good chunk of code required to do it, so let's go through what we need to do as part of the next exercise.

```
┌─────────────────────────────────────────────────────────────────────┐
│                        CREATING THE SLUG PAGE                         │
└─────────────────────────────────────────────────────────────────────┘
```

To create the slug page, follow these steps:

1. First, open a new file in your editor, then save it as [slug].js in a folder called product, which needs to sit under the \pages folder.

2. We have a lot of code to work through, so as in previous examples, we'll go through it block by block, starting with the imports:

```
import React, { useState } from "react";
import {
  AiOutlineMinus,
  AiOutlinePlus,
  AiFillStar,
  AiOutlineStar,
} from "react-icons/ai";

import { client, urlFor } from "../../lib/client";
import { Product } from "../../components";
```

3. Next, miss a line, then add this code – this takes care of the opening lines of our component, as well as defines some constants:

```
const ProductDetails = ({ product, products }) => {
  const { image, name, details, price, sku, ingredients, weight,
  delivery } =
    product;
  const [index, setIndex] = useState(0);
```

4. Next, leave a line blank, then add this as the first half of the return block for our component:

```
return (
  <div>
    <div className="product-detail-container">
      <div>
        <div className="image-container">
          <img
            src={urlFor(image && image[index])}
```

```
        className="product-detail-image"
      />
    </div>
```

5. This next block looks after the array of thumbnail images that sit below the main image:

```
        <div className="small-images-container">
          {image?.map((item, i) => (
            <img
              key={i}
              src={urlFor(item)}
              className={
                i === index ? "small-image selected-image" :
                "small-image"
              }
              onMouseEnter={() => setIndex(i)}
            />
          ))}
        </div>
      </div>
```

6. This next large block looks after the rendering of product details onscreen:

```
        <div className="product-detail-desc">
          <h1>{name}</h1>
          <div className="reviews">
            <div>
              <AiFillStar />
              <AiFillStar />
              <AiFillStar />
              <AiFillStar />
              <AiOutlineStar />
            </div>
            <p>(20)</p>
          </div>
          <h4>Details: </h4>
          <p>{details}</p>
          <p className="price">
```

```
                ${price.toLocaleString("en-US", {
                  maximumFractionDigits: 2,
                  minimumFractionDigits: 2,
                })}
              </p>
              per box of 12
              <div className="quantity">
                <h3>Quantity:</h3>
                <p className="quantity-desc">
                  <span className="minus">
                    <AiOutlineMinus />
                  </span>
                  <span className="num">1</span>
                  <span className="plus">
                    <AiOutlinePlus />
                  </span>
                </p>
              </div>
              <div className="sku">SKU: {sku}</div>
            </div>
          </div>
```

7. The last part displays a "You may like" carousel, along with closing tags for the markup:

```
        <div className="maylike-products-wrapper">
          <h2>You may also like</h2>
          <div className="marquee">
            <div className="maylike-products-container track">
              {products.map((item) => (
                <Product key={item._id} product={item} />
              ))}
            </div>
          </div>
        </div>
      );
    };
```

8. None of the above is of any use to us, without knowing the details of which
    product we want to get! To do this, we place a call to Sanity, this time using the
    slug to identify our chosen product and return static URLs' for each product page:

```
export const getStaticPaths = async () => {
  const query = `*[_type == "product"] {
    slug {
      current
    }
  }
  `;

  const products = await client.fetch(query);

  const paths = products.map((product) => ({
    params: {
      slug: product.slug.current,
    },
  }));

  return {
    paths,
    fallback: "blocking",
  };
};

export const getStaticProps = async ({ params: { slug } }) => {
  const query = `*[_type == "product" && slug.current ==
  '${slug}'][0]`;
  const productsQuery = '*[_type == "product"]';

  const product = await client.fetch(query);
  const products = await client.fetch(productsQuery);

  return {
    props: { products, product },
  };
};

export default ProductDetails;
```

9. Go ahead and save the file, then close it.

10. Switch to a Node.js terminal session, then make sure the working folder is set to our project area.

11. At the prompt, enter npm run dev and hit Enter – this will start the Next.js development server.

12. When prompted, browse to http://localhost:3000/shop, and click any one of the products. If all is well, we should see something akin to the example shown in Figure 3-10, if we scroll down the page (and using the Cranberry Clementine macaron as an example).

Cranberry Clementine
★★★★☆
(20)
Details:
Enjoy the taste of our indulgent Chocolate Orange Macaron:
$18.50
per box of 12
Quantity:
−1+
SKU: MACM003
You may also like

Figure 3-10. Example of an individual product page

Well done if you managed to get this far – I know the site doesn't look that spectacular, but we will change it later in the book! We've covered some important points in the last demo, particularly around fetching data, so let's take a moment to review the changes we made, before continuing with the next task.

Exploring the Changes Made

Although we're only adding one instance of this component, the Product page (or [slug].js) is probably one of the most complex in the entire site! A lot of it is marked up with placeholders, but there is also some GROQ code to call our products.

We started with adding a bunch of imports – most are for icons we use on the page, from the react-icons package; we also import two functions from client.js, along with the Product component we've already built.

The next few blocks consist largely of markup with placeholders for our data values – we first pass in product and products, before destructuring the individual values, such as image, name, and details. At the same time, we set up a state value for index, which we use to create the small image row below the main image. We then display the data in predefined markup, all the way down as far as rendering the SKU value onscreen. It's a lot of markup, but needs must!

To round off the markup, we then insert the "You may like…" carousel – this displays all of our products in a marquee format, using the Product component we created in the previous demo.

Adding the markup is only part of the story though – to bring it all together, we had to add two GROQ queries, plus a function to map the results into something we can use in our page. The first query calls getStaticPaths, which creates basic paths for all entities of type product, using the slug property as a filter (and only displaying current entries). This returns a paths object, which we use in getStaticProps to create static pages based on the slug values we retrieved from the first query. These are returned as instances of Products and product, which we use to render the pages onscreen from our site.

There is however still more to do before we can start to prettify the site; let's start with adding a tabs entry, to display some missing information for our site.

Adding Additional Product Details

Any time you look at product pages, you will frequently find some form of additional information given – it all depends on the type of product, but it might typically be in tab format, as this is a great space saver. Ours will be no different – the information I have in mind to display will be ingredients, weight, and delivery method.

There is no point in creating anything from scratch as a tab component, as there are plenty available already online! With that in mind, I've elected to use react-tabs (available from `www.npmjs.com/package/react-tabs`), as the basis for the last demo of this chapter.

CREATING THE TABS

To add the information tabs, follow these steps:

1. First, open a new Node.js terminal, then make sure the working folder is set to our project area.

2. At the prompt, enter `npm install react-tabs --save` and press Enter to install the react-tabs component.

3. Once done, open a new file in your editor, then save it as `Info.jsx` in the `\components` folder.

4. Inside the file, we have a nice hunk of code to add, so we'll start with the imports:

```
import React from "react";
import { Tab, Tabs, TabList, TabPanel } from "react-tabs";
```

5. Next, miss a line, then add the opening tag for our Tabs component, followed by what will be the tab headers:

```
const Info = ({ ingredients, weight, delivery }) => (
  <Tabs>
    <TabList>
      <Tab>Description</Tab>
      <Tab>Additional Information</Tab>
    </TabList>
```

6. Immediately below that step, add this code – this takes care of the tab panels:

```
<TabPanel>
  <h2>Ingredients</h2>
  <p>{ingredients}</p>
</TabPanel>
<TabPanel>
  <h2>Additional Information</h2>
  <table className="additional-info">
    <tbody>
      <tr>
        <th>Weight:</th>
        <td>{weight}</td>
      </tr>
      <tr>
        <th>Delivery:</th>
        <td>
          <p>{delivery}</p>
        </td>
      </tr>
    </tbody>
  </table>
</TabPanel>
```

7. We'll close out the component, then add the usual export at the end:

```
  </Tabs>
);

export default Info;
```

8. Save the file, then close it. We need to add a reference for this component in the component index file – open index.js from the \components folder, then add this line at the bottom:

```
export { default as Info } from "./Info";
```

9. Save and close this file. With the Info component now in place, we need to call it – go ahead and open the [slug].js file from the previous exercise, then add this import before the line starting const ProductDetails...:

```
import { Info } from "../../components";
```

10.   Scroll down to this line: `<div className= "maylike-products-wrapper">`, then add this call:

```
<Info ingredients={ingredients} weight={weight} delivery={delivery} />
```

11.   Switch to a Node.js terminal session, then make sure the working folder is set to our project area.

12.   At the prompt, enter `npm run dev` and hit Enter – this will start the Next.js development server.

13.   When prompted, browse to http://localhost:3000/shop, and click any one of the products. If all is well, we should see something akin to the example shown in Figure 3-11, if we scroll down the page (and using the Cranberry Clementine macaron as an example).

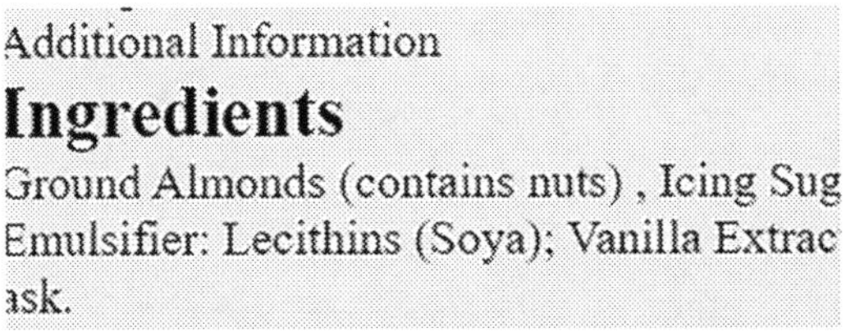

Figure 3-11. *An extract of the Additional Information tabs on the product page*

I have to admit that in its current unstyled state, you might have struggled to see any change in the overall, once we ran it! The change is definitely there, but hidden somewhere around the middle of the page. This will of course change once we style the page, but for now, let's quickly cover off the changes we made in the last demo in more detail.

Breaking Apart the Code

Although this demo did require a few steps, most of the work required is straightforward – much of it depends on the type of tabs component we chose to use at the beginning of this demo. I picked one which is relatively lightweight, as we're only creating a small demo – others are available, so it's worth making sure that we explore options if we wanted to scale up the code.

Leaving that all aside for the moment, we began by first installing the `react-tabs` component. We mentioned before the exercise that there was little point in trying to create something from scratch, as there are plenty of components available online – it makes better sense to use one of them!

Once done, we then set up our component – we started with adding the imports, before laying out the markup for the component. We then finished it off by adding an import into the barrel import file (the index file in the components folder), before calling it in from the `[slug].js` file. To finish it off, we ran up the site in our browser and checked to make sure that the tabs were displaying correctly on the site.

Summary

We've now reached an important milestone – we've created the basic code for our site and are now ready to add one of the key elements, which is the checkout process! Over the last few pages, we've covered a lot of code, with plenty of useful tips and features; let's take a moment to review what we have learned.

We started way back when (it does seem a long time ago!), by working through the architecture for our site, before exploring any security concerns we might have with using third-party systems. Next up, we then installed Sanity and worked through the steps required to configure it for use in our site.

We then moved on to adding products into our data store, before hooking the Sanity setup into our site and updating the pages to display details from the newly created data store. For the remainder of the chapter, we then created the shop page, along with the product card, followed by the product details pages. It means that we can now display products in the shop and set them so that customers can click on individual links to display more details in their browser.

We're not done though with creating our site – there is still plenty more to cover! Although we can display products, we need a means to select and pay for them – without it, our site won't be any good! For this, we need to add a checkout process and add a payment processor; stay with me, and I'll take you through all the details in the next chapter.

CHAPTER 4

Checkout and Order Processing

In the previous chapter, we worked on building our basket – no e-commerce site is any good without some means to pay for our products! It's time for us to add in a checkout and payment process – the question is, what will that look like?

Several different providers are available, so for this chapter, we will look at some of the options available before implementing a suitable solution for our shop. We have a lot to cover, so let's crack on – the first task is to take a quick look at how the process of checking out will work in more detail.

Breaking Apart the Process

For any checkout process, customers will follow a set list of steps – this will differ if we host the payment provider process or use a hosted service from our provider.

In our case, I've elected to use Stripe, as it is an easy tool to implement, even if we have to run through a fair few steps, as you will no doubt see later in this chapter! Each customer who completes the checkout process on our site will have to follow these steps:

- When customers are ready to complete their purchase, your application creates a new Checkout Session.

- The Checkout Session provides a URL that redirects customers to a Stripe-hosted payment page.

- Customers enter their payment details on the payment page and complete the transaction.

- After the transaction, a webhook fulfills the order using the `checkout.session.completed` event.

© Alex Libby 2023
A. Libby, *Practical Next.js for E-Commerce*, https://doi.org/10.1007/978-1-4842-9612-7_4

It looks pretty straightforward, but it is a high-level view though – there are more steps involved. To show you what I mean, I've included a PDF that reproduces a more detailed set of steps to show the different touch points we have to go through each time a customer purchases from our site – as you will see, there is a bit more to it than the four steps listed just now!

I've included a more detailed diagram of the process in a PDF in the code download for this book – it's called `Checkout process.pdf`.

The critical point to note is that the process I've outlined is specific to Stripe – other providers will operate similar methods, albeit with their API methods and functions.

Suppose I had not decided to go with Stripe and used a different provider. In that case, I could have chosen any one of dozens of other companies – including those based solely in my country, such as PaySimple (`www.paysimple.com`), or ones with a more global reach, such as Shopify. You may already have one you've used before, which suits your needs; if not, then here are a handful to get you started:

- Shopify: `www.shopify.com`

- PayPal: `www.paypal.com/`

- AmazonPay: `https://pay.amazon.co.uk/`

- GooglePay: `https://pay.google.com/about/`

- Square: `www.squareup.com`

- Adyen: `www.adyen.com/`

Of course, these are available for use in my home country – this may not be the case for you. Choosing a provider, if you don't already have one, will require lots of research – it's also important to remember that if you're working for a client, they may already have selected one. That means choosing one may be a moot point, but since selecting providers is a minefield anyway, that's probably no bad thing!

Dealing with Security

We've talked about which provider we will be using, but there is one supercritical topic that I am sure will be on top of any developer's list: security.

Security is a vast topic – so big that to really make a dent in it would be outside of the scope of this book. However, I want to bring up one part: using Stripe. As it is an external service, it's essential it does not present a security risk and compromise our site.

Fortunately, Stripe takes security extremely seriously – they use best-in-class tools and practices to maintain security, which has helped them to achieve PCI Service Provider Level 1 status (the highest level available in the payments industry). Some of these practices include the following:

- Using 3D Secure authentication for online payments within the EEC, as required by the Strong Customer Authentication regulations.

- HTTPS is enabled throughout, using TLS – this includes the account dashboard. Nothing is served by HTTP, and your browser console will even flag a warning about not using HTTPS during development!

- Libraries, including `Stripe.js`, are only served via TLS and use TLS certificates to verify each connection.

- Encryption uses AES-256, with keys held on servers in a separate hosting environment. The infrastructure used for encrypting, storing, or decrypting card numbers is held on separate systems from the primary services and does not share any credentials.

These are just a few of the practices Stripe use – it's safe to say that we shouldn't have any problem with security, at least in terms of using their payment solution! Of course, we still need to be mindful that this is a small part of the whole security piece we will need to implement, but that falls outside of the scope of this book.

Finishing the Buttons

Okay – enough of the theory: it's time we added some code! We have a fair bit to add, but there is one set of code changes we must complete first:

Hopefully, you will remember from the last chapter that we didn't add the Buy Now or Add to Cart buttons on the product page – there was a reason for not doing so. Adding them would require a lengthy context component; we had already made many changes, and it seemed sensible to get to a point where the site could load and display the products without issue. It seemed more practical to deal with the context piece in this chapter, as it ties in nicely with Stripe; we will do both later in this chapter.

Before we can do that, though, we need to add some missing code that will use the context – let's take a look at what we need to do in more detail.

FINISHING THE BUTTONS

To finish the product page, follow these steps:

1. First, crack open [slug].js from within the \pages\product folder, then add this line immediately after the imports at the top of the file:

```
import { useStateContext } from "../../../context/StateContext";
```

2. Next, look for the line beginning with this: const [index, setIndex...]; immediately after this line, go ahead and add this statement:

```
const { decQty, incQty, qty, onAdd, setShowCart } = useStateContext();
```

3. Leave a line blank, then add this function – this will take care of any clicks on the Buy Now button that we will add shortly:

```
const handleBuyNow = () => {
  onAdd(product, qty);
  setShowCart(true);
};
```

4. With these definitions in place, we can add some extra markup to help select the quantity we want to add to our basket. First, look for this line of code: <h3>Quantity:</h3>.

5. Once you've found it, amend the next nine lines of code, so they look like this (changes in bold):

```
<p className="quantity-desc">
  <span className="minus" onClick={decQty}>
    <AiOutlineMinus />
  </span>
  <span className="num">{qty}</span>
  <span className="plus" onClick={incQty}>
    <AiOutlinePlus />
  </span>
</p>
```

6. We have one more feature to add: the Add to Cart and Buy Now buttons. Scroll down until you find this line of code:

    ```
    <div className="sku">SKU: {sku}</div>
    ```

7. Next, add this block of code immediately after it:

    ```
    <div className="buttons">
      <button
        type="button"
        className="add-to-cart"
        onClick={() => onAdd(product, qty)}
      >
        Add to Cart
      </button>
      <button type="button" className="buy-now"
      onClick={handleBuyNow}>
        Buy Now
      </button>
    </div>
    ```

8. Save and close the files for now.

You will see from that last demo that I've deliberately not asked you to run up the demo in a browser. Don't worry, there's a good reason for not viewing the site just yet.

Although we have added the relevant buttons to allow us to add products to our basket, it will still fail – our basket doesn't exist yet! To do that, we need to add that missing state context for the site I mentioned at the start of this section. It will require adding a somewhat lengthy component which we will do shortly, but before we do that, let's review the changes we made to add the cart buttons to our site in more detail.

Understanding the Changes Made

It might seem odd to have to do more work to finish off something from a previous chapter, but without it, the site won't run – instead, you'll get an error message flagged and very little to show for it in the browser! We must make sure the site is as prepared as it can be, ready for when we add the code that creates the basket and allows customers to check out and pay for their goods.

Fortunately, the work we had to do was minimal – we first had to add a call to a new component, `StateContext`, which we will add later in the chapter. We then had to destructure a set of variables (`decQty`, `incQty`, etc.) from this component, ready for use first by a new `handleBuyNow` function (which adds products and shows the cart), followed by markup for two buttons to add or remove products from the basket.

To finish it off, we added two buttons, "Add to Cart" and "Buy Now" – these won't fully work just yet, as we have to configure state context throughout the site first! However, we now have everything in place – this means we can now add the component we need to help persist data throughout the site.

Okay – let's crack on: although we now have the majority of our markup in place, there is one key element we now need to add. We've touched on it briefly already; I'm referring to state context. This isn't a visual change, but one that will maintain data in the background throughout the site. It's best to think of it as a large storage bucket: if you put something to the basket, you can then reference those values elsewhere in the site. Implementing this is quite a meaty change, so without further ado, let's crack on and add it to our site.

Persisting Data Through the Process

Now that we have the relevant buttons in place, we need to focus on adding a critical component – context.

This is critical as it will manage various counts for us – this includes the total number of products we select, the total price, the number of different products we have in the basket – and whether we want to add or remove any! As a result, we have a lot of code to cover, so let's dive in and take a look as part of the next exercise.

Note   This is a large component, so don't worry about writing it out by hand: all of the code is available in the download for this book.

ADDING CONTEXT TO OUR SITE

To add the context component, follow these steps:

1. First, create a new folder called `context` – this should be at the root of the project folder.

2. Next, crack open a new file in your editor, then save it as `StateContext.js` in the folder we created in step 1.

3. We need to add a sizeable chunk of code to create this component. As before, we'll do it in sections, beginning with two imports:

```
import React, { createContext, useContext, useState, useEffect } from
"react";
import { toast } from "react-hot-toast";
```

4. Next, leave a line blank, then add a `const` to declare `Context`, the opening tag for our component, and more constant declarations:

```
const Context = createContext();

export const StateContext = ({ children }) => {
  const [showCart, setShowCart] = useState(false);
  const [cartItems, setCartItems] = useState([]);
  const [totalPrice, setTotalPrice] = useState(0);
  const [totalQuantities, setTotalQuantities] = useState(0);
  const [qty, setQty] = useState(1);

  let foundProduct;
  let index;
```

5. The next function is onAdd – this takes care of adding products. We check to make sure the product exists; if it does, we adjust the count and totals or add it as a new product:

```
const onAdd = (product, quantity) => {
  const checkProductInCart = cartItems.find(
    (item) => item._id === product._id
  );
```

```
setTotalPrice(
  (prevTotalPrice) => prevTotalPrice + product.price * quantity
);
setTotalQuantities((prevTotalQuantities) => prevTotalQuantities +
quantity);

if (checkProductInCart) {
  const updatedCartItems = cartItems.map((cartProduct) => {
    if (cartProduct._id === product._id)
      return {
        ...cartProduct,
        quantity: cartProduct.quantity + quantity,
      };
  });

  setCartItems(updatedCartItems);
} else {
  product.quantity = quantity;

  setCartItems([...cartItems, { ...product }]);
}

toast.success(`${qty} ${product.name} added to the cart.`);
};
```

6. We can't have an onAdd event handler without its opposite number – this is onRemove, which takes care of removing products from the basket and adjusting totals accordingly:

```
const onRemove = (product) => {
  foundProduct = cartItems.find((item) => item._id === product._id);
  const newCartItems = cartItems.filter((item) => item._id !==
  product._id);

  setTotalPrice(
    (prevTotalPrice) =>
      prevTotalPrice - foundProduct.price * foundProduct.quantity
  );
  setTotalQuantities(
    (prevTotalQuantities) => prevTotalQuantities - foundProduct.
    quantity
```

```
  );
  setCartItems(newCartItems);
};
```

7. We need to add `toggleCartItemQuantity` next – this will take care of adjusting quantities (and values) of items already in the cart:

```
const toggleCartItemQuantity = (id, value) => {
  foundProduct = cartItems.find((item) => item._id === id);
  index = cartItems.findIndex((product) => product._id === id);
  const newCartItems = cartItems.filter((item) => item._id !== id);

  if (value === "inc") {
    setCartItems([
      ...newCartItems,
      { ...foundProduct, quantity: foundProduct.quantity + 1 },
    ]);
    setTotalPrice((prevTotalPrice) => prevTotalPrice +
    foundProduct.price);
    setTotalQuantities((prevTotalQuantities) =>
    prevTotalQuantities + 1);
  } else if (value === "dec") {
    if (foundProduct.quantity > 1) {
      setCartItems([
        ...newCartItems,
        { ...foundProduct, quantity: foundProduct.quantity - 1 },
      ]);
      setTotalPrice((prevTotalPrice) => prevTotalPrice -
      foundProduct.price);
      setTotalQuantities((prevTotalQuantities) =>
      prevTotalQuantities - 1);
    }
  }
};
```

8. We're almost done – the last two functions are helper functions to increase or decrease quantities, which we use elsewhere in this component:

```
const incQty = () => {
  setQty((prevQty) => prevQty + 1);
};
```

```
    const decQty = () => {
      setQty((prevQty) => {
        if (prevQty - 1 < 1) return 1;

        return prevQty - 1;
      });
    };
```

9. To finish this lengthy component, we need to add the return block that passes all of these functions into our `Context.Provider`:

```
    return (
      <Context.Provider
        value={{
          showCart,
          setShowCart,
          cartItems,
          totalPrice,
          totalQuantities,
          qty,
          incQty,
          decQty,
          onAdd,
          toggleCartItemQuantity,
          onRemove,
          setCartItems,
          setTotalPrice,
          setTotalQuantities,
        }}
      >
        {children}
      </Context.Provider>
    );
  };

  export const useStateContext = () => useContext(Context);
```

10. Go ahead and save this file, then close it – the changes for this file are complete.

    With the Context component set up, we now need to call it at the appropriate points on our site.

11. Go ahead and open the file `Footer.jsx` from the `\src\components` folder –
     add this line of code below the last import statement at the top of the file:

     ```
     import { useStateContext } from "../../../context/StateContext";
     ```

12. Move down a few lines, then add this const declaration immediately after the
     opening tag of our component:

     ```
     const Footer = () => {
       const { showCart } = useStateContext();
     ```

13. Save and close the file. Next, open `NavBar.jsx` from the same folder and add
     this import statement below the last of the import declarations at the top of
     the file:

     ```
     import { useStateContext } from "../../context/StateContext";
     ```

14. Immediately after the opening tag for the component, add this line, so it looks
     like this:

     ```
     const NavBar = () => {
       const { showCart, setShowCart, totalQuantities } =
       useStateContext();
     ```

15. After the closing `</button>` tag, modify the call to `<Cart />`:

     ```
     {showCart && <Cart />}
     ```

16. Save and close this file. We have one more file to update, which is `_app.js` –
     open this file, and add this declaration in the same way:

     ```
     import { StateContext } from "../../context/StateContext";
     ```

17. Just a few lines down, we need to add calls to the `StateContext`
     component – insert the highlighted lines as shown in the following code:

     ```
     <StateContext>
       <Layout>
         <Toaster />
         <Component {...pageProps} />;
       </Layout>
     </StateContext>
     ```

18.   Save and close the file.

19.   Fire up a Node.js terminal – make sure the working folder is set to our project folder.

20.   At the prompt, type npm run dev, then press Enter. Browse to http://localhost:3000/shop, click the product image, and scroll to below the second image. If all is well, we should see something akin to this extract if we click the Add to Cart button a few times (Figure 4-1).

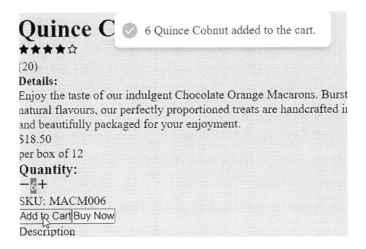

Figure 4-1. *Notification of products added to the basket*

Phew – we've covered a lot of content in this last demo; that is for sure! Context is a critical part of the site, though: without it, we can't pass values around efficiently and would have to pass a lot more as props which will get messy. The Context component contains many valuable examples of how we can manage values, so let's take a moment to review the code in more detail before moving on to adding our carts.

Exploring What Happened

I must confess that this last demo was probably one of the largest so far in this book – it covers a lot of content, with touchpoints throughout the site. We made some significant changes, so let's take a moment to review them in more detail.

We began by creating the core Context component – after the usual imports, we set several constants, most of which were based around state. We then added an `onAdd` event function – this determines if the product exists; if it does, we up the count or add it as a new product to our basket. We perform something similar with the `onRemove` function, but this removes the product.

At the same time, we created a `toggleCartItemQuantity` function – this takes care of finding the selected item; if it exists in the basket, and we passed `inc` as a value, we increase the `foundProduct.quantity` property by 1 (which effectively updates the item in the basket). If we passed `dec` as a value instead (to decrease the selected quantity), we would reduce `foundProduct.quantity` by 1.

Next up, we added a couple of helper functions – these do something very similar, but the key difference here is that we trigger them from the add or subtract buttons from the product page.

Moving on, we inserted references to the Context component from various places throughout the site, such as in the Footer and NavBar components, before saving the changes and previewing the results in our browser. At this stage, we won't see the items in the basket just yet; we had to set up the Context as a necessary dependency before seeing the products added to the cart. As you can see, this required a lot of changes – a necessary evil, but needs must!

Okay – let's move on: this brings us nicely into the part I know you've all been waiting for, which is the cart itself. Adding the cart is where things get interesting, as we're going to add not one but two carts – it might seem a little odd, but I will explain why very shortly.

Constructing the Cart

Hold on – *you said "carts." Surely sites only have one cart, right?*

This is indeed correct, but in our case, we have two cart components, one as the main cart and a second as a minicart – at least for now. They are largely identical, so there is an opportunity to improve on this – for now, though, let's get them installed and working as part of the next demo.

As this demo is quite large, we'll do it as a two-part exercise – the first part will be to construct the main cart component. We'll tie it into the site in part two of this exercise later in this chapter.

ADDING THE MAIN CART – PART 1: THE COMPONENT

To set up the main cart, follow these steps:

1. First, crack open a new file in your editor, saving it as `Cart.jsx` in the `\src\ components` folder.

2. We have a lot of code to add, so as before, we will add it in sections – let's start with the imports:

```
import React, { useRef } from "react";
import Link from "next/link";
import {
  AiOutlineMinus,
  AiOutlinePlus,
  AiOutlineLeft,
  AiOutlineShopping,
} from "react-icons/ai";
import { TiDeleteOutline } from "react-icons/ti";
import toast from "react-hot-toast";

import { useStateContext } from "../../context/StateContext";
import { urlFor } from "../../lib/client";
```

3. Next, we need to add a set of `const` declarations – one of these will be as an object, while the others we will deconstruct from `StateContext`:

```
const Cart = () => {
  const cartRef = useRef();
  const {
    totalPrice,
    totalQuantities,
    cartItems,
    setShowCart,
    toggleCartItemQuantity,
    onRemove,
  } = useStateContext();

  const eUSLocale = (x) => {
    return x.toLocaleString("en-US", {
      maximumFractionDigits: 2,
```

```
      minimumFractionDigits: 2,
    });
  };
```

4. The next section is key – this is the core of the component. Leave a line blank after the previous section, then add the following lines:

```
return (
  <div className="cart-wrapper" ref={cartRef}>
    <div className="cart-container">
      <button
        type="button"
        className="cart-heading"
        onClick={() => setShowCart(false)}
      >
        <AiOutlineLeft />
        <span className="heading">Your Cart</span>
        <span className="cart-num-items">({totalQuantities}
        items)</span>
      </button>
```

5. This next block takes care of displaying an appropriate notice if the cart is empty:

```
{cartItems.length < 1 && (
  <div className="empty-cart">
    <AiOutlineShopping size={150} />
    <h3>Your shopping bag is empty</h3>
    <Link href="/">
      <button
        type="button"
        onClick={() => setShowCart(false)}
        className="btn"
      >
        Continue Shopping
      </button>
    </Link>
  </div>
)}
```

6. The first half of this next, somewhat lengthy block looks after displaying chosen products in the basket, along with a thumbnail image:

```
<div className="product-container">
  {cartItems.length >= 1 &&
    cartItems.map((item) => (
      <>
        <div className="product" key={item._id}>
          <button
            type="button"
            className="remove-item"
            onClick={() => onRemove(item)}
          >
            <TiDeleteOutline />
          </button>
          <img
            src={urlFor(item?.image[0])}
            className="cart-product-image"
          />
          <div className="item-desc">
            <div>
              <span>{item.name}</span>
              <span>
                {item.quantity} @ ${eUSLocale(item.price)}
              </span>
            </div>
```

7. We'll finish off that block with this code, which contains the buttons for increasing or decreasing quantities in the basket:

```
<p className="quantity-desc">
  <span
    className="minus"
    onClick={() => toggleCartItemQuantity(item._
    id, "dec")}
  >
    <AiOutlineMinus />
  </span>
  <span
```

```
                    className="plus"
                    onClick={() => toggleCartItemQuantity(item._
                    id, "inc")}
                >
                    <AiOutlinePlus />
                </span>
              </p>
            </div>
          </div>
        </>
      ))}
    </div>
```

8. Next, add this last block immediately below the code from the previous step – this will display the total price, provided the cart has one or more items in it, and add the finishing tags for our component:

```
        {cartItems.length >= 1 && (
          <div className="cart-bottom">
            <div className="total">
              <h3>Subtotal:</h3>
              <h3>${eUSLocale(totalPrice)}</h3>
            </div>
          </div>
        )}
      </div>
    </div>
  );
};

export default Cart;
```

9. Save and close the file.

Excellent – that's the main cart component done! It, of course, won't be any good unless we can reference it on our site; we will do that as the second part of this demo. Go grab a drink, pause for a moment to catch your breath, and when you're ready to continue, let's take a look at what we need to do.

ADDING THE MAIN CART – PART 2: REFERENCING THE COMPONENT

To tie the cart component to our site, follow these steps:

1. With the cart component created, we now need to add a reference to the component index file, making it easier to call when needed. Open the `index.js` file from the `\src\components` folder, then add this line at the bottom of the list:

    ```
    export { default as Cart } from "./Cart";
    ```

2. We have two changes to make in one more file – save the component index file, then close it; when that's done, go ahead and open `NavBar.jsx` in your editor.

3. First, add an import to the Cart component to the bottom of the list of imports:

    ```
    import { Cart } from "./";
    ```

4. Next, just after the opening tag for our component, go ahead and add this line, as highlighted:

    ```
    const NavBar = () => {
      const { showCart, setShowCart, totalQuantities } =
      useStateContext();
    ```

5. Scroll down the page until you see this line:

    ```
    <Link href="/contact">Contact</Link>
    ```

6. Immediately below it, go ahead and add this block:

    ```
                    <button
                      type="button"
                      className="cart-icon"
                      onClick={() => setShowCart(true)}
                    >
                      <AiOutlineShopping />
                      <span className="cart-item-qty">{totalQuantities}</span>
                    </button>
                    {showCart && <Cart />
    ```

7. Save and close any files you have open in your editor.

8. Switch to a Node.js terminal session, then make sure the working folder points to our project area. At the prompt, enter npm run dev and press Enter, then browse to a product: I've chosen http://localhost:3000/product/quince-cobnut as my example. Click the Add to Cart button toward the bottom of the page – if all is well, we should see the quantity change to a 1 against the Contact link, as shown in Figure 4-2.

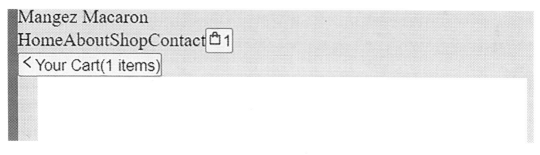

Figure 4-2. The updated quantity indicator from our basket

9. Click the 1 shown in Figure 4-2, and we will see this view – this shows our item has been added to the basket, along with the quantity and subtotal values displayed (Figure 4-3 and Figure 4-4).

Mangez Macaron
HomeAboutShopContact 🛍1
‹ Your Cart(1 items)

Figure 4-3. The updated basket view, showing the top half…

⊗
Quince Cobnut1 @ $18.50
— +
Subtotal:
$18.50

Figure 4-4. The bottom half of the updated cart, with the product details

If you scroll down that page, you might wonder why we see two more product images that look the same. Don't worry – this is intentional: this will change when we style the page in Chapter 5. The view seems odd, as we will show the cart as a slide-in panel over the top of the main image (second in the list) and what will be a thumbnail image (third image in the list).

Phew – that might have been a long demo, but nevertheless an important one! We can see the site starting to act as it should – of course, we still have to add a checkout method, but we can at least add products to the cart. We've covered a lot of useful tips and code in both demos, so let's take a moment to explore the code changes from both demos in more detail.

Breaking Apart the Code Changes

Adding the cart to our site is an important step forward – we already have the product pages working, but seeing products added and ready for checkout is a sure sign we are getting closer to completion!

To get us there, we created our cart component as `Cart.jsx` – this was a lengthy component, but this is necessary, owing to the number of functions it does throughout the site. We began with a series of imports for components such as the five icons, react-hot-toast, and of course, React itself. We followed this by creating a series of constants, destructured from StateContext, before starting to build the markup for our component.

The markup (and JavaScript) splits roughly into two parts – the first part takes care of whether `cartItems.length` returns less than 1; if it does, we can assume that there are no products in the cart, so show an appropriate message. If this is not the case, though (and `cartItems.length` is equal to or greater than 1), we know we have at least one item. We can then iterate through them before rendering details onscreen and provide an option to increase or decrease the quantity required at the same time.

We then round out the first part of this lengthy demo by displaying the total cost onscreen – this we format to US locale, but this is easy to change to accommodate different countries. Most importantly, though, we only display this total cost if the cart has items in it!

After a quick break, we first added a reference to it from the component index file before linking to it in the NavBar component. This is so the site knows when to show or hide the cart, based on what is set in the showCart constant. We then finished by running through a quick test – we added a product, then checked to ensure that both the count was updated and displayed the new product in the basket on our site.

Okay – let's move on: we've added the first of the two carts, so we now at least have somewhere customers can put their chosen products. I did say that we would be adding two carts, though, so let's go ahead and add that second cart in the upcoming demo.

Adding a Minicart

Remember how, a few pages ago, I said we would have not one but two carts in our demo?

Many sites only work with one cart – there's nothing technically wrong with this approach, but you must keep checking the cart page to see what you've ordered. This checking isn't always a good thing – customers are time-poor and (dare I say it) often lazy; the more we can do to simplify their experience, the better!

One of the ways we can help is to show a minicart in the footer – it might not have all of the details and options of its bigger brother, but it will at least indicate the number of items selected, along with a running total. There are some disadvantages to this approach which I will cover later, but for now, let's have a look at what we can do to implement something as a starting point for our customers.

DEMO – ADDING THE MINICART

To add the minicart component to our site, follow these steps:

1. First, crack open a new file in your editor, saving it as MiniCart.jsx in the \src\components folder.

2. We have a lot of code to add, so as before, we will add it in sections – let's start with the imports:

```
import React from "react";
import { AiOutlineShopping } from "react-icons/ai";
import toast from "react-hot-toast";
```

```
import { useStateContext } from "../context/StateContext";
import { urlFor } from "../../lib/client";
import getStripe from "../../lib/getStripe";
```

3. Next up, leave a line blank, then add the opening tag to our component, along with some destructured constants:

```
const Cart = () => {
  const { totalPrice, totalQuantities, cartItems } =
  useStateContext();
```

4. This next part will take care of showing a default message and image if the cart is empty:

```
return (
  <div className="mini-cart-container">
    <span className="heading">
      Your Cart contains {totalQuantities} item
      {totalQuantities > 1 || totalQuantities === 0 ? "s" : ""}
    </span>

    {cartItems.length < 1 && (
      <div className="empty-cart">
        <AiOutlineShopping size={150} />
        <p>Your shopping bag is empty</p>
      </div>
    )}
```

5. For any products we add, we need to display their details – that's handled by this longer block of code:

```
<div className="product-container">
  {cartItems.length >= 1 &&
    cartItems.map((item) => (
      <div className="product" key={item._id}>
        <span>
          <img src={urlFor(item?.image[0])} className="mini-
          cart-image" />
        </span>
        <span className="item-desc">
          <span>{item.name}</span>
```

112

```
            <span className="totals">
              <span>{item.quantity}</span>
              <span className="multiply">x</span>
              <span>
                $
                {item.price.toLocaleString("en-US", {
                  maximumFractionDigits: 2,
                  minimumFractionDigits: 2,
                })}
              </span>
            </span>
          </span>
        </div>
      ))}
    </div>
```

6. For the last part of this component, we need to display a subtotal value formatted to two decimal places. This is taken care of by this block of code:

```
    {cartItems.length >= 1 && (
      <div className="mini-cart-bottom">
        <div className="total">
          <h3>
            Subtotal: $
            {totalPrice.toLocaleString("en-US", {
              maximumFractionDigits: 2,
              minimumFractionDigits: 2,
            })}
          </h3>
        </div>
      </div>
    )}
  </div>
  );
};

export default Cart;
```

7. Save and close the file. We need to make one more change, which is to the footer –
    crack open `Footer.jsx` from the `\src\components` folder, then add this import:

    ```
    import MiniCart from "./MiniCart";
    ```

8. Scroll down the page a little until you see the list of Link entries, followed by a
    closing `</div>` tag.

9. Immediately after that closing `</div>` tag, modify the code so it looks like this:

    ```
            <Link href="/contact">Contact Us</Link>
        </div>
        <div>Contact: hello@macaronmagic.com</div>
        <MiniCart />
    </div>
    ```

10. Save and close any files you have open in your editor. Switch to a Node.js
    terminal session, then make sure the working folder points to our project area.
    At the prompt, enter `npm run dev` and press Enter, then browse to a product:
    I've chosen http://localhost:3000/product/quince-cobnut as my example.

11. Notice first how we have an empty basket showing in what will be the footer
    (Figure 4-5).

Figure 4-5. *The empty minicart*

12. Click the Add to Cart button a little further up the page – if all is well, we should
    see the basket change to show the details listed in Figure 4-6, where it shows
    a partial image alongside the selected quantity.

Figure 4-6. *The updated minicart, showing a (partial) image and quantity*

13. Below the image, we can see that the description and subtotal values have been added (Figure 4-7).

Subtotal: $18.50

Quince Cobnut1x$18.50

Figure 4-7. *The subtotal and description of our selected product*

Perfect – we now have a cart in place, so our shop is pretty much working as it should! Okay, it's true that we can't get customers to pay for products, at least not just yet; we'll change that momentarily. For now, though, let's review the code changes we've made in more detail and discuss why our minicart may not be the best approach for our site.

Exploring the Code Changes

Although we added the second cart in the last demo, one might be forgiven for feeling a sense of déjà vu – they would be correct: much of the minicart code is identical to the original! It was intentional, though, as this is just a demo – it made better sense to take an MVP approach to get something working before iterating on and fine-tuning the final version.

That said, it still serves as a helpful reminder of the changes we made for our component – we started with a set of imports similar to those we used in the main-cart component. Next up, in much the same way as we did before, we added markup that displays a message to say the cart is if `cartItems.length` is less than 1. Otherwise, it shows each item, quantities, totals, and a count of how many items we have. We then added a call to this component from the Footer component; for now (as in other instances), we only display the markup, but we will soon style it to something more aesthetically pleasing.

115

To round off our demo, we navigated to a product of our choosing (I chose the Quince Cobnut macaron, but any would have worked) before checking that the basket was empty. We then proved that the cart worked by adding an instance of the macaron to our basket, after which it displayed our chosen product in the minicart on our site.

Onward we go – you might have noticed something about this cart, in addition to that sense of déjà vu, I mentioned just now. It looks like our minicart component has a bit of an identity crisis: I've called it MiniCart here and in the code, but the name is just Cart! It's something we should rectify (even if only for clarity), but – is that the only thing we can do here?

Refactoring the Cart

When writing code, I'm a great believer in the MVP, or minimum viable product, approach – we focus on the basics first, then come back to finesse the code using an iterative process. It means we can get more out quickly: it may not look perfect, to begin with, but we can push code out that works and identify or exclude features that may need adapting if they won't work as expected.

For this next part, I've tried to use this approach to see what we could refactor for the two carts, as both use very similar code. However, all is not plain sailing – while they use identical code in places, it wasn't as easy as I expected! I'll go through the details in a moment, but let's first see what I could do as an initial pass in the next demo.

REFACTORING THE CART CODE

To implement the changes, follow these steps:

1. First, crack open MiniCart.jsx, then copy these lines:

```
const eUSLocale = (x) => {
  return x.toLocaleString("en-US", {
    maximumFractionDigits: 2,
    minimumFractionDigits: 2,
  });
};
```

2. Next, open the `utils.js` file from within the `\lib` folder, and scroll to the bottom. On a new line, add the word export, then paste in the copied lines – you should have this:

```
export const eUSLocale = (x) => {
  return x.toLocaleString("en-US", {
    maximumFractionDigits: 2,
    minimumFractionDigits: 2,
  });
};
```

3. Save the file and close it.

4. We need to adapt the carts to use this new function – in `MiniCart.jsx`, replace any instance of this code:

```
${item.price.toLocaleString("en-US", {
  maximumFractionDigits: 2,
  minimumFractionDigits: 2,
})}
```

… with this:

```
${eUSLocale(totalPrice)}
```

5. Change the markup around this function to `<span>` for the first instance, then `<h3>` for the second.

6. Repeat steps 4 and 5 for `Cart.jsx`, but this time replace the markup around each instance with `<span>`.

Note I've included the updated code in the code download, so you can see what it should look like if you get stuck!

---

7. Next, create a new folder called Cart in the `\src\components` folder. Inside this folder, create a new file called `EmptyCart.jsx`.

8. Go ahead and add these lines to that file, then save and close it:

```
import React from "react";
import { AiOutlineShopping } from "react-icons/ai";

const EmptyCart = ({ children }) => {
  return (
    <div className="empty-cart">
      <AiOutlineShopping size={150} />
      <p>Your shopping bag is empty</p>
      {children}
    </div>
  );
};

export default EmptyCart;
```

9. Open the index.js file in the \src\components folder, then add this reference:

```
export { default as EmptyCart } from "./Cart/EmptyCart";
```

10. Revert to the Minicart component, then look for this line:

```
{cartItems.length < 1 && (
```

11. Adapt the block to this:

```
        {cartItems.length < 1 && (
          <EmptyCart>
            <Link href="/shop">
              <button type="button" className="btn">
                Go to Shop
              </button>
            </Link>
          </EmptyCart>
        )}
```

12. We need to do something similar for Cart.jsx, so open that file and change that block to this:

```
        {cartItems.length < 1 && (
          <EmptyCart>
```

```
<Link href="/">
  <button
    type="button"
    onClick={() => setShowCart(false)}
    className="btn"
  >
    Continue Shopping
  </button>
</Link>
</EmptyCart>
)}
```

13.   Save and close the files. Fire up a Node.js terminal – make sure the working folder is set to our project folder.

14.   At the prompt, type npm run dev, then press Enter. Browse to http://localhost:3000/shop, click the product image, and click on it. Click Add to Cart – if all is well, we should see the 0 by the basket icon in the NavBar change to a 1. A quick check at the bottom of the page should show a product in the basket in the footer.

Oops – sorry: another long demo! In my defense, though, I would say the changes are improvements to the original code and should give you a flavor of what we could do in future iterations.

These kinds of updates are less around *what we change* but more the process of *why and how* we do it. With that in mind, let's take a moment to review the changes we made and talk a little about some of the pitfalls we might see when using a cart of this design on our site.

Breaking Apart the Code Changes

Refactoring code can be a double-edged sword – it can open up lots of opportunities but equally prove to cause more problems later if we find something isn't as refactorable as we would like! As it so happens, that was the case here – despite some of the similarities of the code, it wasn't as easy to refactor as first thought. Before we get into that, let's quickly go through the changes I was able to make in the last demo.

We kicked off by creating a new eUSLocale function in the utils file to replace the existing one used in MiniCart, but not yet introduced to Cart. The function was a direct copy in the main, but we had to add the export tag to it so we could call it from both components. Once in the utils.js file, we then updated references to it from both cart components while at the same time altering the markup – the latter being a step closer to making the markup the same in both cases (where possible).

We then moved on to creating a new EmptyCart component to replace the markup used in both files – this wasn't a large change, but it will help reduce the duplicate markup in both components. We copied over the markup into this file, then added a {children} tag, and referenced it from both components. The {children} tag is essential, as while the markup is the same in both carts, they each have different child components which need to sit inside the parent tags from the EmptyCart component. We then rounded out the demo by running a quick check to ensure that if we added a product to the cart, the correct details still appear in both cases.

Okay – let's crack on: this refactoring has highlighted a few things we should explore in a little more detail, particularly as they will affect how we refactor more code in this demo. Let's take a look at these in more detail.

Making More Changes: A Postscript

When making the changes in the last demo, a few questions came to mind: how we might refactor the code or whether we should change elements in our site.

We should probably have picked up some of these sooner in the design process, so it's important to be aware of that; sometimes, you may not find things out until much later! With that in mind, here are the questions I think we should ask:

- The code around the plus or minus buttons is similar but not used elsewhere; should we refactor it, given that it might reduce some code but only be used in this file?

- I tried moving the handleCheckout function into a separate file, but this caused all sorts of problems, particularly around using the react-hot-toast component. Can we still move it, or do we need to change to using a different notification before we can hive it off into a separate file?

- Although the code in both cart components is very similar, the designs are different; could we change to using one for both the footer and main cart, or will this use too much space in the footer? Could we adapt the design to only show the bare minimum in the footer (such as the number of products and running total)? This would reduce the size of the minicart component and potentially make it easier to use the main cart component but show or hide elements as appropriate.

- We could refactor the end blocks that show the totals, as they are both very similar in each cart component – can we handle the handleCheckout function, even though this caused problems elsewhere (see next point)?

These are just a small selection of the questions that came to mind – I am sure you will find more! The key here, though, is to keep challenging the status quo: make the site as efficient as possible, but at the same time maintain a balance between what you want to do against what is sensible to do within the timeframes you have and the resources available at your disposal.

Integrating a Payment Provider

We've almost reached the end of the initial build process – this is where things get critical: it's money time!

Yes, we've created a shopping cart where customers can add products, but we have no means for people to check out and pay for those products. It's time we fixed that by tying in our chosen payment provider – I've elected to use Stripe, but as we mentioned earlier, we could use any as long as they fit our requirements.

Let's look at what we need to hook in Stripe as our payment provider in more detail.

HOOKING IN THE PAYMENT PROVIDER – PART 1: INITIAL CONFIGURATION

To configure our site for use with Stripe, follow these steps:

1. The first step is to get two keys from Stripe – log into your Stripe account at `https://dashboard.stripe.com/login`, then click Developers to the right.

2. Click the API Keys in the left menu – you will see a section marked Standard Keys.

3. In this section, you need to take a copy of the keys under the Token section – both are long strings of random characters, and for one, you will need to click the Reveal secret key to view it. Keep these safe – you will need these in the next step.

Tip   Once you see the keys, clicking them will send them to your clipboard automatically, so there is no need to try to highlight them!

---

4. Next, create a new file at the root of your project called `.env` (note the spelling). In this file, add two lines – please insert the relevant key as shown:

    ```
    NEXT_PUBLIC_STRIPE_PUBLISHABLE_KEY = <enter your PUBLISHABLE key
    value here>

    NEXT_PUBLIC_STRIPE_SECRET_KEY = <enter your SECRET key value here>
    ```

5. Save and close the file. Open a new file in your editor, then add this code – this takes care of telling your project about how to initiate Stripe:

    ```
    import { loadStripe } from "@stripe/stripe-js";

    let stripePromise;

    const getStripe = () => {
      if (!stripePromise) {
        stripePromise = loadStripe(process.env.NEXT_PUBLIC_STRIPE_
        PUBLISHABLE_KEY);
      }
    ```

```
    return stripePromise;
};

export default getStripe;
```

6. Save this project as getStripe.js in the \lib folder in the project area.

7. We have one more file to add, stripe.js – for this, go ahead and extract this from the code download that accompanies this book and save it into the \src\pages\api folder.

8. Save and close this file – the initial changes are complete.

This last demo might not have been a very long one, but it's vital to getting Stripe configured on our site and ready for us to use in the appropriate places. With that code now in place, we can move on to adding calls to Stripe in various places around the site so that people can begin to check out and pay for goods once we release the site into production.

HOOKING IN THE PAYMENT PROVIDER – PART 2: ADDING STRIPE

We have a few changes to add to both the Cart and MiniCart components – to make those changes, follow these steps:

1. The first change is in Cart.jsx – go ahead and open that file in your editor, then add these two imports at the end of the imports at the top of the file:

    ```
    import getStripe from "../../lib/getStripe";
    import toast from "react-hot-toast";
    ```

2. Next, scroll down the page to just after the eUSLocale function, then leave a line blank and add this function:

    ```
    const handleCheckout = async () => {
      const response = await fetch("/api/stripe", {
        method: "POST",
          headers: {
            "Content-Type": "application/json",
          },
          body: JSON.stringify(cartItems),
        });
    ```

```
    if (response.statusCode === 500) return;

    const data = await response.json();

    toast.loading("Redirecting...");

    stripe.redirectToCheckout({
      sessionId: data.id
    });
  };
```

3. There is one more change we need to make in this file – scroll down to the bottom of the page, and look for these two lines of code:

```
        <h3>${eUSLocale(totalPrice)}</h3>
      </div>
```

4. Immediately after the second line, add this markup:

```
        <div className="btn-container">
          <button type="button" className="btn"
          onClick={handleCheckout}>
            Pay with Stripe
          </button>
        </div>
```

5. Save and close the file. Next, crack open MiniCart.jsx, then add these two lines immediately below the imports at the top of the file:

```
import getStripe from "../../lib/getStripe";
import toast from "react-hot-toast";
```

Some of these upcoming steps will look familiar; this is deliberate, and I'll explain why and what we can do about it later in the chapter.

---

6. Go ahead and repeat steps 2-4 in this file to add the same handleCheckout function and button markup to the minicart component.

7. Save and close the file. We have one more file to get, success.js – go ahead and download this from the code download and put it into the \pages folder.

At this point, we're ready to test our checkout process – we'll start on this shortly. This is where it can either make or break our site; touch wood, it will all go without a hitch. We're only going to do a quick litmus test to ensure it works, though, enough to prove we can get a sale through to Stripe.

It's important to note, though, that we will do more complete testing later in Chapter 9 – before we do any of that, let's take a moment to review the changes we made in more detail.

Understanding What Happened

Adding a payment provider can be a lengthy process, depending on which provider you use – each will have its own process, but there will be some common elements, such as obtaining API keys or adding them to the codebase. Setting up Stripe for us was no different – to make it easier, we split it into two parts and focused on the initial configuration in Stripe first.

We first logged in to get the API keys, which we added to a .env (or environment) file in our codebase. It's worth noting that this is the recommended way to do this, as it stores the values in a file away from the main codebase. We then used one of the keys in this file, NEXT_PUBLIC_STRIPE_PUBLISHABLE, to create a component to load Stripe into our codebase. At the same time, we extracted a copy of the stripe.js file from the code download – this is a lengthy file, so it was easier to add from the code download rather than manually enter it!

In the second part, we started to add references to Stripe in the relevant places throughout our codebase. The first file to target was Cart.jsx; here, we added imports for the getStripe.js file we created earlier and react-hot-toast (which we use to show notifications when we add products to the cart). We also created a handleCheckout event handler, which we trigger when clicking the Pay by Stripe button (added in step 4 of this part of the exercise). This handler redirects the customer to Stripe while passing in their sessionId value so that Stripe knows what the customer's total amounts are at the point of paying for their goods.

We then repeated the first part of the second demo, but this time for MiniCart.jsx – we added the same imports, handleCheckout event handler, and the markup for the "Pay by Stripe" button.

In this instance, there are no changes we need to make to allow for the second cart – this did create some duplication, but we can fix and optimize the code. I've discussed this in the section marked "Refactoring the Cart" earlier in this chapter.

We then round out the demo by adding the success.js file, which provides a return page for Stripe to confirm that the payment has been successful and that we can dispatch the goods to the customer.

Excellent – we now have Stripe enabled and configured for use on our site! One more important step we need to complete before we can say we're done with this part is to test the results of our work. It's at this point where things can get a little nerve-wracking, as we're not sure what will happen – let's dive in and take a look. Did we get everything in place, I wonder?

Testing the Checkout Process

Now that we have set up Stripe, it's time to test our site – will it work as we expect?

Of course, it will – I have every faith in you, my dear readers! I know this can be nerve-wracking, as we're never quite sure if everything is in place or if we've missed anything. The time has come, though, to rid ourselves of some of that doubt – let's put our site through its initial test.

TESTING THE SITE

To perform an initial test of the site, follow these steps:

1. First, fire up a Node.js terminal session and ensure the working folder points to our project area. At the prompt, enter npm run dev and press Enter, then browse to a product: I've chosen http://localhost:3000/product/quince-cobnut as my example.

2. Click Add to Cart – notice that we should see a toast message appear toward the top of the page, like the one shown in Figure 4-8.

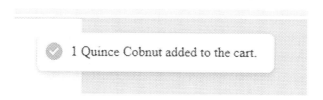

Figure 4-8. *A toast message to confirm the product is now in the cart*

3. Next, click the 1 by the Contact link at the top of the screen, then on the next page, scroll down to the Pay with Stripe button and click it. Wait for it to redirect to the next page (Figure 4-9).

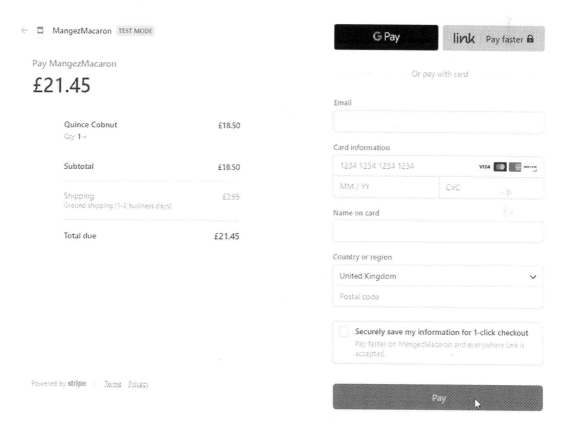

Figure 4-9. *An example of the Stripe payment page*

4. On this page, go ahead and enter any details you like for the email, name on the card, zip (or postal) code, and country fields.

The exact details are not critical for this part, but I would suggest keeping them realistic – for example, an email address that looks like a standard one, but it doesn't have to work!

5. For the card fields, use these:

Field	Value
Card number	4111 1111 1111 1111
CVC field	370
MM / YY field (date of expiry)	11 / 27

Stripe does have documentation available for testing – you can see some examples at `https://stripe.com/docs/testing`. You can choose to use any of these – they will give different results in Stripe based on the country/card number used.

6. Next, hit the Pay button and let it process – if all is well, we should see the Success page with a confetti animation.

7. With the transaction complete, go ahead and log into your Stripe account at `https://dashboard.stripe.com/login`, then click Payments.

8. Take a closer look at the list of payments – I have a fair few as I've been testing, but you will only have one. It should look like the one shown in Figure 4-10 (where I've blanked out the email address for the customer):

	AMOUNT		DESCRIPTION	CUSTOMER	DATE	
	£21.45	Succeeded ✓	pi_3MbTXNIG1cktkZ0R1hdw6k56	███████████	14 Feb, 18:47	•••

Figure 4-10. *An example of a successful order*

9. Click Succeeded to view the order – you will see details such as when the payment started, the customer, the amount, and the products they ordered.

If you scroll down, you will even see a Risk Management entry – this is a feature of Stripe to help you determine if an order is suspicious and should, therefore, not be fulfilled. It is only available once you go live, though – sorry!

If you manage to reach this stage, congratulations – you have completed your first purchase in your shop! Our demo site is operational since we can choose a product, add it to the cart, and "pay" for it (yes, I know it's not real, but that will come in time…).

Summary

Adding a checkout process to any e-commerce site is an important milestone – it brings home the point that we now have something that works and can start to earn income for us. We still have a long way to go in adding styling, polishing, and testing the site, but the site is complete functionally. We've covered a lot of changes in this chapter, so let's take a moment to review what we have learned in more detail.

We started way back when (it seems a long time ago!) by breaking down the process into a high-level view. This was so we could understand how the different elements will work and explore some of the security concerns we might have when using third-party tools in a Jamstack environment.

We then moved on to finishing off the buttons and a few other tasks from the last chapter so we could preview the results at the end of the previous chapter and get everything ready for the upcoming changes in this chapter.

Next up came a key part – we had to add context around the site so that changes persist from the site into the cart and Stripe and vice versa. Following this, we constructed the main Cart and MiniCart components before hooking both into our site. We also briefly explored some changes we could make to refactor the code and remove some of the duplication.

For the last part, we then added Stripe to our site – we worked through configuring the Stripe setup first before updating the code to hook an instance into our site. At the same time, we ran a quick test to prove we could add products to our site, see them in the cart, and check them out as a customer before seeing the order results appear in our account in Stripe.

Phew – a long chapter, but well worth it! We've pretty much built the core site, so things will get easier from here onward. Our site does look like an ugly duckling, though, so I think it's time for us to fix that before our Cinderella heads out to the ball. Okay, I know some of you might not get that reference, but don't worry – stay with me, and I'll explain all in the next chapter.

CHAPTER 5

Styling the Site

This is where things begin to get more interesting – we've built the basis for our shop, but it looks a little rough and ready!

It's time we turn our ugly duckling of a site into something more attractive – the question is, what tools should we use? Do we have a preference – how will it look? Next.js makes it very easy to add styling using one of a handful of ways – let's begin with a quick exploration of the options open to us when adding styles to our site.

Exploring the Options

Hands up, how many of you still rely on the old-school way of adding CSS?

You know what I mean – creating a long stylesheet, importing it into our site's `<head>` section, and manually refreshing the browser to see the changes. Oh, and hoping that you did get those changes right too...

Sound familiar? There's nothing wrong with old-school methods – they are tried and tested and work well. However, time has moved on: when it comes to styling Next.js sites (and others, too), we have a few options in addition to using standard CSS stylesheets. Table 5-1 lists a few that are supported out of the box by Next.js – we'll use two of them in our demo site.

© Alex Libby 2023

A. Libby, *Practical Next.js for E-Commerce*, https://doi.org/10.1007/978-1-4842-9612-7_5

Table 5-1. *Some of the options available when styling a Next.js site*

Tool	Details
Sass (using Dart Sass)	Available from `www.sass-lang.com`. Ideal for supporting older browsers, if necessary, outside of those not supported by Next.js.
CSS modules	This option is available in the browser by default and needs minimal configuration.
CSS-in-JS	CSS-in-JS is a more advanced option, using tools like Styled Components, Tailwind, or Emotion. See `https://nextjs.org/docs/basic-features/built-in-css-support#css-in-js` for some examples of how Next.js can work with these frameworks.
PostCSS	Available from `www.postcss.org` –this comes with some transformations already baked into the default setup, such as Autoprefixer and Flexbox. For more details and an example, head over to `https://nextjs.org/docs/advanced-features/customizing-postcss-config`.

The next question I hear coming is, which one do we choose? As always, the short answer in scenarios like this will nearly always be, "it depends." It might sound like a bit of a cop-out, but don't worry: there is a reason for saying this – let me explain what I mean. Although Next.js has options for styling sites in several different ways, the one you choose will ultimately depend on your circumstances, skillset, and experience.

The simplest one to use (but not always the most practical) is standard CSS – we can add this into one or more stylesheets as long as we import the files into the `_app.js` file. Where it gets less practical is the size – did you see the 600+ lines of code in the stylesheet we added in the last demo? Sure, it's a relatively small site, but even still: that is a lot of code to manage!

We can get around this lengthy code using one of two methods (technically three, but I'll return to method number 3 shortly) – Sass or CSS Modules. If you've not used either, they can help split large stylesheets into smaller individual files based on specific areas, features, or components. We can choose how to split – however we do it, it makes the files shorter and easier to manage. Sass offers a lot more than this, such as variables, mixins, and the like; we'll go through each option later in this chapter.

The next option is CSS-in-JS, where we can add the styles inline to a targeted element or as an inline stylesheet – I'm thinking of examples such as Emotion (from `www.emotion.sh`), Styled Components (`www.styled-components.com`), or Tailwind (`www.tailwindcss` or `www.tailwindui`). Although these libraries are great tools in their own right, they are somewhat overkill for our small site! We could even use a tool such as PostCSS to process our styles, although that takes a lot more work to set up, so it is only practical if you already have something in place.

The critical point here is that Next.js isn't opinionated when it comes to styling – while you might have a few steps to work through when it comes to setting up styles, you are free to choose whichever method suits your needs. Yes, you might have to put styles in certain places, but only if you decide to use that option – it's up to you!

OK – let's crack on with some more technical matters. Before we get into the realms of adding styles, I want to cover a couple of things that relate to how we will style our site.

Taking the Mobile-First Approach

I have a small confession to make at this point – conventional wisdom says we should take a mobile-first approach when it comes to designing our site. However, as you are about to see, I'm going to break that rule.

Taking a mobile-first approach is strongly recommended in this modern age of e-commerce, as more people buy from portable devices. Indeed, as of 2022, those who buy from mobiles outweigh desktop users by a factor of 2 to 1!

It, therefore, makes for no excuse when it comes to styling – we should focus on mobiles first, then expand to cover tablets and later desktops. However, when you spend as long as I do, researching and writing books, squinting at a small screen isn't practical – it means I have to style the other way round, that is, desktop to mobile.

With this in mind, we will start with styling for desktops but go through adapting for mobiles and tablets later in Chapter 6. I know we could choose from a host of devices, but to start with, I will use iPad and iPhone 12 – both are available in Chrome's Responsive Mode, making life easier, when it comes to development.

Designing the Theme

This next part is probably the most fun part of the process – we can choose our color scheme!

Okay, so for some people, this might be dictated by existing brand colors we would have to use, so choosing may be a moot point. However, if this is not the case, we can select a suitable color palette for our site.

Choosing one can be tricky, as the psychology of color can affect people's buying habits. I could go into some length as to how we might create different types of color palettes, but that would be outside of the scope of this book. Suffice it to say, there are two tricks I like to use for occasions such as this, where colors are not critical (as we're running a proof of concept).

Keep the choice simple: a site with a dozen colors will look busy and cluttered, whereas you will get more of an impact with a smaller palette. Try to keep to four to five colors plus black and white (or suitable equivalents, if you prefer to use a grayer black and not pure white).

If you have a suitable photo you want to include as media on the site, then use this as the basis for your palette. Plenty of sites on the Internet can generate suitable palettes based on dominant colors from a photo, such as this example: `https://coolors.co/774726-caa34d-a6a99c-7e8b44-bebeb3`.

Note   If you use one of these sites, then make sure you get the URL of your palette and keep it safe. If you lose it, be prepared – you may find the site doesn't create a palette with the same colors from the photo you used the first time! (I know from experience…)

There is one last takeaway, though, which applies to this chapter – for reasons of space, we'll be focusing on the mechanics of how you add color and styling to our site, not the specific details. With that in mind, let's finish with the theory and turn our attention to getting down and dirty with making our site look… well… just a little more presentable!

Applying the Changes

OK – we've explored some of the options for styling and worked out our theme: let's start applying some color!

Adding basic styles in a Next.js application is a cinch – as we've already seen, we can make our site look a little more attractive in several ways. The most straightforward (but perhaps not the most practical) is to apply standard CSS styling – owing to the global nature of styling in Next.js, it's best to do this by importing it from the _app.js file in the pages folder.

I know it's not ideal, as it means we can't scope styles this way (at least not easily or cleanly). But, it is a valid method we can use and is a great launching point for applying more optimized styling at a later date. Let's dive in and look in more detail to see what I mean.

APPLYING STYLES

Adding styles to a Next.js application is easy – to do so, follow these steps:

1. First, go ahead and delete globals.css from the \src\styles folder – we'll replace it with a new one shortly. Do the same for home.module.css – it's in the same folder.

2. Next, extract a copy of frontimage.jpg, and drop it into a new folder called images under the /public folder.

3. You may see some additional SVG images in the same images folder – next. svg, vercel.svg, and thirteen.svg. We don't need any of them, so go ahead and delete them. (They come from the default build for a Next.js site, so they are easily replaceable if needed.)

4. Copy across a copy of globals.css from the code download for this book – drop it into the \src\styles folder.

5. We're almost done – before we check the site, look at /src/pages/_app.js; if all is well, we should already see an import for globals.css somewhere in the block of imports at the top of the file.

If, for any reason, it is not there, add this line before the opening function call:
```
import "../styles/globals.css";
```

---

6. Save and close all open files. Fire up a Node.js terminal, then change the working folder to our project area if it is not already set.

7. At the prompt, enter npm run dev and press Enter – if all is well, we should see this screenshot when browsing to http://localhost:3000/, as shown in Figure 5-1.

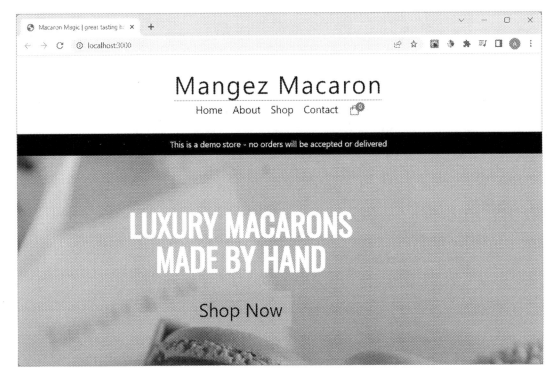

Figure 5-1. *A screenshot of the homepage with styling applied*

Yes – that looks better compared to that dull gray layout, huh? Granted, it will probably not win any style awards anytime soon, but it at least looks half-decent.

It does show that it's straightforward to add styles – this effectively boils down to two things: putting the stylesheet in the right place and adding the import to the correct file. There are a couple more interesting points I want to bring up about our stylesheet, so before we look at alternative styling methods, let's dive in and explore the changes we made in more detail.

Understanding What Has Changed

So, what changes did we make in the last demo?

To prove a point, I deliberately kept them simple – when styling a Next.js application, adding styles follows the same steps as any static site. Add the stylesheet, and import it into the correct file: in this case, _app.js.

OK, I might be oversimplifying things here, but you get the idea – we didn't have to set or change any configuration settings; everything just worked out of the box.

It is worth pointing out, though, that if you take a look at the styles for the Tabs component used on the individual product pages, you will notice a slightly different style (pun intended). I've used BEM, or Block Element Modifier – a popular method that helps with writing cleaner class names in CSS and getting around instances where we might have multiple layers of CSS. Although BEM is a practical methodology in its own right, it's not consistent with the other styles I've used, so we should probably refactor this code to make it more consistent. At the same time, I recommend renaming the stylesheet – globals.css isn't the most appropriate name here, as we have styles that are not meant to be global!

For anyone curious about BEM as a methodology, I would recommend heading over to the BEM website for more details at https://getbem.com/introduction/.

The only other change we made was to add a new frontimage.jpg (which the stylesheet references) and remove some redundant images added when we created the initial site. As they say, job done...

Or is it? Sure, we can stay with a standard stylesheet – there is nothing wrong with using this approach, at least from a technical perspective. But if we did, then we won't be making full use of what Next.js can offer us – plus, we'd have to deal with a stylesheet that will get larger and eventually become too unwieldy to manage!

To get around this, we should look at some alternative methods that Next.js supports – CSS Modules, Sass, CSS-in-JS, or even PostCSS. Given that our site isn't that big, I will focus on the first two, but I will touch on CSS-in-JS and PostCSS toward the end of this chapter. With that in mind, let's start with CSS Modules to see how this will make our lives a little easier when managing styles in a Next.js site.

Taking Alternative Approaches

If you've spent time developing with React, you will likely be familiar with a key tenet of this framework: we don't need to put all of the styles in one file. The same applies to Next.js – there are a few ways to do it, but the basic principle is the same: we can split our styles into multiple smaller files.

Why would we do this? Well, for one, it makes files smaller and easier to manage – styles will only apply to the feature or component where we reference the stylesheet file and remove any risk of conflicts (unless we put the same styles in by mistake!). We can also make the transition bit by bit – as long as we have the fundamentals in place, then we can convert styles over a period of time and not have to take a big-bang approach.

To achieve this, there are two ways we can do this: via CSS Modules (the modern, new-school way of doing it), or if you need to support older browsers, you can go old school and use Sass. Let's take a look at the first to see what's involved in more detail.

Using CSS Modules

There are two things I love about CSS Modules – Next.js supports them out of the box and will automatically compile them into what we could call namespaced styles, so there should be little or no risk of them conflicting with other styles! How does this work?

At face value, our styles in CSS Modules will be the same, albeit split into smaller files. The key to making it work, though, is that Next will concatenate these files into minified smaller files that are code split – it makes sure that we only load the minimum styles needed for our application to render onscreen. To see what I mean, I will convert the styles we used for the Footer component to work as a CSS module as our starting example. This will show you how easy it is to transition while keeping the original styles running until we can convert them to the new process.

USING CSS MODULES

Adding CSS Module support is easy – to do so, follow these steps:

1. First, go ahead and create a new folder called Footer in the `\src\components` folder – we'll use this to store our updated styling and component.

2. Next, create a new file called `Footer.module.css` inside the Footer folder from step 1.

3. Open the `globals.css` stylesheet, then search for Footer – you should see a block of styles relating to the Footer component. Copy that section into `Footer.module.css`, then comment out the original styles in `globals.css`, so Next doesn't try to use them during compilation. Save and close the files.

In the `globals.css` file, you'll see a series of comment lines – these are the starting point for each block. Copy down as far as the next comment line.

---

4. We need to move the Footer component into the Footer subfolder we created in step 1 – this will help keep styles (and components) separate and manageable. Go ahead and update any references to `Footer.jsx` in `Layout.jsx`, to point to the file in its new location.

5. Next, open `Footer.jsx`, then in the return block, change any references in CSS rule names that have -c to C. For example, you will see footer-container – change this to `footerContainer`. Your updated code will look like this:

```
return (
  <>
    <div className={styles.footerContainer}>
      <div className={styles.footerContent}>
        <div>
          <Link href="/delivery">Delivery</Link>
          <Link href="/privacy">Privacy</Link>
          <Link href="/terms">Terms and Conditions of Sale</Link>
          <Link href="/contact">Contact Us</Link>
        </div>
        <div>Contact: hello@macaronmagic.com</div>

        <MiniCart />
      </div>
      <div className={styles.iconContainer}>
        <PaymentIcons />
        <div className={styles.icons}>
          <AiFillInstagram />
          <AiOutlineTwitter />
        </div>
```

```
        </div>
      </div>
      <p className={styles.copyright}>2022 Macaron Magic All rights
      reserved</p>
    </>
  );
};
```

6. Save and close the file. We need to repeat the same change in the new stylesheet we created – go ahead and change any instance of -c to C; the affected rules should look like this:

```
.footerContainer {
  color: #caa34d; background-color: #000000; text-align: center;
  margin-top: 20px; padding: 30px 10px;
font-weight: 700; display: flex; flex-direction: column; align-items:
center; gap: 10px; justify-content: center; border-bottom: 1px solid
#c7c7c7; }

.footerContainer .footerContent { display: flex; margin-left: auto;
margin-right: auto; width: 800px;
}

.footerContainer .footerContent div { flex-direction: column; display:
flex; text-align: left; min-width: 250px; margin-right: 20px; }

.footerContainer .footerContent div:last-child {
  margin-right: 0; }

.footerContainer .mini-cart-bottom { width: 100%; }

.footerContainer .icons { font-size: 30px; display: flex; gap: 10px; }

.footerContainer .iconContainer { width: 800px; display: flex;
justify-content: space-between; }
```

I've compressed the styles for space reasons. The properties will be identical; only the CSS rule names will change.

7. Save and close all open files. Fire up a Node.js terminal, then change the working folder to our project area if it is not already set.

8. At the prompt, enter npm run dev and press Enter – if all is well, we should see the footer looking the same as before when browsing to http://localhost:3000/, as shown in Figure 5-2.

Figure 5-2. *The Footer component, after changing over to using CSS Modules*

9. You will not see any immediate change, which is to be expected – after all, the properties haven't changed: only the rule names! However, if we look in the browser console, we should see a different set of styles appear, as shown in Figure 5-3.

```
▼<footer> == $0
  ▼<div class="Footer_footerContainer__J8Mug"> flex
    ▼<div class="Footer_footerContent__YH3WT"> flex
      ▶<div>…</div> flex
        <div>Contact: hello@macaronmagic.com</div> flex
      ▶<div class="mini-cart-container">…</div> flex
      </div>
    ▼<div class="Footer_iconContainer__OgVk_"> flex
      ▶<div class="payment-icons">…</div> flex
      ▶<div class="Footer_icons__F7g6z">…</div> flex
      </div>
    </div>
    <p class="Footer_copyright__vZZRL">2022 Macaron Magic Al
    </p>
</footer>
```

Figure 5-3. *The new style class names for the Footer component*

Perfect – we've implemented the first example of CSS Modules on our site; this is a great starting point to gradually convert the remaining pages and components to this new format. Although our styles haven't really changed, there are a couple of interesting points we should explore – let's look at the changes we made in more detail.

Breaking Apart the Changes

When it comes to working with CSS Modules (and Sass, for that matter too), it pays to be organized – dropping all of the stylesheets and components into the same folder may work for some, but this can become too unwieldy to manage on a large site!

To get around this, we should split each into smaller groups – typically, we might colocate a stylesheet with its component or page, although this can be tricky if there is a lot of crossover between components. This colocating is what we did in our demo – we started by creating a separate folder for the Footer component before moving it into this new folder and adding a new stylesheet module.

We then transferred a copy of the original styles into this file before renaming some of them – some of the CSS rules had hyphens in them, which throws an error when compiling as this is not supported when creating CSS Modules. To round out the demo, we then fired up a test run of the site to prove all was still working as expected and that we could see the results of the change in the browser console.

You will notice from the screenshots in the last demo that the Payment icons component doesn't show the same naming style as our Footer component. It's still using the original name as we've not converted it yet, even though we're calling it from within the Footer component. It shows that we can do a progressive conversion – Next can still display any styles not yet converted without issue.

Okay – let's move on: CSS Modules are a relatively new way of styling our site and will work for modern browsers released within the last few years.

However, there may be occasions where you might have to support older browsers or want to use existing styles from Sass-based projects, such as color variables or style mixins. No problem: Next.js supports styling through Sass, making it a cinch to add support. To see how easy it is, let's dive in and take a look at converting part of our site to use Sass as part of our next demo.

Using Sass

In the age of the Internet, Sass is old school – it's been around (in various forms) since 2006. There are versions for different environments, such as libSass for C++, jSass for Java – and even phamlp for PHP! Nowadays, when we talk about Sass, we're referring to the version written in Dart, which uses the block formatting more commonly associated with standard CSS.

For those of you who use Sass, you will no doubt have spent time creating mixins, variables, and the like, many of which you will want to keep going when creating sites in Next.js. Adding support is easy, although there is one thing to bear in mind – Next.js works with Dart Sass, so as long as your styles are compatible with that version of Sass, you shouldn't have an issue. (This is important, as node-sass and, by default, libSass have both been deprecated.) Assuming the styles are compatible, let's take a look at how we can convert part of our site over to use Sass.

For this demo, I will use the About page as our initial example; converting the remaining pages and components will use a similar process. I'll come back to this at the end of the demo.

CONFIGURE FOR SASS

To add support for Sass, follow these steps:

1. First, fire up a Node.js terminal, then change the working folder to our project area.

2. At the prompt, enter this command to install Sass:

    ```
    npm install –save-dev sass
    ```

3. Next, crack open the `next.config.js` file at the root of the project, and alter it to update the configuration to support Sass (as highlighted):

    ```
    /** @type {import('next').NextConfig} */
    const nextConfig = {
      reactStrictMode: true,
      sassOptions: {
        includePaths: ["styles"],
      },
    };

    module.exports = nextConfig;
    ```

143

4. Create a second new file — in this file, add this line, then save it as `index.scss` in the `\src\styles` folder:

```
@use "about"; /* About Us page */
```

5. Crack open `_app.js`, then add this new line under the import for `globals.css`:

```
import "../styles/globals.css"; /* common page elements */
import "../styles/index.scss"; /* main styles */
```

6. Save and close the file.

7. We now need to create our smaller stylesheet — create a new file called `about.scss`, and save it in the `\src\styles` folder.

8. Switch to the `globals.css` file, then find this line:

```
/* ABOUT -------------------------------------- */
```

9. Copy the contents of this section, down as far as the next comment, into `about.scss`:

```
.about-us {
  width: 70%;
  margin: 0 auto;
}

.about-us p:nth-child(1) {
  margin: 40px 0 0 0;
  font-family: "Oswald", sans-serif;
  font-size: 42px;
}

.about-us > p:nth-child(2) { margin: 20px 0 20px 0;}
```

10. Next, go through the code and change it to this:

```
.about-us {
  width: 70%;
  margin: 0 auto;

  & p:nth-child(1) {
    margin: 40px 0 0 0;
```

```
        font-family: "Oswald", sans-serif;
        font-size: 42px;
    }

    & > p:nth-child(2) { margin: 20px 0 20px 0; }
    }
```

11. Once you've updated the styles in about.scss, go ahead and comment out or remove the section from globals.css – this is to ensure we don't try to use these when compiling our stylesheet.

12. Fire up a Node.js terminal – make sure the working folder is set to our project folder.

13. At the prompt, type npm run dev, then press Enter. Browse to http:// localhost:3000/about – if all is well, you should not see any *visual* change. If we look at the console, we should see a difference with the stylesheet source files (Figure 5-4).

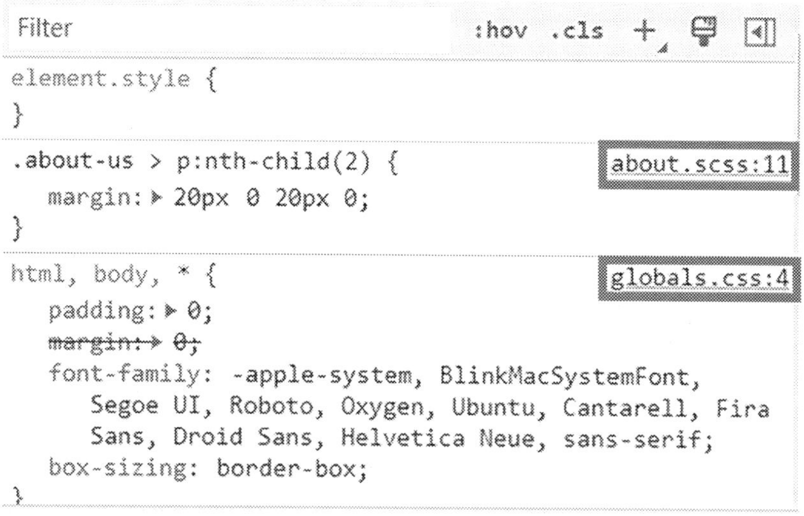

Figure 5-4. The original styles converted to Sass format

Phew – that might have seemed like a lot of steps, but the reality is that adding Sass support isn't difficult; we just have to make a few changes in various places throughout our codebase! The great thing is that if we want to add more styles, we absolutely can – Sass allows us to transfer styles over bit by bit without any problem.

While I appreciate not everyone will use Sass, it's still essential to have an appreciation of what happened in the last demo, just in case circumstances change. With that in mind, let's take a quick look through what we created to understand how it all works in more detail.

Breaking Apart the Code Changes

If you've not worked with Sass before, then at first glance, it might seem we have to go through a lot of steps to get it set up and working in our environment! Don't worry, though – some of these steps are one-offs that we won't need to repeat. To understand what I mean, let's go through the changes we made in more detail.

We first began by installing Sass and adding a setting to the `next.config.js` file. This setting adds the `sassOptions` property to tell Sass which folder contains the source files to use when compiling our code. Next up, we created an index file for our Sass source files – here, we added a `@use` statement for the about page that we are using as our example. At the same time, we had to modify the `_app.js` file to include the new reference to this index file that will automatically import all Sass files contained within our project.

The next part of the demo was the most critical. We transferred a copy of the rules from the original stylesheet into our new individual stylesheets. We also had to comment out the original code so that site would not try and compile two versions of the same code!

Once we completed that transfer, we ran a preview to ensure that everything worked as expected and that we wouldn't see any change visually. However, we would see the difference in the browser console, where we now import Sass files into our demo.

Okay, let's move on: we converted one file as part of this exercise, but the reality is that we can use the same process to split our stylesheet into multiple, smaller files. To do this, we would only need to create new source files (e.g., `navbar.scss`), copy the styles over, and add a `@use` statement into the stylesheet index file. If we completed this, we would have a host of imports in the index file, which would look something like this:

```
@use "navbar"; /* navbar */
@use "marquee"; /* "You may like" */
@use "cart"; /* Main and mini cart */
```

```
@use "shop"; /* Shop page */
@use "tabs"; /* Tabs on product page */
@use "contact"; /* Contact us form */
@use "perfect-message"; /* Perfect Occasions component - home page */
@use "success-cancel"; /* Success and Cancel pages */
@use "email-signup"; /* Email signup component on main page */
@use "footer"; /* Footer */
@use "may-like"; /* May like products component */
@use "payment-icons"; /* Payment icons */
@use "homepage"; /* styles for homepage */
@use "product-page"; /* product page */
```

It seems a lot, but bear in mind that we're now referencing smaller files, making it easier to manage – the styles are scoped for the component or page they refer to, not the whole site!

A minor point – I've assumed that you might already have a certain familiarity with Sass, and in particular, Dart Sass. If you would like to learn more about using Sass, please refer to my book on Dart Sass, published by Apress.

Could We Use Sass Variables?

We've talked briefly about Sass being more of an old-school method of styling, but it also contains much more functionality than CSS Modules. This functionality allows us to run basic math operations such as adding values together or using a `lighten()` command to lighten a shade of color by, say, 10-20%.

One feature Sass has which is particularly useful is variables. For the uninitiated, think of these as placeholder buckets for values. We define a bucket (so to speak) at the start of our code), with a specific value, such as a hex code for a color. If we use that color anywhere in the code, we use the placeholder value instead – should the original definition be changed, then Sass will automatically replace any instance of the placeholder with the updated value.

One of the great things about styling in Next.js is that it supports exporting Sass variables from CSS Module files. For example, we could do something like this, where we use the exported primaryColor Sass variable:

```
/* variables.module.scss */
$primary-color: #64ff00;

:export {
  primaryColor: $primary-color;
}
```

We would then link to this variables file from within _app.js:

```
import variables from '../styles/variables.module.scss'

export default function MyApp({ Component, pageProps }) {
  return (
    <Layout color={variables.primaryColor}>
      <Component {...pageProps} />
    </Layout>
  )
}
```

However, there is one critical problem: we can't use this approach on our site. I tried this approach to style the Footer, with the aim of having a variables.scss file that contained all of the colors we would need to reference in our site. To achieve this (or at least try), I took these steps:

1. Created a new file called variables.module.scss in the \styles folder.

2. Added this code as my starting point:

   ```
   /* color scheme */
   $primary-black: #000000;

   :export {
     primaryBlack: $primary-black;
   }
   ```

3. Modified the imports in `Footer.jsx`, to this:

```
import styles from "./Footer.module.css";
import variables from "../../styles/variables.scss";
<div className={styles.footerContainer} backgroundColor={variables.
primaryBlack}>
```

Here's where things failed – when compiling the styles, I got this error message:

```
./styles/variables.scss
Global CSS cannot be imported from files other than your Custom <App>. Due
to the Global nature of stylesheets, and to avoid conflicts, Please move
all first-party global CSS imports to pages/_app.js. Or convert the import
to Component-Level CSS (CSS Modules).
Read more: https://nextjs.org/docs/messages/css-global
Location: components\Footer\Footer.jsx
```

This approach only works if we reference it from the `_app.js` file and have more components that we style inline, using a CSS-in-JS method. We don't, so unfortunately, this is one approach we must discard for our site, at least for now!

Taking Things Further

Throughout this chapter, we've explored some methods we can use to style our site, such as standard CSS, Sass, or CSS Modules. One thing we can't help but avoid, though, is to acknowledge that some of you may prefer to use a CSS-in-JS tool such as Tailwind or even a tool such as PostCSS.

There is nothing wrong with these tools – they are perfectly valid options, but probably suited to larger sites where scoping CSS styles is more important. At the same time, setting up PostCSS will take a bit of effort; we can use it to perform all manner of tasks outside of just compiling styles, such as appending vendor prefixes, so we need to make sure we get the most out of it if we were to go down this route.

Ultimately, it's up to you to decide what you want to use; it's important to choose a tool or method that suits your circumstances, existing knowledge, and any environmental limitations. With this in mind, let's take a quick walk-through converting a tool to use a CSS-in-JS approach to see how we might adapt our codebase. I'll use Tailwind for this following walk-through, but the same principles will apply to other tools such as Emotion or Styled Components.

WALK-THROUGH: CONVERT DEMOBANNER TO USE TAILWIND

To convert the DemoBanner component to using Tailwind, we would need to do something like this:

1. First, install Tailwind in a Node.js terminal using this command:

```
npm install -D tailwindcss
```

2. Next, we would need to create a tailwind configuration file using this command:

```
npx tailwindcss init
```

3. With the config file in place, we would need to update it to pick up our new component:

```
/** @type {import('tailwindcss').Config} */
module.exports = {
  content: [
      './components/**/*.{js,ts,jsx,tsx}',
    ],
    theme: {
      extend: {},
    },
    plugins: [],
  }
```

4. Next, we would need to add the Tailwind CSS imports to globals.css, like so:

```
@tailwind base;
@tailwind components;
@tailwind utilities;
```

5. In a Node.js terminal, we would need to start the Tailwind CLI build process to scan for any Tailwind classes:

```
npx tailwindcss -i ./src/input.css -o ./dist/output.css –watch
```

6. Finally, we would need to update the component to use Tailwind classes, not standard CSS styles – I've highlighted the affected code from this extract:

```
const DemoBanner = () => {
  return (
    <div className="background-color-black color-white text-
    center pt-10">
      <span>
        This is a demo store - no orders will be accepted or
```

7. As part of updating DemoBanner, we would need to remove the old styles from `global.css` so we don't import them into the updated stylesheet:

```
.demo-banner-container {
  background-color: #000000;
  color: white;
  text-align: center;
  padding: 10px 0;
}
```

At this point, we would save and close anything open, then run the usual `npm run dev` process to rebuild the site – if all is well, we should end up with a Tailwind-enabled demo. The critical point here is that we should not feel obliged to use a framework such as Tailwind – it's up to you to choose the right tool that suits your needs; if that happens to be using an old-fashioned single stylesheet, then so be it!

Summary

I love it when we start to add styles to any site – being a visual person myself, it's great to see things come alive, experiment with what looks good, and discard anything that we clearly know won't work! In this last chapter, we've applied styling to our site, so it's now looking presentable, as well as experimented with using a couple of different ways to apply these styles. We've covered a lot of valuable tips in the last few pages, so let's take a moment to review what we have learned.

We started by briefly exploring the options open to us when it comes to applying styles in a Next.js site – this could be as simple as using a standard CSS stylesheet, or we could kick things up a notch by using Sass, CSS Modules, or even a CSS-in-JS tool such as Tailwind. At the same time, we talked a little about the approach – I mentioned that we should go "mobile-first" but that this makes it harder to develop the site during the writing phase, so I would cover this later in the book once we've added the desktop styles.

We then worked our way through applying a standard stylesheet to see how easy it was to add styles before looking at using Sass or CSS Modules. We explored some of the benefits of using these two tools, with the best one being that we can progressively update the site and not have to do it in one go. To finish, we came back to discuss how we could take things further – we ran through a quick walk-through to see what it would be like to convert to using a tool such as Tailwind should we decide that this was the approach we wanted to take for our site.

Phew – a lot covered, but it's all good stuff! With our core styles in place, let's move on to the next task, which, as it so happens, is to adapt our styles for mobile devices! Yes, we should do it the other way around, but I am old-school, and using desktops is easier to see things. We won't worry too much about that, though – let's crack on and see what changes we need to make to adapt our site in the next chapter.

PART III

Wrapping Things Up

CHAPTER 6

Adapting for Mobile

In the modern age of mobile devices, more and more people are purchasing via cell phones or tablets – making our site work on these devices is essential.

In Chapter 5, we started with styling for desktops, but what about mobiles or tablets? We need our site to work across multiple devices, so in this chapter, we'll focus on what we need to do to ensure our site works on various environments, from mobile to PC. Before we get into applying styles, let's first decide which devices we will use to test our site and assess what needs to change in each layout.

Setting the Scene

Okay – so where do we start?

Our first task is to assess what the sites look like if we were to mimic viewing them on mobile devices – it's time to see what they look like. They won't look perfect, but you never know: they could look pretty decent! However they look, we need to make sure they at least look presentable and work out what (if anything) we need to do to improve their layout. With this in mind, I've elected to choose two device types in addition to desktop, which will be

- Google Pixel 5

- iPad Air, in portrait and landscape modes

I could have picked anyone of dozens of different types of cell phones: the principles of what we're about to do are the same for any device type. I've selected these two as they are available in Google Chrome's Responsive Mode tool. The important point here, though, is that it's more about how we check the designs on our chosen devices and that no matter which we choose, we make sure the devices display our site as expected in their browser. Let's put this to the test by checking our first device, which is the Pixel 5 in portrait mode.

© Alex Libby 2023
A. Libby, *Practical Next.js for E-Commerce*, https://doi.org/10.1007/978-1-4842-9612-7_6

It's worth noting that throughout this chapter, we'll focus on making the changes that make the site legible first; any changes to improve the design can come later.

Checking Mobile

So – how will our site appear? Will it look OK, reasonable, or – heaven forbid – a complete mess, I wonder?

At this point, I always wonder how well it will work in a mobile or tablet format. I really should switch to mobile-first, but when you spend as long as I do researching for books and creating sites, looking at the site in a small, cramped view can get a little wearing after a while! But I digress...

For this next task, we need to use Google Chrome – this is important, as we need to use the Responsive Mode tool, which happens to have the preset sizes we need to test our chosen devices. Chrome helpfully shows the sizes of each device we want to use, plus a tool (to the right) that allows us to switch between portrait and landscape modes (Figure 6-1).

Figure 6-1. *The screen sizes for Pixel 5, as shown in Chrome*

If we run up the site (like we do at the end of each demo), then switch to the Pixel 5 view, we can see what our site looks like in mobile mode. I've included two screenshots over the following few pages – the first, in Figure 6-2, shows the top half of our site.

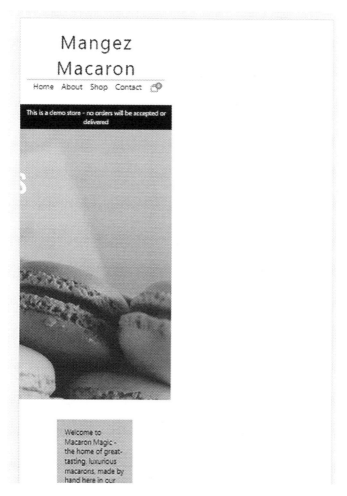

Figure 6-2. *The top of our site in a Pixel 5 view*

If we scroll down to the bottom half (as shown in Figure 6-3), we can see the bottom half of our site.

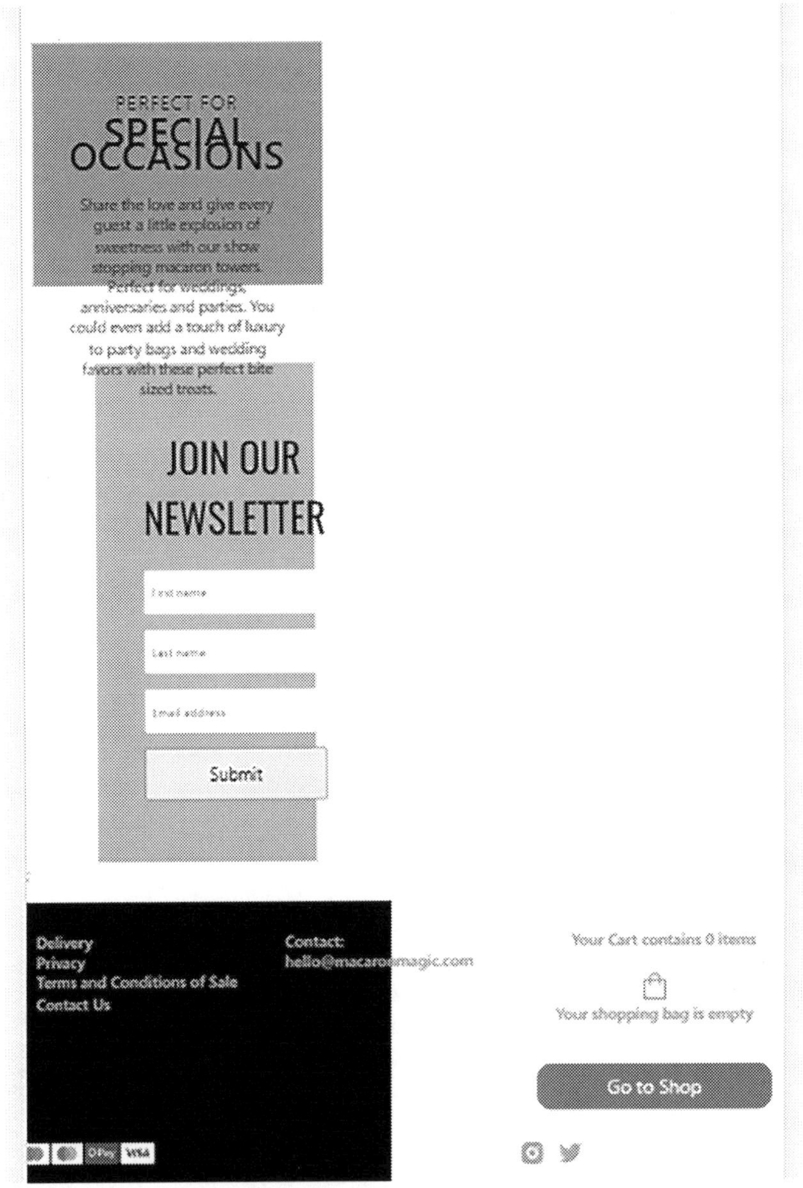

Figure 6-3. *The bottom half of our site in the same Pixel 5 view*

We can see that although all of the content is still there, there are some formatting issues – for example, the header and footer only cover half of the screen width. We could add some padding in the footer and ensure all callout boxes show at the proper width too!

Checking Tablet in Portrait Mode

We've already checked our site on a mobile phone – while this didn't come out too badly, the same may or may not be true of viewing our site on a tablet device. The portrait mode on a tablet will, of course, appear wider, but we also have the added extra of needing to cater for both portrait and landscape modes.

As we did before, we will need to use Chrome to check what our site looks like on a tablet device; this time, we'll use the iPad Air option. We can see what our site looks like in a portrait view in Figure 6-4.

Figure 6-4. *The top half of our site in an iPad Air view*

Don't worry if you can't see it all clearly in the screenshots – at this stage, it's more about the visual positioning of content than the text itself! If we scroll down, we can see what the bottom half of our site looks like in Figure 6-5.

Figure 6-5. *The bottom half of our site in an iPad Air view*

This time, the header and footer appear to cover the entire screen width. There is still a need to adjust some of the formatting in the callout boxes and add some padding to the footer, but this will be a straightforward task to complete. A quick look through the other pages shows that we don't have many changes to make – we'll fix them shortly, but let's first take a quick look at how our site looks on a tablet in landscape mode.

Checking Tablet in Landscape Mode

So far, our designs have come out reasonably well – in both cases, we don't have a lot of changes we need to make. The final design, Tablet in landscape mode, should (in theory) be even better; after all, it's the closest to the desktop layout we've worked on to date, so it should need minimal changes.

To confirm if this is the case, we'll use the same iPad Air setting in Responsive mode, but this time set for landscape – this equates to a layout of 1180px by 820px. We can see what the top half looks like in Figure 6-6.

Figure 6-6. *The top half of our site in iPad Air (landscape) format*

I was expecting some changes to be needed, but if we scroll through various pages, we should see everything looks great! I would even go as far as to say that we don't need to make any changes – at least not initially. We might want to tidy things up later, but for now, the design looks acceptable for what we want at this stage of development.

Okay – now we've been through and assessed the layouts, it's time to apply the fixes we need to get all of them up to scratch. We need to make changes that won't be too large, so let's start fixing the mobile design.

Tidying Up Mobile Design

Okay – so we know our site doesn't look 100% perfect, but it's fair to say it could have been worse!

For a design that wasn't built with a mobile-first approach in mind, it's turned out fairly well; I think this was more through luck than by design. Fortunately, the rest of the pages don't need a lot of changes – let's take a look at what we need to do to get our site looking a little more acceptable as part of the next demo.

FIXING THE PORTRAIT MODE FOR MOBILES

To fix the styling issues for our chosen mobile device, follow these steps:

1. First, go ahead and create a file called `mobile.css` in the `\src\styles` folder.

2. Next, crack open the `_app.js` file in the `\pages` folder, then add this line under the last import statement:

```
import "../styles/mobile.css";
```

Make sure this entry is **below** the one for `globals.css` – this needs to kick in after we apply all of the base styles from this file.

3. We now need to add our styles – open `mobile.css`, then add this code:

```
@media (max-width: 414px) {
  html { display: flex; width: 100%; }

  footer > div:nth-child(1) { padding: 30px; }

  .product-detail-container { margin: 60px; }

  .cart-wrapper { top: 190px; width: 100%; min-height: 2000px; }
```

```
@keyframes movemobile {
  0% { transform: translateY(-40%); }
  100% { transform: translateY(0%); }
}

.cart-container { min-height: 500px; width: 100%;
animation-name: movemobile; animation-duration: 2s;
animation-iteration-count: 1; animation-fill-mode: forwards; display:
flex; flex-direction: column; }
}
```

4. Save and close the file. Next, fire up a Node.js terminal, then change the working folder to our project area.

5. At the prompt, enter npm run dev, and press Enter, then browse to http://localhost:3000 in your browser.

6. Once running, press Ctrl+Shift+I, then Ctrl+Shift+M (or Cmd+Shift+I, Cmd+Shift+M, if running on a Mac) to activate Chrome's Responsive Mode.

7. With the mode activated, choose Pixel 5 from the Dimensions: menu – if all is well, we should see our updated design in Figure 6-7.

Figure 6-7. *The results of our changes to support a mobile device*

Okay, granted – trying to read the text in that last screenshot will be a challenge! Don't worry, though, as this isn't critical – the more important point here is that our pages now look a little more respectable and that we can see elements are correctly laid out on the page.

The irony is that we did not need much extra code to fix the styling; we only had to apply a handful of changes. It does raise an important question, so before we explore that, let's quickly cover off the changes we made in more detail.

Understanding What Has Changed

When adapting designs for different devices, there is always a risk we might have to make significant changes to our code – this time, though, we got lucky! Even though we started with desktop and adapted to mobile, we only needed to add a few changes.

We started by adding a CSS overrides file – there is a reason for this, which I will come back to later – before adding a handful of styles to fix various elements throughout our site, where changing to mobile had affected their positioning.

The critical point to note is that we wrapped all the style changes in a media query for devices with a maximum screen width of 414px. I could have chosen any of several different screen widths (such as 360px or 390px), but given that the Pixel 5 has a width of 393px, I wanted to make sure that our changes applied correctly at our chosen breakpoint with a bit of room to spare.

We also changed how the basket is displayed – the original design didn't extend to the full height and was more suited to desktops than mobile devices. With the new designs in place, we restarted the development server before checking our design in Chrome, using its Responsive Mode and confirming it displayed the changes as expected in our browser.

Okay – so far, so good. We have a working design that suits a mobile device and looks a little more aesthetically pleasing. Keep those thoughts in your mind, as I want to ask you two questions:

1. Should we go horizontal?

2. Given that we didn't have to make many changes to adapt our design, can we retrofit those changes to the base design so we don't need to use overrides?

A couple of interesting questions, I'm sure you will agree! For now, though, keep the second question at the back of your mind – we will answer it toward the end of the chapter. There is a reason for this, which you will see as we update the remaining designs!

The first question raises some important points that we should consider. So without further ado, let's crack on and see if we can provide an answer to the first question.

Should We Go Horizontal?

When designing for mobile devices, the natural inclination would be to cater to portrait and landscape modes, right? After all, we don't know which way round our visitors prefer to use their device, so we need to cater to them – there is bound to be a few people who want to be different...

Therein lies our dilemma: catering for both horizontal and portrait modes is essential, at least for tablets. I am not so sure about mobile devices; while it is possible to *cater* to both modes, I'm not so sure I've seen many people access a site in landscape mode on a cell phone. The only safe way to answer this would be to ensure we have good analytics in place to see how people access our site; this should tell us if the demand is sufficient to incorporate changes to allow for landscape mode on cell phones.

For now, though, I won't update our site to allow for landscape mode on cell phones. I suspect most people will access our site in portrait mode, and given this is a demo, we can always come back to this later if things change!

Adapting for Tablets

We've seen how our site looks for a Pixel 5 as our chosen mobile device – I wonder how it might look if we were on an iPad Air, for example?

To do so, we can use the same principles as we did for the mobile phone device – we create a dedicated override stylesheet, then attach it as an additional resource to the `main _app.js` page. There is a slight wrinkle in this, though, as we don't have just one stylesheet to add, but two!

We need to cater to both portrait and landscape modes – since both require their own media query parameters, we need to add both as separate files. With this in mind, let's start first by exploring the changes we need to implement to fix the layout for portrait mode.

Updating Portrait Mode

So far, we've updated our design to cater to cell phones (albeit in portrait mode only) – we can use the same process to add changes to cater to tablets.

It means we should end up with a CSS overrides file for tablets – this will give us an idea of what needs to change and whether we can merge the styles into core (remember that question I asked earlier?). Let's dive in and look at the steps required in more detail.

FIXING PORTRAIT MODE FOR TABLET

To fix the styling issues for our chosen mobile device, follow these steps:

1. First, go ahead and create a file called `tablet.css` in the `\src\ styles` folder.

2. Next, crack open the `_app.js` file in the `\pages` folder, then add this line under the last import statement:

    ```
    import "../styles/tablet.css";
    ```

Make sure this entry is **below** the one for `globals.css` — we need to make sure this kicks in after all base styles are applied from this file.

---

3. We now need to add our styles – switch to the `tablet.css` file we created in step 1, then add this code:

    ```
    @media (min-width: 414px) and (max-width: 820px) {
      body {
        width: 100%; display: flex;
      }

      .product-detail-container {
        margin: 0;
        padding: 40px;
      }
    ```

```
footer > div:nth-child(1) {
  padding: 30px;
}

.cart-wrapper {
  top: 190px;
  width: 100%;
  min-height: 2000px;
}

@keyframes movemobile {
  0% { transform: translateY(-40%); }
  100% { transform: translateY(0%); }
}

.cart-container {
  height: 0;
  min-height: 500px;
  width: 100%;
  animation-name: movemobile;
  animation-duration: 2s;
  animation-iteration-count: 1;
  animation-fill-mode: forwards;
  display: flex;
  flex-direction: column;
}
}
```

4. Save and close the file. Next, fire up a Node.js terminal, then change the working folder to our project area.

5. At the prompt, enter npm run dev and press Enter, then browse to http://localhost:3000 in your browser.

6. Once running, press Ctrl+Shift+I, then Ctrl+Shift+M (or Cmd+Shift+I, Cmd+Shift+M, if running on a Mac) to activate Chrome's Responsive Mode.

7. With the mode activated, choose iPad Air from the Dimensions: menu – if all is well, we should see something akin to the screenshot shown in Figure 6-8.

Fantastic – we now have a working design for tablet mode! We used the same process as before, with a CSS overrides file that applies the changes after loading the initial core styles into our site. Indeed, the only differences are that we set a different breakpoint (which is to be expected) and that some values assigned to each property might be different compared to those we used for mobile devices.

Keep that in mind, as I will be coming back to that question I asked earlier; for now, though, let's take a look at the final design, which is for tablets in landscape mode.

Figure 6-8. *The updated design for tablet in portrait mode*

Checking Landscape Mode

By now, I'm sure you're probably thinking I know what the process is – we need to add a media query for landscape mode, then add the relevant styles; we can put all of this into the same tablet.css file we created just now, right? Well – hold your horses, dear reader, as we don't need to do anything!

Cast your mind back to the checks we performed earlier – we found that the site works pretty well as is, without any changes needed for landscape mode. It should come as no surprise that as this mode is very close to desktop anyway, there was every likelihood that we wouldn't need to change too much anyway. Granted, we might want to apply tweaks to our design to improve the styling even further, but that can come later – we at least have something presentable. Or do we?

Merging the Styles

Cast your mind back to that question I asked earlier about merging styles and whether we still need to keep separate override files for each device type. With that in mind, take another **closer** look at our styles – notice anything in particular?

Many of the style rules I've implemented in the overrides are the same for tablet and mobile, so we should at least be able to merge most styles into one file. We could probably go as far as bringing these styles into the core so that we can do away with overrides, but that's something we can look at doing at a later date! For now, let's work on reducing the styles into one file as part of the next demo.

MERGING STYLES INTO ONE

To merge the styles into a single file, follow these steps:

1. First, we need to create a new file in the \src\styles\overrides folder – save it as portable.css.

2. Next, crack open _app.js – comment out any imports for tablet.css and mobile.css; we still need globals.css, plus the two stylesheet files for the About page.

3. Immediately below the last stylesheet import, go ahead and add this line of code:

```
import "../styles/overrides/portable.css"
```

4. Open the portable.css file in your editor – we need to add the combined styles from the previous override stylesheets. There is a good chunk of code to add, so we'll do it in blocks, starting with the updated @keyframe needed for the animation:

```
@keyframes movemobile {
  0% {
    transform: translateY(-40%);
  }
  100% {
    transform: translateY(0%);
  }
}
```

5. Next comes the combined media query to serve all changes below 820px, which are the same for both mobile and tablet:

```
@media (max-width: 820px) {
  html {
    display: flex;
    width: 100%;
  }

  footer > div:nth-child(1) {
    padding: 30px;
  }

  .cart-wrapper {
    top: 190px;
    width: 100%;
    min-height: 2000px;
  }

  .cart-container {
    min-height: 500px;
    width: 100%;
```

```
      animation-name: movemobile;
      animation-duration: 2s;
      animation-iteration-count: 1;
      animation-fill-mode: forwards;
      display: flex;
      flex-direction: column;
    }
  }
```

6. Some styles can't be shared between devices, so we need to put them into individual media queries. Let's add the one for mobiles first, using the same max-width media query as before:

```
@media (max-width: 414px) {
  .product-detail-container {
    margin: 60px;
  }
}
```

7. We need to do the same thing for tablets in portrait mode, so go ahead and add the query for this one:

```
@media (min-width: 414px) and (max-width: 820px) {
  .product-detail-container {
    margin: 0;
    padding: 40px;
  }

  .cart-container {
    height: 0;
  }
}
```

8. Save and close the file. Next, fire up a Node.js terminal, then change the working folder to our project area.

9. At the prompt, enter npm run dev and press Enter, then browse to http://localhost:3000 in your browser.

10. Once running, press Ctrl+Shift+I, then Ctrl+Shift+M (or Cmd+Shift+I, Cmd+Shift+M, if running on a Mac) to activate Chrome's Responsive Mode.

11. With Chrome's Responsive Mode enabled, try browsing through the pages – use the selector at the top to flip between different modes. We should see no visual change from before, but we're only using one override stylesheet this time, not two!

Perfect – we've managed to combine our override styles into one file and set it so that both tablet and mobile share most of the styles. This is a great improvement – I suspect we can do more, but I'm a great fan of iterating over time, so we can return to that later.

In the meantime, it's worth going through the changes we made – many will use the same principles from previous exercises but with a few key differences. We've moved the `@keyframe` to the top of the file (and outside the queries). This won't affect desktop, as it is only called from within this file.

The two previous queries are still present, but we've moved most of the code into a single `@media (max-width: 820px)` query. This contains the common styles from both tablet and mobile, so it will apply to any devices with a max-width of 820px, which will be mobiles and tablets (the latter in portrait mode). Any styles that are not common will remain in their original query, which is now significantly reduced in size!

To round off the demo, we ran a quick check through each of the different modes to ensure that the site still operated as expected in our browser.

Summary

Throughout the last two chapters, we've spent time adding styles to our site – back in Chapter 5, we focused on the desktop, with mobile and tablet changes made in Chapter 6. It marks a turning point for us as we move from basic construction into implementing new features and generally tidying up and testing the site. We've covered a fair few changes in this chapter, so let's take a moment to review what we have learned.

We started with a quick look at setting the scene – here, we talked about which device types we would use to check our site. We noted that we could have chosen anyone of different mobile devices (and probably tablets, but the choice isn't so wide) – I chose some that we could mimic from within Chrome to give us a feel for how the site will look.

We then assessed the site in each device type, starting first with mobile, then moving to tablet in portrait mode, and finishing with tablet in landscape mode. Once done, we made some changes to each to correct the design, so it at least worked as expected – we focused on getting the basics right, intending to refine the design at a later date. To round out the chapter, we then tried merging styles into one stylesheet – this was because many styles were shared, so we could get some efficiencies from improving our code.

Excellent – we can move on to the next task with our site now looking half decent. It's at this point we can ask ourselves, what could we do to improve existing features or maybe add that extra candy? I have a few ideas in mind – join me in the next chapter, and I will reveal everything!

CHAPTER 7

Finessing the Site

We've gotten everything in place – our site is running: we have products in store and can now sell them, so is there anything missing?

At this stage, I am sure there will be: before we can test our site, now is an excellent opportunity to consider finessing the user experience. I can think of a few topics to get us started; how about adding that missing cancel page for Stripe or animating content such as an updated add-to-cart button?

There are a few things we can do, but before we get into the detail, there is one thing we should do first, which is to take stock of where we're at and see whether there is anything we should do to tidy up the site before adding more new features.

Taking Stock

Throughout this book, we've added many new features, hooked into a content system for the back end, and can now process sales through the site (albeit in a test capacity only, as I'm sure you will appreciate!).

So, what's next? Now would be a great time to take stock of where we're at – how does our site look? I know we're not yet ready to release into production; there's still more to come, such as adding SEO, language support, and testing features (all of which we will cover in future chapters). Even though this site is a demo, we should make sure it is tidy – have we removed any redundant comments or media we no longer need, for example? What about components – are they all correctly labeled? Do we have all the products we want in the back-end CMS system (i.e., Sanity)?

These might seem odd questions, but there is a serious point to this – while researching and building the demo site for this book, I came across instances where I knew I would need to tidy up or fix little "buggettes" (mini issues) in code that would not be good to have in production. Rather than get sidetracked, I kept a list of them, ready to look at fixing them in this chapter. We can implement several fixes, so let's dive in and look at what I found in more detail.

© Alex Libby 2023
A. Libby, *Practical Next.js for E-Commerce*, https://doi.org/10.1007/978-1-4842-9612-7_7

Tidying Up the Codebase

For our first task, we will work through a few issues I found while creating the demo for this book – none of these are significant, and indeed, customers won't even see some of them! Nevertheless, fixing them is essential to maintain a sound codebase. Let's take a look at the detail.

Note   Some of these bugs you may have already dealt with yourself or may not have: it doesn't matter. The critical point here is to encourage you to look at anything broken or not working 100% and see if you can fix them.

CORRECTING ERRORS/BUGS

To fix the bugs found during development, follow these steps:

1. First, crack open `Minicart.jsx` from the `\src\components` folder. Go ahead and rename Cart in the opening tag and export tag at the end of the file to `MiniCart`. Save and close the file.

2. Next, open `\components\index.js` and add this statement to the bottom of the list:

   ```
   export { default as MiniCart } from "./MiniCart";
   ```

3. We must also rename the name in the opening tag and export for the `PaymentIcons` component. Open `PaymentIcons.jsx` from the `\src\components` folder, and rename both instances of the word `Footer` to `PaymentIcons`.

4. Save and close any files open.

5. Next, go ahead and delete the `favicon.ico` file in the `\public` folder – this is the version from when we provisioned the site, which we will replace.

6. Extract a copy of these files and folder from the code download accompanying this book, and save them to the `\public` folder: `favicon folder`, `site.webmanifest`, and `browserconfig.xml`.

7. While researching for this book, I came across this error:

```
next-dev.js?3515:32 Warning: Prop `id` did not match. Server: "react-
tabs-56" Client: "react-tabs-4"
    at li
    at Tab (webpack-internal:///./node_modules/react-tabs/esm/
    components/Tab.js:47:62)
```

8. To fix it, crack open Info.jsx from the \src\components folder, then add
    this code immediately below the import for React:

```
import dynamic from "next/dynamic";
const Tabs = dynamic(
  import("react-tabs").then((mod) => mod.Tabs),
  { ssr: false }
);
```

9. Next, remove the import for Tabs from this line, so you end up with this:

```
import { Tab, TabList, TabPanel } from "react-tabs";
```

10. Save and close the Info.jsx file.

11. Next, open Cart.jsx – we have a warning that is appearing, which relates to
    a lack of a key tag for each item in the basket:

```
next-dev.js?3515:32 Warning: Each child in a list should have a unique
"key" prop.
Check the render method of `Cart`. See https://reactjs.org/link/
warning-keys for more information.
```

12. Add the key =... tag, as highlighted:

```
{cartItems.length >= 1 &&
            cartItems.map((item) => (
  <div className="product" key={item._id}>
    <button
```

13. Save and close the file. Switch to a Node.js terminal, then ensure the working
    folder points to our project folder.

14. At the prompt, enter cd sanity to change into the Sanity folder; press Enter.

15. To start the Sanity server, enter `sanity dev`, press Enter, then browse to http://localhost:3333 when prompted.

16. Have a good look through the records – do we have all of the fields listed and valid data in them? We need to make sure that what is shown in Shopify matches what is in Sanity. Otherwise, we will have problems with missing data!

17. Assuming all is well with that last step, go ahead and save and close any files still open, fire up a Node.js terminal, then change the working folder to our project area.

18. At the prompt, enter `npm run dev`, and press Enter, then browse to http://localhost:3000 in your browser. Ensure everything looks as it did before we made the changes, and you can browse the pages without issue.

Great – we may have completed some odd tasks in different parts of the site, but that's to be expected: the critical point here is that we've taken time to check over the site, fix any immediate bugs that we can, and generally make sure it is ready for the next task, which will be to add some new features. Before we do that, let's take a moment to review the changes we made in the last demo, so we can understand how they fit into the bigger picture.

Exploring the Fixes Applied

Wow – that was a lot of tidying up! Anyone might think that we'd not taken care over how we did things: in some respects, they may be right. However, I don't look at it that way – I would say that while this is a proof of concept, things won't be perfect. Instead, it's an excellent opportunity to refine what we have to make the code more solid ahead of any plans to create a proper production version. With that in mind, let's look at the changes we made to understand how this will help improve our codebase.

We started first with the `MiniCart` and `PaymentIcons` components – in both cases, these icons had incorrect opening tags, even though they appeared to work fine! We changed them to be correctly named in the code and added a call to `MiniCart` from the `index.js` barrel file.

Next, we added some missing manifest files and changed the favicon file; the former was reported as a 404 error in the browser (i.e., missing), and the latter was still the original file from creating the base site, which we needed to update.

The next two tasks we covered were related to warnings displayed in the console log. The first was a React Hydration error, where there was a difference in how the browser was pre-rendering the React tree for the Tabs component; this was out of sync with the DOM, resulting in unexpected content. The second one is probably more familiar if you've worked with React before – anytime we create lists, we need to add key tags. This is so React can correctly identify if items are added or removed and the order they should be displayed.

We then finished by checking the Sanity CMS system – while researching for this book, I noticed instances where items didn't appear to be present in the back-end database. A quick check through our CMS setup will help identify any missing products; if this is the case, we can add them so that our shop has the correct number of items on display. As a final step, we ran up the site in our browser to ensure everything was still displayed as before and that our changes hadn't had an adverse effect on our site.

Excellent – let's move on with the next task. We'll be looking at what we can add to customize our site, but before we do so, I want to touch on a small point worth mentioning: duplication in the `global.css` stylesheet.

Tidying Up: A Postscript

Although our demo is a proof of concept (and therefore not production ready), there is one thing we should be careful about, which is duplication in our stylesheet.

I know there is a temptation to add code in sometimes for a demo and not worry too much about where it sits in our code. Before long, that will trip us up if we're not careful; now is an excellent opportunity to quickly review the code and ensure we remove any duplication.

For example, I know that I (at least) have some duplication for the `.cart-container` and `.cart-wrapper` rules – I was able to remove this code from the `globals.css` file, along with this:

```
@keyframes move {
  0% { transform: translateX(100%); }
  100% { transform: translateX(0%); }
}

.cart-container {
  height: 100vh;
  width: 600px;
```

```
  background-color: white;
  float: right;
  padding: 40px 10px;
  animation-name: move;
  animation-duration: 2s;
  animation-iteration-count: 1;
  animation-fill-mode: backwards;
}

.cart-wrapper {
  width: 100vw;
  background: rgba(0, 0, 0, 0.5);
  position: fixed;
  right: 0;
  top: 0;
  z-index: 100;
  will-change: transform;
  transition: all 1s ease-in-out;
}
```

I suspect you will find something similar, albeit possibly not in the same places as my version; the important thing is that we check the code and remove any apparent duplication where possible. I'm not expecting it to look perfect for a demo or proof-of-concept site, but we can at least make sure we have one set of reasonably decent rules!

Okay – with that out of the way, we can start with the exciting stuff: customizing our site! We could do all sorts of things, depending on how far we want to take it; I've chosen a few examples to get us started, so let's look at what we will be building in more detail.

Customizing the Site

When it comes to customizing our site, it's tempting to go crazy and add all kinds of different features, but sometimes less is very definitely more!

I'm a great believer in only adding features that make sense and not just for the sake of trying something out. That said, one of the projects we will be tackling will be a real "will it work, won't it work?" choice – you'll see what I mean when we get to it! For now, though, here's a list of what I've chosen:

- Clearing the client browser token warning for Sanity

- Animating elements – add to cart button and flipping product tiles

- Adding a cancel page for Stripe

- Updating the star reviews to be more dynamic on the product page

Most of them are relatively minor changes, with only the review system being a slightly larger update – I've tried to choose ones that I hope will add a little extra sparkle and a sense of completeness to our site. We'll first start with a straightforward change: clearing the browser token warning for Sanity. It might be a small (almost) one-word change, but the size of this change does belie the impact it could have for us!

Clearing the Sanity Token Warning

While researching for this book, I came across a warning in the browser console for our site – it looks like the one shown in Figure 7-1.

Figure 7-1. *Warning about the use of a client token for Sanity in the browser*

For clarity, I've reproduced it here:

> You have configured Sanity client to use a token in the browser. This may cause unintentional security issues. See `https://docs.sanity.io/help/js-client-browser-token` for more information and how to hide this warning.

This is an interesting warning – as it turns out, it's a simple fix to clear it, so you think adding it and restarting our server would be all that is required, right? Mmm… maybe not – there is more to this than at first seems: let's start with clearing the warning, then I will explain why this might open that proverbial can of worms if we're not careful with our security.

CLEARING THE WARNING

To clear the warning, follow these steps:

1. First, go ahead and open \lib\client.js, then look for closing }); about three-quarters the way down the code.

2. Immediately before these closing brackets, add this line of code:

```
ignoreBrowserTokenWarning: true,
```

3. Your code should look like this:

```
token: process.env.NEXT_PUBLIC_SANITY_TOKEN,
ignoreBrowserTokenWarning: true,
});
```

4. Save and close the file. Next, fire up a Node.js terminal and make sure to set the working folder to our project area.

5. At the prompt, enter npm run dev and press Enter – if all is well, we can browse to http://localhost:3000 when prompted. We shouldn't see any warnings about using a token for Sanity in our browser, as shown in Figure 7-2.

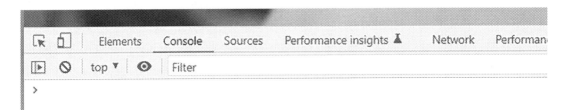

Figure 7-2. *Client token warning for Sanity no longer present*

Although this was a simple change, its simplicity hides a potential can of worms if we're not careful – this isn't a change we should affect unless we know what we're doing!

I've included it here as an example of why we shouldn't dive into tweaking our site unless with good reason – with that in mind, let's spend a moment reviewing the change in more detail and understanding why this isn't one we shouldn't make without due consideration.

Understanding the Significance of This Change

Fools rush in where angels fear to tread...

This proverb, from *An Essay on Criticism* by the English poet Alexander Pope, is a perfect way to describe making the change we discussed in the last demo. It might be a simple one to affect, but it potentially hides a world of pain if we've not been careful!

Why? The answer is simple – we shouldn't use a client token in JavaScript that a browser consumes unless absolutely necessary. If we do, we are leaving the site prone to unauthorized access, particularly if the data exposed is not meant for general public consumption.

You might rightly ask why I've included it here – it's a perfect example of why adding an innocuous-looking property could cause us trouble. I've taken us through this demo not because I would recommend blindly adding the token but to give this whole topic due consideration before implementing this change. Indeed, the better alternative is to use the environment variables file (.env) and add any tags there (as we have done for our project). We might still need to add the tag to clear the warning, but adding the key to the environment file won't expose it in the browser.

Note   You might want to try a similar exercise with the Project ID, too: you can add this line in your client.js file, then put the project ID value into the environment file:

```
projectId: process.env.NEXT_PUBLIC_SANITY_PROJECT_ID,
```

I've not seen any official documentation on this subject, but it seems to work, at least for me!

Okay – let's crack on with the next project. While building the site, have you tried to cancel an order and return to the product gallery? I'll bet that if you have, you might have come across a little problem...

Adding a Cancel Page for Stripe

Unlike our last change, where adding an innocuous-looking tag could cause us a world of pain if we're not careful, this next demo is something we need to implement on our site.

If customers decide to change their minds, we need to give them a way to back out of a potential purchase – Stripe already gives them this opportunity, but if we use it, we will get a 404 error! Don't worry, though, it's a simple fix – we need to add a new page and amend some styles. Let's look at the steps to get our page in place and ready for use.

ADDING A CANCEL PAGE

To add a cancel page for our checkout process, follow these steps:

1. First, open a new file in your editor – save it as `canceled.js` in the `\src\pages` folder.

2. We have a good chunk of code to add, so let's add it block by block, starting with the three imports:

```
import React, { useEffect } from "react";
import Link from "next/link";

import { useStateContext } from "../context/StateContext";
```

3. Next, leave a line blank, then add the opening tag for our component, declare a const for a call to `useStateContext()`, and add a `useEffect()` statement:

```
const Canceled = () => {
  const { setCartItems, setTotalPrice, setTotalQuantities } =
  useStateContext();

  useEffect(() => {
    localStorage.clear();
    setCartItems([]);
    setTotalPrice(0);
    setTotalQuantities(0);
  }, []);
```

4. Leave a line blank, then go ahead and add the return block, which forms the main part of our component:

```
return (
  <div className="canceled-wrapper">
    <div className="canceled">
      <h2>Your order is canceled - you have not been charged.</h2>
      <Link href="/">
        <button type="button" width="300px" className="btn">
          Continue Shopping
        </button>
      </Link>
    </div>
  </div>
);
};
```

5. We need to finish it off with the usual export statement:

```
export default Canceled;
```

6. Save and close the file. Next, crack open global.css, then scroll down until you see this comment:

```
/* SUCCESS-CANCEL COMPONENT ------------------- */
```

7. In this block, you will see three instances of the word cancel – change these to canceled so your code looks like this:

```
.success-wrapper,.canceled-wrapper { background-color: white; min-height: 60vh; }

.success, .canceled { width: 1000px; margin: auto; margin-top: 20px; background-color: #dcdcdc; padding: 50px; border-radius: 15px; display: flex; justify-content: center; align-items: center; flex-direction: column; }

.success .icon { color: green; font-size: 40px; }

.success h2 { text-transform: capitalize; margin-top: 15px 0px; font-weight: 900; font-size: 40px; color: #324d67; }
```

```
.success .email-msg { font-size: 16px; font-weight: 600; text-align:
center; }

.canceled { cursor: pointer; }

.canceled p { font-size: 20px; font-weight: 600; }
```

8. Save and close the file. Next, fire up a Node.js terminal and make sure the working folder is set to our project area.

9. At the prompt, enter npm run dev and press Enter – if all is well, we can browse to http://localhost:3000 when prompted. Browse to a product, then hit Buy Now to add to the basket, and Pay with Stripe when the basket appears.

10. On the next page (which is Shopify's payment page), click the back arrow to the top left (next to Mangez Macaron) – this will cancel the purchase request and return you to a canceled page, as shown in Figure 7-3.

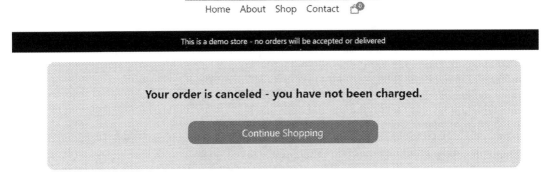

Figure 7-3. *Our new canceled page*

Et voila! Our new page is in place – customers can get out if they cancel a potential purchase. Granted, it probably won't win any style awards anytime soon, but at least it gives a proper way to exit the checkout process. To get here, we've added a good chunk of code, so let's take a moment to review the changes in more detail to understand how they fit into the bigger picture.

Understanding What Happened

Although it's never nice to see customers cancel an order, there will be occasions when it is necessary – we need to be able to handle cancellations when required! You might rightly ask why we've not added this page until now – it's a great question, and I probably don't have a sensible answer for it! Truth be told, I wanted to focus on the core pages to ensure we can push a sale through from start to finish, and the cancel page probably isn't one of those pages, but I digress…

So – what did we achieve? We began by creating a new blank component file, adding a destructure statement to get `setCartItems`, `setTotalPrice`, and `setTotalQuantities` from context. We need these values to work out what they hold at present before resetting all three to either `null` or zero and clearing `localStorage`. You will notice that we wrap these calls in a `useEffect` statement, to which we pass an empty array as the second parameter – this is telling React we don't need to worry about what the values are, as we don't depend on them, and do not need to rerun them.

Moving on, we then add the markup that forms the page – I've left it very basic for now, but I'm sure there will be an opportunity to tweak or add to it at a later date. We then finish off by amending some of the styles – these we added when we created the success page, and given we're reusing some of the markup from that page, it makes sense to use it. The only difference, though, is that I had to change the class name I gave to the Cancel page, so I had to reflect that change in the styling rules. We then started the development server and made a test purchase to verify that when canceling it, we did indeed get the new Cancel page displayed in the browser.

Okay – let's move on: it's time to step things up and get a little animated if you pardon the terrible pun! Over the following two exercises, we will add a little animation to our site. I've lined up two examples of how we can do this – one is to animate the Add to Cart button, and the other is to flip over the images in the product gallery. We'll come to that one shortly, but let's start with the add to cart button demo.

Animating Styles: Add to Cart Button

One of the essential requirements for our site (and indeed any e-commerce site) is to give feedback to our customers for particular tasks, such as adding items to their baskets. We have done this already, but while designing it, it got me thinking – is using the Toast option the best design? This was the perfect opportunity to devise an alternative – let's take a look.

ANIMATING THE ADD TO CART BUTTON

To animate the add to cart button, follow these steps:

1. First, crack open the `[slug].js` file in the `\src\pages\product` folder, then find the words "Add to Cart".

2. Below it, you will see a closing `</button>` tag – go ahead and add this code immediately below that tag, so you end up with something like this:

```
<button
  type="button"
  className="add-to-cart"
  onClick={() => onAdd(product, qty)}
>
  Add to Cart
</button>

{/* NEW BUTTON */}
<button
  className="button btn-cart"
  type="button"
  onClick={() => onAdd(product, qty)}
>
  <span>
    <span>Add to My Bag</span>
  </span>
</button>
```

3. Save and close the file.

4. Next, open `globals.css` from the `\styles` folder and scroll to the bottom of the file.

5. Go ahead and extract a copy of the styles from the code download, then add them to the end of the file. We have a lot to add, so I will go through it in blocks, starting with defining three overrides required for existing styles:

```
/* UPDATED ADD TO CART BUTTON */
.buttons { margin-top: 40px; }
```

```
.buttons .add-to-cart,
.buttons .buy-now { margin-top: 0; }
```

6. Next, we need to add three keyframes for the animation effects:

```
@keyframes shift-left {
  0% { transform: translateX(0); }
  100% { transform: translateX(-40px); }
}

@keyframes shift-left-circle {
  0% { transform: translateX(0); }
  50% { transform: translateX(-40px); }
  100% { transform: translateX(-40px); }
}

@keyframes shift-left-mask {
  0% { height: 7px; transform: translateX(0) rotate(0); }
  50% { transform: translateX(0) rotate(180deg); }
  100% { transform: translateX(-40px) rotate(180deg);}
}
```

7. This block takes care of the base styling for our new button:

```
.btn-cart {
  display: block;
  width: 200px;
  border: none;
  margin: 0 auto;
  background: none;
  background-color: #ffffff;
  font-weight: 500;
  color: white;
  font-size: 14px;
  position: relative;
  cursor: pointer;
  height: 45px;
  border: 1px solid #f02d34;
  font-size: 18px;
}
```

```
.btn-cart:before {
  content: "";
  display: block;
  width: 12px;
  height: 12px;
  position: absolute;
  border: 2px solid #f02d34;
  transform: translateX(0);
  left: 94px;
  border-radius: 50%;
  top: 5px;
  box-sizing: border-box;
}

.btn-cart:after {
  content: "";
  position: absolute;
  top: 0;
  left: 0;
  width: 100%;
  height: 100%;
  background: #f02d34;
  transition: all 400ms cubic-bezier(0.175, 0.885, 0.32, 1.275);
}
```

8. We need to add some styles for when the button has focus – this is taken care of by these styles:

```
.btn-cart:focus {
  outline: none;
}

.btn-cart:focus:before {
  animation: shift-left-circle 800ms forwards;
  animation-delay: 1200ms;
}

.btn-cart:focus:after {
  width: 20px;
  height: 20px;
```

```
  top: 12px;
  left: 90px;
  animation: shift-left 400ms forwards;
  animation-delay: 1200ms;
  transition-delay: 400ms;
}

.btn-cart:focus > span:before {
  animation: shift-left-mask 800ms forwards;
  animation-delay: 800ms;
  height: 7px;
}

.btn-cart:focus > span:after {
  transform: translate(-30%, 0);
  transition-delay: 1600ms;
  opacity: 1;
}

.btn-cart:focus > span span {
  opacity: 0;
  transform: translateY(20px);
}

.btn-cart > span {
  position: relative;
  display: block;
}

.btn-cart > span:before {
  content: "";
  display: block;
  position: absolute;
  width: 12px;
  height: 20px;
  background: white;
  top: 5px;
  left: 94px;
  animation-timing-function: linear;
```

```
    transform: translateX(0) rotate(0deg);
    transform-origin: center bottom;
}

.btn-cart > span:after {
    content: "Added"; color: green; position: absolute;
    z-index: 3; left: 50%; opacity: 0; transition: all 400ms cubic-
    bezier(0.175, 0.885, 0.32, 1.275); transform: translate(-30%, 20px);
    transition-delay: 0; }

.btn-cart span span {
    display: inline-block; position: relative; z-index: 2; transition:
    all 400ms cubic-bezier(0.175, 0.885, 0.32, 1.275); transform:
    translateY(0px); }
```

9. Save and close the file. Next, fire up a Node.js terminal and make sure the working folder is set to our project area.

10. At the prompt, enter npm run dev and press Enter – if all is well, we can browse to http://localhost:3000 when prompted. Browse to a product, then hit Buy Now to add to the basket, and Pay with Stripe when the basket appears.

11. On the next page (which is Shopify's), click the back arrow to the top left (next to Mangez Macaron) – this will cancel the purchase request and return you to a canceled page, as shown in Figure 7-4.

Figure 7-4. *The alternative Add to Cart Button, showing "Added" when clicked*

We now have our alternative button in place – but, before you all point out the obvious, yes, there is a reason why I've not removed the original! For me, I think this version has some benefits, but the design doesn't quite fit – what do you think? While you ponder that over, let's review the changes we made, so we can understand how it works in more detail.

Exploring What We Changed

Buttons are an essential part of any website, as I am sure you will appreciate – getting the design right is crucial. One might hope we don't need a lot of styling for a simple component – in our instance, we've added a considerable amount! Is this a good thing? Before answering that question, let's first dig into the code changes in more detail.

We began by adding our new button's markup to just below the code for the original Add to Cart button in [slug].js – this uses standard HTML markup but with an extra onClick() handler that triggers the same onAdd() function used by original button. We can assess how the new button works while keeping the functionality the same as the original button.

Next up, we added a slew of style rules to the bottom of the globals.css file – this included three @keyframe rules for the animation, plus a host of other styles you might find with any animated button component. To finish, we restarted the Next.js development server before browsing the site and initiating a purchase to see the new button on our product pages.

Right – back to that question I asked earlier: now you've seen the design, what do you think of it and the code we've used? I'm personally not sure about the colors; I know that red is frequently used for primary actions (such as buying – blue would be for secondary, informational actions). However, it seems like we've used a lot of code to style our button; while the action might be great, the amount of code needed is not so good. This is one of those occasions where we shouldn't be tempted to add features such as this without giving it due consideration – I strongly suspect we could improve on the amount of code used in this demo!

Animating Elements: Flip Tile

For our second animation demo, we will focus on the product cards in our shop – at the moment, these are somewhat static, so they feel a little plain!

The effect I'm going to add reminds me of an advertisement for a certain vegetable extract product with the tagline "You either love it or you hate it" (...or at least words to that effect). It's an animation that flips the card over to reveal an information panel when you hover over it – to save reinventing the wheel, I'm going to reuse an effect I found on CodePen, by Ciaran Walsh.

You can see the original at `https://codepen.io/littlesnippets/` `pen/dGbaOp`, with more effects on the LittleSnippets.net website at `www.` `littlesnippets.net`.

For some, it's a great way to provide a bit more information without having to view the product page itself, while for others, it could get in the way of doing just that: viewing the product page! Let's put any doubts about it aside for one moment and take a look at the effect in more detail.

FLIPPING PRODUCT IMAGES

To add the flipping effect, follow these steps:

1. First, crack open `Product.jsx`, from the `\src\components` folder, and find this line:

   ```
   <div className="product-card">
   ```

2. Immediately below, add this line:

   ```
   <figure className="fliptile">
     <img
       src={urlFor(image && image[0])}
       width={250}
       height={250}
       className="product-image"
     />
   ```

3. Next, add these lines immediately below the closing image tag:

   ```
   <figcaption>
     <p className="product-name">{name}</p>
   </figcaption>
   </figure>
   ```

4. Save and close the file. Next, crack open `globals.css` and scroll to the bottom.

5. Extract a copy of `flipping product images.txt` from the code download, and add this to the bottom of `globals.css`.

6. Save and close the file. Next, fire up a Node.js terminal and make sure the working folder is set to our project area.

7. At the prompt, enter `npm run dev` and press Enter – if all is well, we can browse to http://localhost:3000 when prompted. Browse to the Shop page, then hover over a product. You should see the image flip over to reveal that product's name, then flip back when you move the mouse away from it. I've tried to capture part of this effect in the screenshot shown in Figure 7-5.

Figure 7-5. *A product card in mid-flip*

Interesting effect, huh? We can add more information on this page and allow customers to add directly to the cart if we provide this option. I think it does raise a few questions about using it and how we might implement it – we'll answer those shortly, but let's first go through the changes in more detail.

Breaking the Changes Apart

Adding any animation effect can be a double-edged sword – if done with care, it can add a special touch; done haphazardly, it will look terrible! In our case, adding the flip effect to our product cards was pretty straightforward, but at the same time, it has shown up that the images are not of – shall we say – the best quality!

To achieve this effect, we wrapped the image inside a `<figure>` tag; at the same time, we inserted a new `<figcaption>` label, which contained an instance of the `{name}` placeholder, which we sourced from the site's `context`. We, of course, had to add styling – this we retrieved from the code download and added to the foot of our `globals.css` stylesheet.

This is where things got interesting – to finish the demo, we ran a quick check in the browser to see what it looked like. It was immediately apparent that some of the images had a background that got in the way of the effect and made it look less than perfect.

I had to amend the styling used from the original to make the image more visible; at the same time, I think we would have to amend our design so that we didn't include the product name twice. For example, we could add an Add to Cart button, a short description, or some indication of availability, such as "Sold in boxes of 12" instead of the product name. If we use this effect, I'm sure we could develop something more appropriate than simply repeating the product name!

Okay – let's move on to the final demo for this chapter: so far, we've set a static star count to represent a product review. It looks OK visually, but other than that, it doesn't really do anything! I think it's time we started to change that – let's make it a little more dynamic. It might not do everything we want it to do, but it will add a bit of realism to our site. We need to replace the components we've used so far with a new single component – let's dive in and take a look at what we need to do in more detail.

Updating the Product Reviews

I don't know about you, but I depend on product reviews – I frequently buy products online, and having something that helps me to decide what to purchase is essential if only to maintain my sanity!

We could do this in several ways, such as adding social media or customer comments, but one of the more straightforward ways is to implement a star count. It will give the customer a visual representation of what people think of the product – hopefully, the rating won't be too bad, so to speak! In this next demo, we'll focus on replacing the existing star components we've used so far with a new single component; this will form the perfect basis for developing it further at a later date.

DEMO: MAKING THE STAR REVIEW DYNAMIC

To make the star reviews more dynamic, follow these steps:

1. First, open a new file in your editor, and save it as `StarRating.jsx` in the `\src\components` folder.

2. We need to add quite a bit of code, so let's start with importing React and setting the opening tags and constants:

```
import React, { useState } from "react";

const StarRating = () => {
  const [rating, setRating] = useState(0);
  const [hover, setHover] = useState(0);
```

3. Next, miss a line and add the first half of our component:

```
  return (
    <div className="star-rating">
      {[...Array(5)].map((star, index) => {
        index += 1;
        return (
          <button
            type="button"
            key={index}
            className={index <= (hover || rating) ? "on" : "off"}
            onClick={() => setRating(index)}
```

4. Immediately below, let's add the second part of the component and finish it off with the usual export statement:

```
            onDoubleClick={() => {
              setRating(0);
              setHover(0);
            }}
```

```
                onMouseEnter={() => setHover(index)}
                onMouseLeave={() => setHover(rating)}
            >
                <span className="star">&#9733;</span>
            </button>
          );
        })}
      </div>
    );
  };

  export default StarRating;
```

5. Save and close the file. Next, crack open \components\index.js, and add this line to the bottom of the list:

```
export { default as StarRating } from "./StarRating";
```

6. Save and close the index.js file. Switch to [slug].js from within the \src\pages\product folder, and strip out the highlighted lines:

```
        <div className="reviews">
          <div>
            <AiFillStar />
            <AiFillStar />
            <AiFillStar />
            <AiFillStar />
            <AiOutlineStar />
          </div>
          <p>(20)</p>
        </div>
```

7. Replace them with a call to our new StarRating component so the code looks like this:

```
        <div className="reviews">
          <StarRating />
          <p>(20)</p>
        </div>
```

8.   As a last step, we need to add some styling to `global.css` in the `\styles` folder – go ahead and add this to the foot of that file:

```
.star-rating button { background-color: transparent;
border: none; outline: none; cursor: pointer; }

.star { width: 16px; height: 16px; display: flex; }

.on { color: #f02d34; fill: #f02d34; }

.off { color: #d3d3d3; fill: #ffffff; }

.on > path { color: #f02d34; fill: #f02d34; }
```

9.   Save and close any open files. Next, fire up a Node.js terminal and make sure the working folder is set to our project area.

10. At the prompt, enter `npm run dev` and press Enter – if all is well, we can browse to http://localhost:3000 when prompted. Browse to the Shop page, then click a product. You should see an updated star count below the main product title, as shown in Figure 7-6.

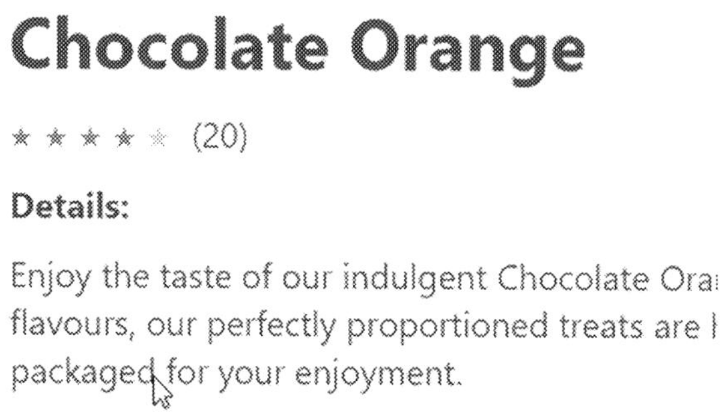

Chocolate Orange

★ ★ ★ ★ ☆ (20)

Details:

Enjoy the taste of our indulgent Chocolate Ora
flavours, our perfectly proportioned treats are l
packaged for your enjoyment.

Figure 7-6. *The updated star count below the product name*

Try hovering over the stars, then move your cursor left or right – you will see the stars change color, depending on whether you want to be mean and select one star or kind and set all five to red!

Perfect – that works better! Granted, it's not maintaining the state of the star count between visits, and we could do something better about averaging the count based on reviews, but that is for another time! In the meantime, it would be a great opportunity to go through the changes we've made in more detail and maybe cover some of the ways we can update this component in the future.

Understanding What Has Changed

So – what did we change in the last demo? We started updating our star review block by creating a replacement star review component – this we use first to iterate through an Array of 5 slots, where we store both the star state and index.

We use this first to set the className of on or off, depending on whether we're hovering over a star in a button. At the same time, we set both onMouseEnter and onMouseLeave event handlers to set the appropriate state of our star, which changes as we hover over the relevant button.

To implement the button, we removed the static SVG icon components from react-icon and replaced them with one component. We applied some extra styling in globals.css to ensure the star appears correctly on the page after restarting the development server.

Thinking further afield – how could we improve on what we've done so far? The obvious choice would be to maintain state so that values persist between visits; should this be by using localStorage, or do we call from the database? Alternatively, we might want to calculate the average based on the reviews from all customers and use this to set the star count. We'd probably want to do this only when the number of reviews changes and probably when we're displaying customer comments, too, to maintain transparency with our customers!

Summary

Until now, we've created a working demo of an e-commerce site suitable for small to medium businesses (SMEs). This demo works well – granted, it's not as complete as it should be, but that will come with time. One of the critical tasks we've had to perform is what I euphemistically called finessing our site – I suspect, though, it's really an excuse to make sure we tidy up our codebase before implementing any more features! On that note, let's take a moment to review what we have learned.

We started way back when by taking stock of where we are with our development – to kick this off, we worked our way through several bugs and issues that I found while developing the site for this book. We covered issues such as adding the correct name tags to two components, adding an updated favicon, and fixing some issues in the browser console.

With those out of the way, we then moved to add some new featurettes – these were not particularly large, although the styles required for one of them might say otherwise! We first explored how to clear a warning from Sanity before adding a cancel page for Stripe and working through two animation examples for our site.

Phew – we've covered quite a bit there! There's still more to do, though; it's time we turned our attention to looking at one of NextJS' strengths – it comes with three letters: S, E, and O. Intrigued? I suspect some of you might twig where I'm going with them, but if not – stay with me, and I will explain all in the next chapter!

CHAPTER 8

Implementing SEO

One of the key features of Next.js is search engine optimization, or SEO.

SEO is essential to help promote a site and get it in front of more people – while it can seem to be something of a black art, there are still things we can do at a starting level. These tasks won't replace in-depth tweaking but will at least give us a good grounding – as I'm sure someone once said, we do have to start somewhere!

Over the following few pages, we'll look at what's required to set up a basic configuration for SEO, work through some of the limitations and considerations around using Next.js, and explore what we could do in future development. First, let's ask a simple question to help set the scene: why is SEO important?

The Importance of SEO

Our website deserves a bigger audience.

Let's face it – without more people, our site would be lost in a sea of minnows! Although we can make it look stunning over time, without those extra people, we'll fight a losing battle without one tool: SEO.

SEO, or search engine optimization, is crucial in attracting more customers – it helps them find us and reach the top spot in search engine listings. The trouble is, improving any site's SEO is frequently seen as an opaque process. If we're successful, I suspect many people will see it as black box magic and yet not be 100% sure how to repeat it, let alone understand what has contributed to the success.

Fortunately, Next.js has several tools available to help make SEO easier to manage on our site – the developers treat it as a critical priority, allowing us to implement good SEO practices and patterns. We may never get to the 88.4 billion (yes, billion) visits each month that Google had as of November 2022, but with some work, we can undoubtedly get onto the long road toward success!

© Alex Libby 2023
A. Libby, *Practical Next.js for E-Commerce*, https://doi.org/10.1007/978-1-4842-9612-7_8

Over the next few pages, we'll focus on the basics to get ourselves started – SEO is an ongoing process that will only finish if we have no further need for our website. To get us started, we'll look at topics such as setting up default SEO values, applying Open Graph tags, structured data, and more. We'll even take a look at one of the more advanced topics related to SEO, which is internationalization – that's a big topic, so you'll have to wait until Chapter 11 before we can give our site more international flair!

In this chapter, we'll focus on the basics but include a bonus PDF covering adding OpenData tags and structured data support to our site.

Although there is plenty for us to do, there are a few things we need to be aware of with SEO and Next.js. Before getting stuck into code, let's begin with defining our strategy to see where to focus our efforts.

Defining Our Strategy

Creating a strategy should be pretty straightforward, even for SEO – after all, our vision is to see SEO set up on the site, with appropriate tags in place and pages optimized where possible. However, for us, it's not going to be quite as simple as that – let me explain what I mean:

I must admit I'm not an SEO expert by any means, so we'll focus on the *mechanics* of how we get tags into our site and **not** whether they are the most appropriate for that page. We are, after all, only running a proof of concept, so there will be more work to do before we can release – for now, it's more important to ensure we can get the tags in place.

This isn't our only challenge – at the time of writing, Next has just released version 13.2 recently. Ordinarily, I'm not a fan of adding specific versions in text, but in our case, there is a reason for doing so:

- Before version 13, we would have typically added tags to the `<head>` section of `Layout.jsx`, which works very well; we could also inject structured data simultaneously.

- With the advent of version 13, Next decided (initially) to use the `head.js` component. As a component, it worked in the same way as `next/head` and would replace the traditional method of adding tags manually.

- However, the head.js option was deprecated in version 13.2 and will likely have been removed when this book goes into print. In its place, we should use the recommended solution, which is the generateMetadata() function, but this only works for server-based components, not for pages.

These little quirks aren't going to make things any easier for us! It means we must use a combination of methods to inject tags into our site. The next-seo component will work fine for pages, but we'll have to add some custom code as the generateMetadata() function won't work for us: we're not using TypeScript, which means the changes won't get picked up on our site.

It's not helped by a shortage of decent documentation and examples for this new function, although hopefully, this will change over time.

With all of these trip hazards in mind, this is the strategy we'll use:

- We won't support the app folder introduced in version 13 – this (at the time of writing) is still experimental and unnecessary for our project. It did present something of a dilemma, as we could have used app and the generateMetaData() function. I'm not a fan of using experimental features, particularly if they don't (yet) have much documentation available. Instead, we will use a mix of methods to get data: this is probably less clean but more reliable.

- We need to ensure no duplication is showing in the head tags.

- We'll focus on a quick setup but then revisit to explore what options we can add as a second pass.

- Next-seo has lots of options – we'll use enough to get the site going but will cover some of the options we can use to refine the setup.

- We'll use the next-seo plug-in wherever possible, but we will need some custom code to make dynamic pages work.

Hopefully, this will make some sense as we work through this chapter – we may not start with the best approach, but the great thing about this is that it gives us cause to iterate and improve the setup. There are a few areas we can concentrate on getting our initial configuration in place; these include

- Adding a default setup and exporting to a custom configuration file

- Overriding options – how can we customize the configuration?

- Adding support for structured (or JSON-LD) data and Open Graph tags

At the same time, we'll take a look at other SEO options available to use, as well as some of the common meta tags we might use when working with SEO in a Next.js environment.

Okay – enough chitchat: let's crack on! The first task is to get a basic SEO configuration in place; to do this, we'll use the next-seo plug-in Available from `https://github.com/garmeeh/next-seo`, we can use this to add basic tags to the head of our site and as a basis for additional options such as Open Graph and structured data tags. This plug-in is straightforward to set up, so let's dive in and take a look in more detail as part of our next demo.

Adding Default SEO to Our Site

For our first task, we will set up a basic SEO configuration – this will primarily be what's available out of the box, with little or no configuration. Before we do this, it's worth looking at what we've already inserted manually – some tags are present, which we added when we created `Layout.jsx`, which we can see in Figure 8-1.

```
▼<head> == $0
   <meta charset="utf-8">
   <meta name="viewport" content="width=device-width">
   <title>Macaron Magic | great tasting home-made macarons</title>
   <meta name="msapplication-TileColor" content="#da532c">
   <meta name="theme-color" content="#ffffff">
   <link rel="apple-touch-icon" sizes="180x180" href="/favicon/apple-touch-ico
   <link rel="icon" type="image/png" sizes="32x32" href="/favicon/favicon-32x3;
   <link rel="icon" type="image/png" sizes="16x16" href="/favicon/favicon-16x1(
   <link rel="manifest" href="/site.webmanifest">
   <link rel="mask-icon" href="/favicon/safari-pinned-tab.svg" color="#5bbad5":
   <meta name="next-head-count" content="10">
```

Figure 8-1. *The current setup, based on tags added in Layout.jsx*

Let's improve on this by installing the next-seo plug-in, which we will use throughout this chapter, to set our SEO tags for us.

ADDING NEXT-SEO

To set up basic SEO support for our site, follow these steps:

1. First, fire up a Node.js terminal session, then change the working folder to our project area.

2. At the prompt, enter `npm install next-seo -D`, then press Enter to install the `next-seo` plug-in.

3. We can now add the component – we'll start with the homepage. Crack open `index.js` from the `\src\pages` folder, then find the line starting with `const Home = () => (`.

4. Immediately below it, add an opening React fragment and then the call to NextSEO, so the opening code for the component looks like this:

```
const Home = () => (
  <>
    <NextSeo
      title="Macaron Magic"
      description="Great tasting home-made macarons"
    />
```

5. Scroll down to the end, then just before the closing) ; add a closing React fragment tag:

```
    </div>
  </>
);
```

6. Save and close the file. Switch to a Node.js terminal, then at the prompt, change the working folder to our project area.

7. Enter npm run dev and press Enter to fire up the Next.js development server. Wait for the server to fire up, then browse to http://localhost:3000. Press Shift+Ctrl+I (for Windows or Shift+Cmd+I for Mac) to bring up the browser console. If you expand the <head> tag, you can see the entries, as shown in Figure 8-2.

```
<!DOCTYPE html>
<html lang="en"> flex
·· ▼<head> == $0
    <meta charset="utf-8">
    <meta name="viewport" content="width=device-width">
    <title>Macaron Magic</title>
    <meta name="msapplication-TileColor" content="#da532c">
    <meta name="theme-color" content="#ffffff">
    <meta name="robots" content="index,follow">
    <meta name="description" content="Great tasting home-made macarons">
    <meta property="og:title" content="Macaron Magic">
    <meta property="og:description" content="Great tasting home-made macarons">
```

Figure 8-2. *Confirmation of the new SEO tags on the homepage*

Perfect – we now have a basic SEO setup in place! You will notice from the screenshots that the original tags we had in the <head> tags in Layout.jsx are no longer present: these have been superseded by the new plug-in, so we can now remove the original <title> tag. Although this was a simple change to make, it opens up quite a few possibilities for us – let's take a moment to quickly review the changes we made before cracking on with customizing the setup.

Understanding What Happened

For the first task in this chapter, we started with something straightforward – installing the next-seo plug-in into our site.

It uses the normal `npm install` process, which is the same for all other npm-based plug-ins; we then added a call to the plug-in, into which we passed the title and description parameters. The only step left to complete was to run up the site locally and confirm that the browser rendered the newly added NextSEO block in the header of our site.

With our plug-in installed and configured, we've started adding SEO support. However, there is a small problem: it's only appearing on one page! We don't want to duplicate this setup across every page manually, even if we only have a handful of pages as we do on our site. What can we do?

Setting and Overriding Defaults

We need a better alternative – enter DefaultSEO. This is a function available from the same next-seo plug-in we've just used that works in a similar manner to the NextSEO function we've just used but with one difference. It does as it says on the tin – we can use this to create a default SEO setup across all pages automatically; if needed, we can override this configuration by providing specific values where needed on each page. Let's dive in and take a closer look.

OVERRIDE DEFAULT SETTINGS

To set a default SEO configuration, ready to override as needed, follow these steps:

1. First, go ahead and stop the Next.js development server if it is running – this is critical to rebuilding the pages for this demo.

2. Next, crack open `_app.js` from within the `\src\pages` folder, then add this import before the stylesheet calls:

   ```
   import { DefaultSeo } from "next-seo";
   ```

3. Scroll down a little, and look for the opening `return (` tag. Immediately below, add this code – notice that the closing tag for this block must be before the call to `<StateContext>`:

```
<>
  <DefaultSeo
    title="Next SEO Example"
    description="Next SEO is a plug in that makes managing your
    SEO easier in Next.js projects."
    twitter={{
      handle: "@handle",
      site: "@site",
      cardType: "summary_large_image",
    }}
  />
```

4. Go to the end of the component, then add the closing React Fragment tag so
    your code looks like this:

```
    </StateContext>
  </>
  );
}
```

5. Save and close the file. Next, switch to a Node.js terminal, then at the prompt,
    change the working folder to our project area.

6. Enter npm run dev and press Enter to fire up the Next.js development server.
    Wait for the server to fire up, then browse to http://localhost:3000. Press
    Shift+Ctrl+I (for Windows or Shift+Cmd+I for Mac) to bring up the browser
    console. If you expand the <head> tag, you can see the newly added title tag,
    as shown in Figure 8-3.

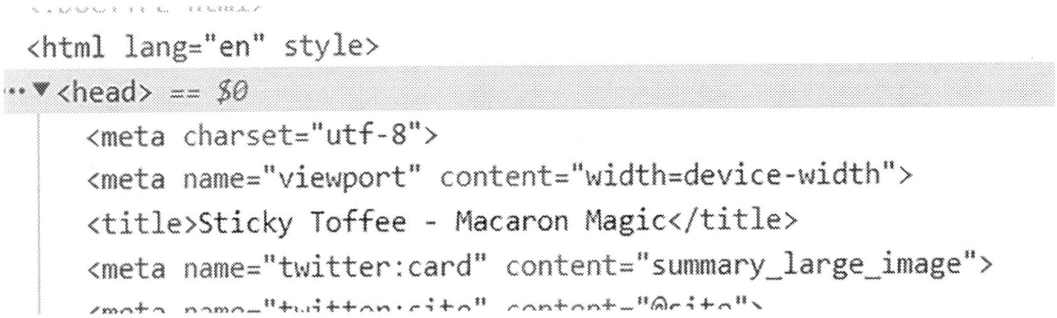

```
<html lang="en" style>
▼ <head> == $0
    <meta charset="utf-8">
    <meta name="viewport" content="width=device-width">
    <title>Sticky Toffee - Macaron Magic</title>
    <meta name="twitter:card" content="summary_large_image">
    <meta name="twitter:site" content="@site">
```

Figure 8-3. *The updated SEO tags for the homepage*

7. Now, browse to http://localhost:3000/about, then press Shift+Ctrl+I (for Windows or Shift+Cmd+I for Mac) to bring up the browser console. If you expand the <head> tag, you can see the entries, as shown in Figure 8-4.

```
▼ <head> == $0
    <meta charset="utf-8">
    <meta name="viewport" content="width=device-width">
    <title>Macaron Magic | great tasting home-made macarons</title>
    <meta name="robots" content="index,follow">
    <meta name="twitter:card" content="summary_large_image">
    <meta name="twitter:site" content="@site">
    <meta name="twitter:creator" content="@handle">
    <meta name="msapplication-TileColor" content="#da532c">
    <meta name="theme-color" content="#ffffff">
    <link rel="apple-touch-icon" sizes="180x180" href="/favicon/apple-touch-icon.png">
    <link rel="icon" type="image/png" sizes="32x32" href="/favicon/favicon-32x32.png">
    <link rel="icon" type="image/png" sizes="16x16" href="/favicon/favicon-16x16.png">
    <link rel="manifest" href="/site.webmanifest">
    <link rel="mask-icon" href="/favicon/safari-pinned-tab.svg" color="#5bbad5">
    <meta name="description" content="Next SEO is a plug in that makes managing your SE
    easier in Next.js projects.">
    <meta property="og:title" content="Next SEO Example">
```

Figure 8-4. *The SEO tags for the About page*

8. Notice how the tags are slightly different? We overrode some of the tags for the first example by specifying our version; in the second example, we're using the default tags set in _app.js.

Note   I've focused on getting SEO tags implemented and working; there's a good opportunity to move the <DefaultSEO.../> block into its own component if we felt this was right. It's worth noting that doing this probably won't give us any efficiencies; it's more likely to make reading the contents of the _app.js file easier!

Perfect – with the basic SEO configuration in place, we're ready to start going to town and really start to customize our setup... or can we?

I have a small confession: this was only partially true when I said we overrode some of the settings. If you take a closer look at the screenshot in Figure 8-4, you will hopefully notice that we still have the original `<title>` tag showing from prior to us installing next-seo for the first time. If we include this tag, we can expect that to override our next-seo setup. It's perhaps time we made sure this doesn't happen and remove that old `<title>` entirely!

Breaking Apart the Changes

With that done, let's take a closer look at the changes we made – we first added an import for the DefaultSEO function from the next-seo plug-in before creating a DefaultSEO block.

Inside this block, we've set the `title`, `description`, and `twitter` parameters – notice that I've set them to text that is not what we would put into a production site! It might look a little odd, but there is a reason for this: we can use it as a check to see if the text is coming through correctly, as we did in step 7. It means that if we don't override, the default text will automatically permeate through all the page components on our site. It won't filter through to components, but that's the other part of our challenge – we'll rectify it later in this chapter.

Okay – let's move on and look at ways we can customize our setup. We've mentioned features such as structured data and Open Graph support – what about also making some of the tags in our pages more dynamic? I'm sure there will be occasions when we want to include product names in our tags; we will explore this shortly. For now, let's revisit some of the ways we can update our configuration before taking a look at some of the commonly used tags for our next-seo plug-in in more detail.

Updating Our Configuration

So far, we've been through the process of setting up the next-seo plug-in and exploring how we might override default settings in our code. This is all well and good, but – what if we end up with a lot of settings we need to pass to the component, particularly if we need to use the same values in multiple places?

There is an answer to this thorny problem – we can use a configuration file. The next-seo plug-in supports using a `next-seo.config.js` file to dump all of the default entries. It keeps our code clean – we only need to add entries where it overrides a specific entry in our code. Let's look at what's involved and explore some of the settings we can add to the updated configuration.

SWITCHING TO A CONFIGURATION FILE

To switch to using a configuration file, follow these steps:

1. First, we need to create the config file – for this, crack open a new file in your editor, then add this code:

```
export default {
  openGraph: {
    type: "website",
    locale: "en_IE",
    url: "https://www.url.ie/",
    siteName: "SiteName",
  },
  twitter: {
    handle: "@handle",
    site: "@site",
    cardType: "summary_large_image",
  },
};
```

2. Save it as `next-seo.config.js` in the root of our project folder.

3. Next, open `_app.js`, then add this import at the bottom of the imports list:

```
import SEO from "../../next-seo.config";
```

4. We now need to update the configuration in _app.js – go ahead and add this prop immediately after the opening <DefaultSEO tag, like this:

```
<DefaultSeo
  {...SEO}
  title="Next SEO Example"
```

5. Next, alter the block so that we only introduce `title`, `description`, and `twitter` parameters – the rest will come from the newly added default configuration file:

```
<DefaultSeo
  {...SEO}
  title="Next SEO Example"
```

```
              description="Next SEO is a plug in that makes managing your
              SEO easier in Next.js projects."
              twitter={{
                handle: "@handle",
                site: "@site",
                card: "summary_large_image",
              }}
            />
```

6. Save and close anything you have open. Next, switch to a Node.js terminal, then at the prompt, change the working folder to our project area.

7. Enter npm run dev and press Enter to fire up the Next.js development server. Wait for the server to fire up, then browse to http://localhost:3000. Press Shift+Ctrl+I (for Windows or Shift+Cmd+I for Mac), to bring up the browser console. If you expand the <head> tag, you can see the newly added title tag, as shown in Figure 8-5.

```
<meta name="viewport" content="width=device-width">
<title>Next SEO Example</title>
<meta name="robots" content="index,follow">
<meta name="description" content="Next SEO is a plug in that
anaging your SEO easier in Next.js projects.">
<meta name="twitter:card" content="summary_large_image">
<meta name="twitter:site" content="@site">
<meta name="twitter:creator" content="@handle"> == $0
```

Figure 8-5. Confirmation that the new configuration file is working

So what did we achieve in this last demo?

Adding a configuration file is a great way to save time when it comes to SEO – we can set up the site to reference any SEO tags required for a page from a central file. This leaves us to add any that are extra or specific to a page – it makes the page content shorter, easier to manage, and reduces the risk of missing a common tag!

To get there, we created the next-seo.config.js file, which sits at the root of our project folder. Inside this file, we added Open Graph and Twitter tags, two tools useful for maintaining SEO. We then updated the _app.js page to include the configuration via a spread operator – if any tags which appear in the configuration file are then included again, the later tags will take precedence; all other tags will come from the main configuration file.

We've used a few of the more commonly used tags, but the next-seo component has a host of others we could easily include in our setup! To give you a flavor, I've listed some of these tags in Table 8-1.

Table 8-1. *A list of commonly used tags for the Next-SEO plug-in*

Common options and meta tags	Purpose
defaultTitle	If no title is set on a page, this string will be used instead of an empty title
noindex	Option to set whether the page should be indexed or not
nofollow	Option to set whether the page should be followed or not
canonical	Set the page's canonical URL
facebook.appId	Add Facebook app ID to your page to receive Facebook Insights data
additionalMetaTags	Additional meta tags like title and content
additionalLinkTags	Additional meta links like favicons

It's worth noting that a longer list of tags that are supported in the Next-SEO plug-in is available at `https://github.com/garmeeh/next-seo#nextseo-options`.

Okay – let's crack on: so far, our setup has been pretty straightforward, but there is a wrinkle we need to deal with in our plans. The issue I'm thinking of is related to the dynamic pages we use for products – try looking at the SEO tags in a developer console, and you might notice a problem. We cannot ignore it if we go into production, so let's look at the issue in more detail.

Making Page Headings Dynamic

So far, we've added tags to each of the pages in our site using the next-seo plug-in – while this may work for static pages such as our About page, we have a problem with dynamic pages.

Our issue is that the next-seo plug-in will rapidly iterate through each of the products in our shop and insert what is likely to be the final product it sees as our SEO title tag. The net result is that while the main title on the customer-facing page will be correct, the one in the `<title>` tag will be anything but!

There is a solution: the official route is to use a new `generateMetadata()` function, but we've already talked about this won't work for us, owing to our setup. We need a different way.

Fortunately, we can achieve the proper effect by still using the next-seo plug-in, but we need to iterate through each product and only use it when it matches the URL used for our product. Let's take a look at how as part of our next demo.

ADDING DYNAMIC NAMES

To add dynamic names as SEO tags, follow these steps:

1. First, crack open `Product.jsx` in your editor – we need to add a fair bit of code, which we will do in sections, starting with importing the SEO plug-in, and the `useRouter` plug-in from Next.js:

```
import { useRouter } from "next/router";
import { NextSeo } from "next-seo";
```

2. Next, we need to add a helper function – this will convert our chosen product name into title case, ready for inserting into the title. Leave a line blank, then add this function:

```
function toTitleCase(str) {
  return str.replace(/\w\S*/g, function (txt) {
    return txt.charAt(0).toUpperCase() + txt.substr(1).toLowerCase();
  });
}
```

3. Next, we need to pick the right name and make sure it matches what's shown in the URL – for this, add the following code after the opening line of our component and before the return tag, as shown:

```
const Product = ({ product: { image, name, slug, price } }) => {
  const { asPath } = useRouter();

  let seoProductSlug = asPath.split("/")[2];
  let seoProductName = "";

  if (seoProductSlug != null) {
    seoProductName = seoProductSlug.replace("-", " ");

    if (seoProductSlug === slug.current) {
      seoProductName = toTitleCase(seoProductSlug.replace("-", " "));
    }
  }

  return (
```

4. We can now use the results of that code to create our dynamic tags – scroll down further until you see the title parameter in the NextSeo component, and amend as shown:

```
<>
  <NextSeo
    title={`${toTitleCase(seoProductName)} - Macaron Magic`}
    description="Great tasting home-made macarons"
  />
```

5. Enter npm run dev and press Enter to fire up the Next.js development server. Wait for the server to fire up, then browse to http://localhost:3000/products/cranberry-clementine. Press Shift+Ctrl+I (for Windows or Shift+Cmd+I for Mac), to bring up the browser console. If you expand the <head> tag, you can see the entries, as shown in Figure 8-6.

```
<!DOCTYPE html>
<html lang="en" style>
▼<head>
    <meta charset="utf-8">
    <meta name="viewport" content="width=device-width">
    <title>Cranberry Clementine - Macaron Magic</title>
    <meta name="twitter:card" content="summary_large_image">
    <meta name="twitter:site" content="@site">
    <meta name="twitter:creator" content="@handle">
    <meta property="og:url" content="https://www.url.ie/">
```

Figure 8-6. *Checking that the Product name displays in the SEO tags*

6. Let's make sure that our tag is indeed dynamic. To do so, choose a different product in the shop – I've chosen Chocolate Orange in my example – and bring up the Developer Console area as before. If we expand the <head> tag, we should see a different name appear, as shown in Figure 8-7.

```
\!DOCTYPE html>
<html lang="en" style>
···▼<head> == $0
    <meta charset="utf-8">
    <meta name="viewport" content="width=device-width">
    <title>Chocolate Orange - Macaron Magic</title>
    <meta name="twitter:card" content="summary_large_image">
```

Figure 8-7. *A second example: Chocolate Orange*

The key here is to ensure that the URL, name on the page, and the <title> tags all match – we can always look at optimizing this solution later!

Perfect – that looks better now that we have the right product name on each product page! Not doing so will not help us when searching for our products on Google – customers will be confused and probably walk away if they can't find the right product.

That aside, we've made some important changes in this exercise, so we should spend a few minutes reviewing the code to understand how these changes work and give us the results we need in our pages.

Exploring the Code Changes

Although adding the next-seo plug-in to our site was easy, it left us with one issue – what about our product pages?

As we've already seen, we don't have physical individual product pages but use a template to generate each during the build time. We clearly can't have the same SEO tags appear for each; otherwise, it will lead to problems! To fix that, we had to make some changes – we first installed the `next/router` plug-in, so we could use `useRouter` to work out which routing the customer took (and, therefore, what the page URL would be).

Moving to the central part of the component, we added a call to `asPath`, which gets the browser URL, then split it and extracted the final part (i.e., the page slug). We then check to make sure that this returns a non-`null` value – if it does, we then check to make sure it matches `slug.current` and reformat the result if it returns `true`. We can then use it as an interpolated value in the title property that we pass into the next-seo component.

We round off by checking it shows as expected in the browser before testing a new page and confirming that the name shown is different (but still matches the product rendered on the page).

Perfect – we're a step closer to having a basic setup in place for SEO. There is still more we can do – some of this will come with time, but for now, there are a few things I want to cover before we switch to using Lighthouse to improve our SEO, performance, and accessibility scores (all good for SEO!).

Taking Things Further for SEO

SEO is a vast topic in its own right – we've only scratched the surface of what is possible, particularly with Next.js! There are, however, a couple of things we can do to develop our setup further – let's take a look at them:

- We've used the next-seo plug-in throughout this chapter; while this works well enough, it's not using the latest recommended method. We should consider switching to/enabling the app feature in Next and using the new `generateMetaData()` function. I would have liked to have used it here, but it was still very new, and documentation was sparse. One of the priorities would be to keep checking for documentation and consider switching to using it once it has become more stable and mature.

- We should consider adding OpenData tags: I've included a bonus PDF in the code download that will start us off for this, but there will be more to do as time goes on. The same applies to structured data, or JSON-LD, tags.

- One tool that we've not had space to cover is a sitemap; this is an essential tool for SEO! Adding one now might be premature in some respects, given that we may want to add more content before moving into production. Whatever happens, we need to put this at the top of the list so one is implemented before that move.

I'm sure there will be more we can do – indeed, Vercel have an interesting article on their blog site, at `https://vercel.com/blog/nextjs-seo-playbook`, that details some of the areas to consider when it comes to implementing SEO. Granted, some of it might be tied to Vercel's platform, but there are some great ideas to work through to help develop our SEO capability!

Using Lighthouse

Performance is critical for any site in this modern age of the Internet – I've lost count of the number of times I've heard someone talk of "sub-2 seconds" when referring to loading time!

The truth is that we need our sites to be fast. Otherwise, people will walk – getting them back is hard, so we must be 100% on our game when assessing how fast our site runs. One way we can do this is by using the Lighthouse tool, which is available in Chrome – it might only do a page at a time, but I suspect once we start fixing issues, it will fix it automatically for other pages, and the issue count will fall.

When it comes to using Lighthouse, there are a few assumptions we need to work under to get the best use of the tool:

- We need to switch off anything else that might be running, so don't fire up that YouTube music video while you wait for the results! The results depend on available processing power, so you must ensure your PC isn't running anything that is really intensive.

- The same applies to plug-ins in your browser – you need to switch them off, as they can affect the results. Chrome will assess these as part of auditing the page, so you may end up with odd results that have no bearing on the site.

- It's important to realize that you may get a different view – this is about assessing what kind of things to expect and how we might fix them.

- Above all – don't expect the results to be consistent: they can change! The following fixes I outline are based on what I got, not necessarily what you will see in your browser.

Given the limitations, I know this might sound a bit draconian, but getting as accurate a result as possible is essential. We must assess the issues as examples of what we might see, not necessarily specific to our PCs. Okay – enough of that: let's crack on with testing!

Assessing Desktop Performance

To test our site, we need Google Chrome – the results won't be 100% as we're working locally, but it will give us a few areas to focus on before pushing our code into production.

For the following two demos, we'll cover testing for desktop and mobile devices; the focus will be on the homepage as our example, but the same principles will appear for other pages on our site.

ASSESSING LIGHTHOUSE PERFORMANCE: DESKTOP

To check our homepage using Lighthouse, follow these steps:

1. The first task is to create a production build – we won' get accurate results on a nonproduction build. Fire up a Node.js terminal, then change the working folder to our project area.

2. At the prompt, enter npm run build and press Enter to start the process.

At this point, you might find you get some errors appear when the build process has been completed, similar to this example:

```
./src/pages/index.js
```

```
39:25  Error: `'` can be escaped with `&apos;`, `&lsquo;`, `&#39;`,
`&rsquo;`.  react/no-unescaped-entities
```

I got this and one other example – I had to replace ' with ' in both /src/pages/index.js and /src/pages/contact.js, as well as fix the import for StateContext in ./src/pages/canceled.js.

The key here is to fix those flagged as errors for now – we can always come back and resolve warnings later.

---

3. Assuming the build is complete and no other issues have appeared, we must run the production server. At the prompt, enter npm run start, and press Enter.

4. Browse to http://localhost:3000/, then bring up the Developer Console by pressing Shift+Ctrl+I (Windows or Linux) or Shift+Cmd+I (Mac).

5. Go ahead and click the Lighthouse tab. Next, click the Desktop option and deselect the Progressive Web App option – we can leave all others as default.

6. Click the Analyze page load, then wait for the results to appear, which will look like those shown in Figure 8-8.

Figure 8-8. *Results from the Lighthouse desktop test*

7. You should see three dots above the result circles at the top of the report to the right – click this, then Open in Viewer to show the results. This will allow us to run the mobile test without losing our results.

It's important to note that you may not get identical results – this doesn't matter. Many factors can affect this test, such as processing power, the hardware used, and so on: it's more important to understand what we need to attend to and how to fix the issues. Before we investigate how to fix the problems, let's first turn our attention to running the same scan on a mobile device – who knows, we might get some similar issues there?

Assessing Mobile Performance

Checking our site on a mobile device uses the same steps as we did for desktop – we created a production build (or used the original one if we had just done it), then chose some options, and fired off the check to see what comes back.

In our case, the results were very similar – not perfect (which isn't great), but at least consistent with desktop devices! Let's take a look at the steps we need to do as part of the next exercise.

ASSESSING LIGHTHOUSE PERFORMANCE: MOBILE

Before we get stuck in, make sure you've run the steps to create a production build, as shown in the last exercise – once you've done that, follow these steps:

1. Assuming the build is complete and no other issues appear, we need to run the production server. At the prompt, enter npm run start, and press Enter.

2. Browse to http://localhost:3000/, then bring up the Developer Console by pressing Shift+Ctrl+I (Windows or Linux) or Shift+Cmd+I (Mac).

3. Go ahead and click the Lighthouse tab. Next, click the Desktop option and deselect the Progressive Web App option – we can leave all others as default.

4. Click the Analyze page load, then wait for the results to appear, which will look like those shown in Figure 8-9.

Figure 8-9.   The Lighthouse results for mobile devices

Perfect – the results don't look too bad for what is effectively a first pass! Sure, we have some work to do, but one thing to bear in mind: it is hard to get 100%, particularly in a production environment. We also may have constraints that mean we can't get it anyway – it's essential to be realistic about what we can and can't fix and potentially review troublesome areas regularly to see if we can improve on this in the future.

Responding to Issues

At this point, we should see a host of issues appear – don't worry: some we can fix, and some we won't be able to do anything about (at least not immediately), so don't be too alarmed!

The great thing about our test is that we only have two areas with less than 100% coverage for the homepage. SEO is almost 100%, and I know that with a quick fix, we can easily get it there. We don't need to concern ourselves with the PWA result, as our site doesn't use that feature.

So – what do we need to fix on our site? I've put together a list of issues that appeared, along with some comments as to whether we can fix them:

- Accessibility – We have a contrast issue on both Desktop and mobile, where the background and foreground colors do not have a sufficient contrast ratio.

- In the Performance tab, Chrome is flagging an issue with two resources from Stripe, where we're not serving static assets with an efficient cache policy. They were `https://js.stripe.com/v3` and m.stripe.network/out-4.5.42.js, respectively.

- An issue came up on both Desktop and Mobile for images being displayed with an incorrect aspect ratio – in this case, it was the `perfect.jpg` image of stacked macarons (Figure 8-10).

Figure 8-10. *The incorrect aspect ratio error reported by Lighthouse*

- Stripe threw up some issues, too, in the Issues log, around the use (or lack thereof) of cookies to denote if they are coming from the same site or not and should be secured (Figure 8-11).

> ▶ ▦ ② Audit usage of navigator.userAgent, navigator.appVersion, and navigator.platform
> ▼ ▣ ④ Indicate whether to send a cookie in a cross-site request by specifying its SameSite attribute
>
> Because a cookie's SameSite attribute was not set or is invalid, it defaults to SameSite=Lax, which prevents the coo
>
> Resolve this issue by updating the attributes of the cookie:
>
> → Specify SameSite=None and Secure if the cookie should be sent in cross-site requests. This enables third-party u
> → Specify SameSite=Strict or SameSite=Lax if the cookie should not be sent in cross-site requests.
>
> AFFECTED RESOURCES
> ▶ 2 cookies
> ▶ 2 requests
>
> ⊙ Learn more: SameSite cookies explained

Figure 8-11.   *Chrome reporting issues around cookies not set*

- I saw comments about the Largest ContentfulPaint element found on our site. The LCP was for the div.frontlogo element (or the banner image at the top). Although this isn't an issue, it's worth checking to ensure it has been optimized and maybe exploring whether we can serve this better (currently set as a background image).

- Lighthouse also threw up an issue around the lack of a Content Security Policy (CSP). We should always have it, but it will apply across the whole site and should be applied once the site is operational.

- The Mobile audit also flagged a problem with four links: the width and height were below recommended guidelines for buttons/links on mobile devices, as shown in Figure 8-12.

Tap targets are not sized appropriately — 69% appropriately sized tap targets   ⌃

Interactive elements like buttons and links should be large enough (48x48px), and have enough space around them, to be easy enough to tap without overlapping onto other elements. Learn more.

Tap Target	Size	Overlapping Target
a	250x21	a
a	250x21	a
a	250x21	a
a	45x27	a

Figure 8-12. *Report of tap targets not being sized correctly*

- In this case, the issue affects three links in the footer (Delivery, Privacy, Terms and Conditions, and Contact Us), plus the Shop link in the top header navigation – we need to adjust the size of both when rendering for mobile mode.

- In addition, I saw a few issues around using a standard `<img>` tag instead of Next's Image component. This also included a few warnings around missing alt tags, such as this one:

```
26:13  Warning: img elements must have an alt prop, either with
meaningful text, or an empty string for decorative images. jsx-
a11y/alt-text
```

- In both Desktop and Mobile, several reports around removing unused JavaScript came up; this is something we should attend to in our development process. I will pick up this in Chapter 10, as we can add a GitHub action that will help in this respect.

- The Mobile audit raised an issue around the image format we should use; Google prefers next-generation formats such as WebP. It is an easy change to make, but we must be mindful of supporting all of our target browsers – this is worth investigating further.

Great – an excellent selection of issues we can work with! Chrome did flag up other entries, but these were informational only, so they are not ones we need to worry about on this occasion. It doesn't mean we can treat this exercise as a one-off, though: we should continually monitor it in case other issues arise.

For now, though, let's turn our attention to working through these issues – we can highlight the ones we want to fix and work out which we can or can't fix as part of the migration into production.

Fixing the Issues

For the final demo of this chapter, we'll work through the issues flagged by Lighthouse and attempt to fix them or improve the code to reduce the impact.

We'll take a slightly different approach on this occasion and work through the highlighted issues as a checklist – it means some of them we can't fix, but we can at least explore why and see if there is anything we can do to mitigate the effect of the issue. With that in mind, let's take a look at them in more detail.

WALK-THROUGH – DEBUGGING LIGHTHOUSE ISSUES

Lighthouse flagged a good selection of issues – let's walk through some of them:

- Lighthouse flagged several Stripe assets as not having an efficient cache policy for static assets with a "Serve static assets with an efficient cache policy" warning. We can't do anything about this, as Google expects static assets to have a cache policy of at least 30 days; Stripe has indicated they need to keep the caching for no more than five minutes, as they may need to release updates quickly.

- We need to reduce unused JavaScript – Lighthouse indicated cases where we had excess code that we could remove. The best way to handle this is as a GitHub action; we can use the plug-in available from `https://github.com/vercel/next.js/tree/canary/packages/next-bundle-analyzer`.

This task is something we will cover later in Chapter 10.

- The frontimage.jpg image used as the banner image is very large at 213.7kb – this was flagged as the Largest Content Paint (LCP) element at 4.2 seconds. In this case, I don't think compressing the image is enough – we should reconsider a different approach. We set this image as a background image; I think part of the problem is that Chrome can't easily find the source of the stylesheet, so affecting the LCP score. Chrome advises that we should have a minimum of 75% or more for a good customer experience – we need to do some work here!

There is an interesting article on optimizing LCP on the WebDev website at `https://web.dev/optimize-lcp/`. It would be worth exploring it if we wanted to push this site into production.

- The next issue is (thankfully) easier to fix – Lighthouse reported problems with insufficient contrast on the "Go to Shop" button in the footer (Figure 8-13).

Figure 8-13. *The Go to Shop button, which failed a Lighthouse test*

- This issue resulted in a Contrast value of 4.09, which is too low – We need to have a minimum of 4.5 (Figure 8-14).

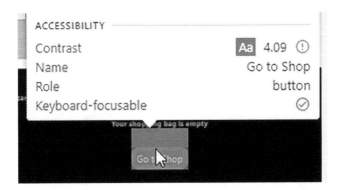

Figure 8-14. *Contrast ratio too low for the Go to Shop button*

- To fix the contrast issues, crack open `globals.css` from the `\src\styles` folder, and search for `background-color: #f02d34`. Change this value to `#d5272e` to resolve the problem – Figure 8-15 shows it is now fixed, as the value is above 4.5.

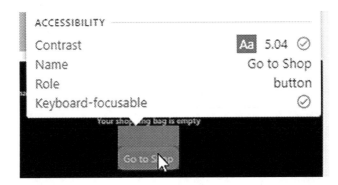

Figure 8-15. *An improved contrast ratio for the Go to Shop button*

- Lighthouse reported several missing alt tags in our code – This is an easy fix. Crack open the files where Lighthouse has seen this issue, and add `alt="..."` or `alt={...}` where required. Replace the ... with either a hard-coded name or the value from the product object (in the case of the Product component).

- We have one image Lighthouse reports as displaying an incorrect aspect ratio: `perfect.jpg`. The issue here is that the actual size of the image (640x640px) does not match the rendered size, which needs to be 442px x 532px, hence the warning. To fix this, we need to resize the image to 442px x 532px, which Chrome reports as the rendered size.

- We used `<img>` tags instead of the `next/image` component in a few places – This was flagged more as a warning in Lighthouse, and the recommendation would be to switch over to using that component instead of standard `<img>` tags. I tried this while researching for this book but came across some issues around using the `urlFor` function (required to ensure we get the right image). The code using `<img>` tags needs reworking as a more involved step.

- The last issue we want to look at is image format – For mobile devices (at least), Lighthouse is recommending using more modern formats such as WebP. WebP is ideal, as it is lighter than others, such as JPEG or PNG; all recent browsers support it. It's worth noting, though, that for our POC, using a JPEG image was acceptable – if we push into production, we should convert to using WebP throughout the site.

Phew – there were quite a few issues there, but fixing them will all help improve our Lighthouse scores. For example, fixing the incorrect aspect ratio issue resulted in a jump from 83% to 92% for me – it's worth taking the time to resolve issues where we can! Every fix we can implement will help improve the scores, resulting in a faster, smoother experience for our customers when browsing our site.

Summary

Implementing SEO is a super critical part of any website – this helps give us a leg up (so to speak) when it comes to attracting customers and appearing at the top of search engine listings. Fortunately, Next.js makes adding SEO tags easier and less of a black box exercise – we've covered some valuable tips in this chapter, so let's review what we have learned.

We started with a quick dive into the importance of SEO before defining our strategy and working through the steps to add a basic setup to our site.

Next, we worked through how to override the defaults, to display values that are more tailored to each page, and not display the same throughout each page. At the same time, we explored some of the limitations of our approach and how we had to work around them to add dynamic tags to our product pages. We then finished with a quick look at what we could do to take SEO further if we were to push the site into production.

Next up, we turned our attention to using Chrome's Lighthouse feature – we understood that we would focus on the homepage for this chapter but that any fixes could filter through to other pages and gradually reduce the number of issues found by Lighthouse.

We then assessed the desktop and mobile platforms before arriving at a list of issues we should fix from the audit. We then considered which issues could or could not be corrected (such as changing files not owned by us). We then explored some of the problems to see how we could fix them and improve our Lighthouse scores.

Phew – we covered a lot there, but it's all useful! We've completed the last of the development tasks, at least for now: what's next? Ah, yes – it's time, folks, to push our site into production. Yikes – this is where it gets very real...! But don't worry – it's not as difficult as you might think: stay with me, and I'll take you through everything in the next chapter.

CHAPTER 9

Testing the Site

Until now, we've concentrated on building our site, and it appears to be working as we expect – is this the case, though, or are there any tweaks we need to perform? Over these pages, we will explore how to perform unit testing. It will be very much with an e-commerce theme, but ultimately help guide the reader through some of the steps they should work through to ensure our site works as expected and is optimized before release.

We'll focus on the setup of our testing suite and start to create some tests – the latter will include both component and end-to-end (E2E) tests, so we can see if the site is working as expected. We have to start somewhere, so let's begin with setting expectations around how we will test our site and the tests we will create in this chapter.

Setting Expectations

When it comes to testing, there is a temptation to go over the top and test everything; indeed, if we did that, we would almost fill this book. Instead, we need to be more selective with what we test as our starting point. We'll set up some fairly simple tests so you can get a feel for how Cypress works; we can then explore other tests we might want to add later to increase code coverage.

At the same time, we'll touch on a few issues that might pop up and cause us problems; it will be an excellent opportunity to see where we could improve our site if we were to push it live. With all that in mind, I've elected to create the following tests (in no particular order):

- Adding products to the cart
- Clicking the review stars
- Visiting a chosen page
- Rendering the Credit Card images component

© Alex Libby 2023
A. Libby, *Practical Next.js for E-Commerce*, https://doi.org/10.1007/978-1-4842-9612-7_9

- Removing products from the cart

- Rendering the Payment Icons component

- Mocking and rendering the Product card component

- Displaying the Info component (used in product pages)

I will go through some of these tests in the book, but all will be available in the code download for this book.

There is something we do have to consider – at some point, we will be pushing our code into a repository, ready for release. We need to ensure that whatever tests we run can also be executed from the CI pipelines. I'm going to split this over two chapters – in this one, we'll create all of the tests we need and get them ready; we'll push execution of those tests in the pipeline to Chapter 10 when we look at releasing the site into production.

Okay – let's crack on: now we have determined which tests we will create, let's turn our attention to the most important task: selecting a testing suite for our site.

Choosing Our Testing Suite

When choosing a testing suite, we could use any one of a handful of different testing suites – these might include React Testing Library, Jest, Jasmine, or even something like Enzyme. All are perfectly valid in their own right and will work with React (as the basis for Next.js). However, I've elected to go with something different – Cypress.

Available from `www.cypress.io/`, this test suite is younger than some of its older siblings. It's a tool I've been using for a few years, and I have been impressed by what it offers – there are three reasons why it's become my preferred tool of choice:

- Unlike other tools, Cypress bundles all the tools applicable to us into one package, with an abstracted command layer to reference each feature. It makes it easier to run the required command without thinking about which package to import!

- When running tests, I've always found it harder to reference elements in the DOM – it's usually a case of what I think I should be targeting is not necessarily the same as what tool X thinks it should be! Cypress uses Chai-jQuery under the hood to reference elements in the DOM, which makes it easier to select elements when creating tests.

- Next has a page on their website with a few testing tools that they don't explicitly recommend as such, but they break down the steps we need to install each tool. Cypress is one of these tools, so it makes sense to go with something they recommend, even if it isn't official!

Of course, if you have your tool of choice, please feel free to use it – there are occasions where we, as developers, have to fit in with existing processes if they exist or where you might already have tools in place for testing that you need to use. Right – enough of that: let's get stuck into installing Cypress!

Installing Cypress

As a tool, Cypress offers both unit (or component) and end-to-end testing – both are available from a single UI but do require us to go through separate steps to configure both for use. Over the following few pages, we'll cover both setups needed to configure each before working through a handful of example tests as a basis for reviewing our site.

One of the great things about Cypress is that it will configure its testing suite automatically – it adds the files it needs and updates any configuration files where required for us. We'll explore this when we review the changes shortly, but for now, let's get the package installed and ready for its initial use.

SETTING UP CYPRESS

To set up Cypress, follow these steps:

1. First, open a Node.js terminal, then change the working folder to our project area.

2. At the prompt, enter `npm install --save-dev cypress` and press Enter to install Cypress.

3. While Cypress installs, open the `package.json` file in your project folder, and add the highlighted line as shown:

```
"scripts": {
  "dev": "next dev",
  "build": "next build",
  "start": "next start",
  "lint": "next lint",
  "cypress": "cypress open"
},
```

4. Save and close the file. Next, go ahead and open the `cypress.config.js` file in your editor and add the bolded line as shown:

```
module.exports = defineConfig({
  e2e: {
    setupNodeEvents(on, config) {
      // implement node event listeners here
    },
    baseUrl: "http://localhost:3000",
  },
});
```

5. Save your change, then revert to the Node.js terminal session from step 2, and at the prompt, enter this command to open the Cypress GUI:

```
npm run cypress
```

6. When open, click the E2E option to initialize the setup for end-to-end testing. Cypress will go away and configure our setup with some additional files; once the process completes, we will see the changes shown in Figure 9-1.

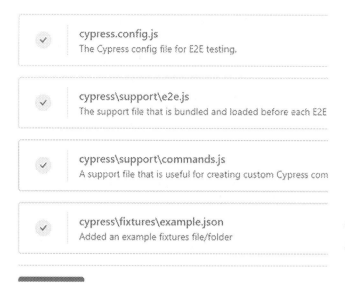

Figure 9-1. *The E2E testing option, ready for use*

7. Once ready, hit Continue, select Chrome as our chosen browser, and click Start E2E Testing in Chrome to begin testing. If all is well, we should see this page appear (Figure 9-2).

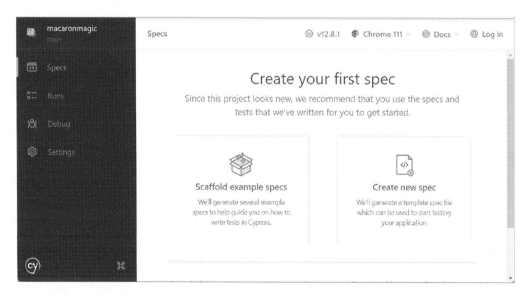

Figure 9-2. *The Cypress UI is ready for us to add tests*

8. Keep this running for now, as we will come back to it shortly – for now, though, feel free to minimize the window.

Perfect – we now have a partly configured Cypress set up, ready to do some testing. I say partially, as we'll be testing some components later, which requires a different setup. For now, though, let's review our changes to understand how they fit into the bigger picture of testing our site.

Understanding the Changes

Although Cypress bundles a host of tools as part of its package, we only need to install it using one command – each package comes already preconfigured, or Cypress automatically handles any configuration changes for us. Cypress is npm-based, so we use a typical npm install command to install it as a `devDependency` in our `package.json` (we don't need it in production, only development).

We then added an entry to the script block to make it a little easier to open the package – at the same time, we added the `baseUrl` property to cypress.config.js. It makes it easier to reference URLs in our tests – we can use relative URLs instead of providing the full path. Once done, we fired up Cypress for the first time; it runs through a configuration process, which adds a handful of files, such as `e2e.js` and `commands.js`, in the `\cypress\support` folder. Once complete, we hit Continue to be presented with a screen ready for us to create our first testing spec file.

Although most of the configuration process for Cypress is automatic, it's worth looking at the files in your editor to see what they look like.

Okay – now that we've been through the changes, let's move on to our next task. We've already seen that Cypress offers two types of testing at present, one of which is component testing. We'll explore that in more detail later in this chapter, but for now, let's dive in and look at the other option Cypress offers, which is end-to-end testing.

Creating E2E Tests

When it comes to testing, it's important to note which type of tests we want to complete. Some of you may have heard of unit testing, integration testing, or – as we're about to do – end-to-end testing. It's easy to get confused between each; while we want to test as much as is sensible to do, we might test areas of the site in a less-than-optimal manner!

For our first set of tests, we will focus on end-to-end, or E2E, testing. Starting with E2E testing first might seem odd, as we'd typically do component or unit testing first. However, as it happens, E2E testing tends to be easier to implement when using Cypress – I also know that some of our components may throw some issues that make unit testing harder, but this is something I'll return to later in the chapter.

There are plenty of ways to test journeys through our site, but we'll focus on some to get you started; we can return to others later. As part of the next demo, let's begin with a test for simple navigation around the site.

Note   To run E2E tests in Cypress, you must run the Next.js development server. Fire up a terminal, change the working folder to our project, and run npm run dev at the prompt before beginning with the next demo.

CREATING THE E2E TESTS

To create the E2E tests, follow these steps:

1. First, go ahead and create a folder called e2e in the \cypress folder.

2. Next, crack open a new file and add this code:

```
describe("Navigation", () => {
  it("should navigate to the about page", () => {
    // Start from the index page
    cy.visit("http://localhost:3000/");

    // Find a link with an href attribute containing "about" and
    click it
    cy.get('a[href*="about"]').click();

    // The new url should include "/about"
    cy.url().should("include", "/about");

    // The new page should contain an h1 with "About page"
    cy.get("div.about-us").contains("About Macaron Magic");
  });
});
```

3. Save the file as app.cy.js in the \cypress\e2e folder. If all is good, then you should see the Specs window (at the end of the previous demo), the change to that is shown in Figure 9-3.

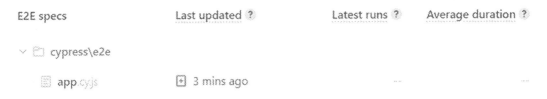

E2E specs   Last updated ?   Latest runs ?   Average duration ?

∨ 🗀 cypress\e2e

    🗐 app.cy.js   ⊕ 3 mins ago   ···   ···

Figure 9-3. *Updated Specs window with our first E2E test*

4. Go ahead and click the name of the test in Figure 9-3 – this will launch the test; if all is well, we should see a successful result, similar to the extract shown in Figure 9-4.

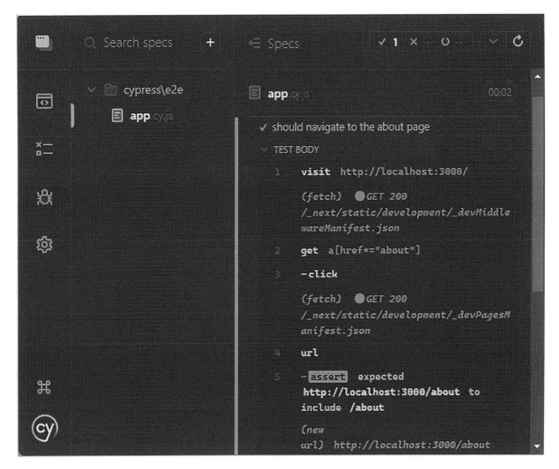

Figure 9-4. *A successful test run in Cypress' UI*

5.   Try clicking one of the steps against the number in the right column – you will see the image update on the right to show what the test was doing at that step (Figure 9-5).

Figure 9-5.   *The site at a specific point in the test process*

6.   Once the test has completed running, you can close the runner window to exit.

Don't worry if you can't see the detail – screenshots of Cypress' GUI don't always render well in print!

The critical detail, though, is that we see the green vertical line and a number against the green tick; both are indicators that the test was successful. Although this was a simple test, it is nevertheless worth spending a moment or two just going through the changes in more detail. Cypress uses similar testing commands to other tools, such as Jest, but there are some differences we should be aware of when testing our site.

Understanding the Changes Made

Writing tests can be a double-edged sword sometimes – some may be very easy to put together, while others can often leave you scratching your head around exactly how we should test that feature. Most developers will say we should test everything, but sometimes we must be realistic – it might not always be possible! (If this is the case, I would argue whether we should include or rework that feature, but that's a discussion for another time.)

Returning to reality, our first test was simple – one more for proving Cypress works than anything else! We added a new folder called `e2e` in the `\cypress` folder – this we will use to store our E2E tests. We then created the test spec itself – inside the usual `describe` statement, we first instruct Cypress to `visit` the URL of our site (`localhost:3000`) before getting the link that contains a URL of `/about` and clicking it. We then navigate to the `/about` page to confirm that there is a div on the page with a class of `.about-us`. At the same time, we also check that it contains the words "About Macaron Magic".

To round off the demo, we saved the test before clicking the name in the main Specs window, confirming that it executes as expected and that we get a positive result in our browser.

Great – we've completed our first end-to-end test and got Cypress set up! There are more tests we can (and should) do – I have a few examples in mind to help get you started, but feel free to add more if you desire. Before we take a look at the ones I have in mind, as part of our next demo, there are a couple of important points I want to touch on that relate to how we can improve the test we created in the last demo.

In the Spirit of Kaizen

Kaizen. I'll lay pretty good odds that this isn't something you've heard of before, so in the hope that I've not lost that bet, it is Japanese for "good change" or "improvement."

Strictly speaking, this would be a process that you would typically use for the benefit of customers – the five pillars of this process relate to topics such as getting to know your customer, empowering people, and beginning transparency.

However, I think that we can use the spirit of kaizen to improve our tests. While researching for this book, I came across an article about several ways we can do this to help step up our testing to the next level.

One of the points that stood out was not referencing elements directly in the DOM but using an alternative – data attributes. Don't get me wrong – there's nothing technically wrong with how we've done our test. However, there is always a chance that others might change references in code, which could potentially break our test! For this reason, we should use something like a data attribute so that the test should still work if we change the selector. Here's how that change might look, with the changes highlighted:

```
cy.get('a[href*="about"]').click(); -> cy.get('[data-cy="about"]').click();

cy.get("div.about-us").contains("About Macaron Magic"); -> cy.get('[data-cy="about-us"]').contains("About Macaron Magic");
```

It's worth noting that if you choose a unique selector of this type in Cypress, it will automatically prefer elements that begin with `data-cy`, `data-test`, or `data-testid`. The first one is more specific to Cypress, but the latter two are useful, particularly if you have colleagues using different testing suites!

On a separate note, cast your mind back to when we first set up Cypress. We added a `baseUrl` value to the `cypress.config.js` file – but we missed an excellent opportunity to use it! Instead of specifying the full root URL in the `cy.visit` statement we used, we could easily have used "/" instead. Cypress is clever enough to know that this equates to the base URL value we set up, so it will use this if it sees a relative link in a test.

If you are interested in reading more about the best practices to use with Cypress, there is a good article on the main Cypress website at `https://docs.cypress.io/guides/references/best-practices`.

Okay – let's move on: we've added our first test, which Cypress successfully executed. We should add more tests to expand our test coverage – I have a few ideas to get us started, so let's dive in and take a look in more detail.

Adding More Tests

When it comes to writing tests, it's essential to be clear as to what we want to test – it's all too easy to come up with an initial idea but then get carried away and end up testing more than you expect! That said, I have a few ideas to get us started:

- Testing the add/remove process for items in or out of our cart

- Checking the credit card images all exist

- Clicking the review stars to ensure we can select a target number

The middle one is very straightforward – indeed, this one should be in the component stack, as it is a component in its own right! The last one – clicking the review stars – is more akin to an end-to-end test, as although we could mount it, customers will click on the ratings stars at some point in their journey.

The test that is of more interest to us is probably the one of more interest to us – adding or removing products from the cart. It encompasses a lot of steps, many of which are similar; we can also take the opportunity to view what shows in the cart as part of the test. Let's dive in and closely examine the code required for this test.

For this book, I will go through the adding items to cart test in detail – the others will be available in the code download for you to have a look at your leisure.

ADDING ITEM TO CART

We can break this test down into three distinct parts – they are

- Navigating to our target product

- Adding the product to our cart and setting the correct quantities

- Verifying that the cart and minicart display the right product and quantities

To create the test, follow these steps:

1. We first need to correct an error in the MiniCart component – this is displaying the incorrect unit price! To do this, crack open `MiniCart.jsx`, then find this line of code:

   ```
   <span>${eUSLocale(totalPrice)}</span>
   ```

2. Change it to this, then save and close the file:

   ```
   <span>${eUSLocale(item.price)}</span>
   ```

3. Next, open a new file in your editor, then add the following code – we have a lot to add, so we'll do it in blocks, starting with the opening describe tag and step to navigate to the site:

```
describe("Adding Products", () => {
  it("should navigate to the home page", () => {
    // Start from the index page
    cy.visit("http://localhost:3000/");
```

4. Next, leave a line blank, then add these four lines – then click the Shop link and verify that we're on the Shop page.

```
    // Click on the Shop link
    cy.get("div.navbar > a:nth-child(3)")
.click(true);

    // The new url should include "/shop"
    cy.url().should("include", "/shop");
```

5. This step takes us to the Spiced Pumpkin macaron page:

```
    // Click on a product - Spiced Pumpkin
    cy.get('a[href*="spiced-pumpkin"]').click();
```

6. We need to increase the desired quantity to 2, so the test clicks on the plus symbol to do that:

```
    // Increase product quantity by 2
    cy.get("span.plus").click();
```

7. At this point, we're ready for the test to add the chosen product to our cart – we then verify that once done, we have two items in our basket:

```
    // Click on Add to Cart
    cy.get("button.add-to-cart").click();

    // Verify that cart icon shows 2
    cy.get("span.cart-item-qty").contains(2);
```

8. This last block takes care of checking the cart and minicart to verify that the details shown are as expected:

```
    // Open cart - verify details
    cy.get("span.cart-item-qty").click();
    cy.get("span.cart-num-items").contains("2 items");

    // Verify mini cart shows relevant details
    cy.get("span.cart-num-items").contains("(2 items)");
    cy.get("span.item-desc > span").contains("Spiced Pumpkin");
    cy.get("span.totals").contains("$18.50");
    cy.get("div.total > h3").contains("$37.00");
  });
});
```

9. Go ahead and click the name of the test in Figure 9-3 – this will launch the test; if all is well, we should see a successful result, as shown in Figure 9-6.

Figure 9-6. *A partial extract of the results from the adding products test*

The results in Figure 9-6 don't show all the details – the key point here is that we get the green light to the left to indicate a successful test.

10.   Once the test has completed running, you can close the runner window to exit.

Excellent – that might have seemed like a few steps, but it's important to note that customers could easily go through as many steps in a journey, so we need to reflect this in our testing!

Breaking Apart the Code Changes

We began by fixing a minor issue I found while creating the site for this book – I had inadvertently used `totalPrice` for the unit price, which clearly won't show the correct value! Fortunately, this was an easy fix – we swapped it out for `item.price` to correct the issue.

We could then start creating our test – we kicked off by adding a `describe()` statement to open our test before adding a `cy.visit` to navigate to our site's homepage. Next up, we added a click event to continue onto the shop page before verifying that we had reached this page; once done, we clicked on a chosen product (Spiced Pumpkin, but I could have chosen any as all will work).

The test increased the quantity on the product page to 2 before clicking the Add to Cart. We then verified that the basket did indeed contain two items. We finished by checking the details in the minicart component to ensure they were what we expected to see on the page.

Before we continue with the next round of testing, there is one important point I wanted to pick up, in the spirit of kaizen. It's how we've created the 2 x $18.50 shown in the minicart – the data itself is not at fault, but we could (and should) look to improve how we render it onscreen. When creating the tests, I had wanted to do something like `cy.get("span.totals").contains("2 x $18.50")`, but if you look carefully, you will see that this would never work! (The text elements, 2, x, and $18.50, are spread over three different elements and so are inaccessible using my desired tag.) It's a small change, but one that will definitely make testing easier!

Okay – let's crack on: we've completed the E2E testing, so it's time to turn our attention to testing the other side of the proverbial testing coin: individual components.

Testing the Components

So far, we've focused on end-to-end testing – we use this to help prove the happy paths through our site or where customers are likely to visit and that we can confirm these areas work as expected.

It's time for us to turn our attention to testing components – this is where things get a little more interesting. Although we have components we (in theory) can and should test, there are some caveats with testing components created with Next.js. We'll go through these shortly, but let's concentrate on setting up our testing suite to perform component tests.

CONFIGURING FOR COMPONENT TESTING

To set up Cypress ready for component testing, follow these steps:

1. First, we need to fire up Cypress, so switch to a Node.js terminal and enter npm run cypress to open the GUI.

2. When open, click Component Testing to start the configuration process.

3. Cypress will prompt us to choose the Front-end framework we want to use (Figure 9-7) – Next.js should already be selected, so hit Next step.

Figure 9-7. *Choosing the framework for component testing*

4. Cypress will then install any dependencies it needs – once done, we should see confirmation that we've installed all the dependencies for component testing, as shown in Figure 9-8.

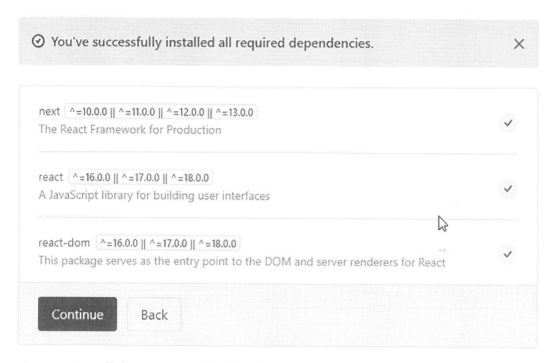

Figure 9-8. *All dependencies installed for component testing*

5. At this point, Cypress will have also updated some of the configuration files required for testing – Figure 9-9 shows the changes Cypress has made.

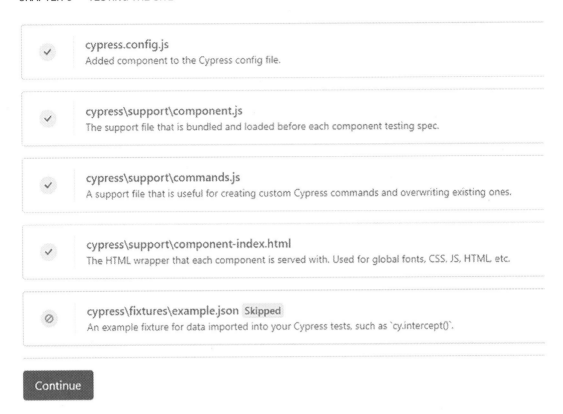

Figure 9-9. *The updated list of configuration files*

6. Once the list has been displayed, click Continue, then wait for the initialization process to complete. When prompted, choose Chrome ➤ Start Component Testing in Chrome to begin testing our site.

At this point, we're ready to begin testing – leave the window open but minimize it; we'll start adding tests shortly.

Great – we've set up Cypress, ready for component testing! It's a quick process with some similarities to the previous task; the only real difference is that we have to choose which framework to use so that Cypress can set up the correct dependencies for testing. The irony here is that Cypress even does some of this for you – it can tell which framework you want to use, so all we have to do is hit Continue, as long as it is the right one! Let's crack on and add some component tests to our suite to prove it all works as expected.

Adding Tests

For this next demo, I've chosen three examples of component tests that we can perform in Cypress.

The components we'll test for are DemoBanner, Info, and Product – I've chosen these as they don't fall foul of some caveats associated with testing Next.js components in Cypress. Let's dive in and look at how to create the tests as part of the next exercise.

ADDING COMPONENT TESTS

To add our example component tests, follow these steps:

1. First, crack open a new file in your editor – we'll start with setting up the DemoBanner component test. For this, add the following code, beginning with importing the component and defining a mockText constant:

   ```
   import DemoBanner from "../../src/components/DemoBanner.jsx";

   const mockText =
       "This is a demo store - no orders will be accepted or delivered";
   ```

2. Next, leave a line blank, then add this opening describe tag and mount block:

   ```
   describe("<DemoBanner />", () => {
     it("should render and display expected content", () => {
     cy.mount(<DemoBanner />);
   ```

3. Next up, we need to add our assertions – the first one checks that the div with the class of demo-banner is visible on the page:

   ```
       cy.get("div.demo-banner-container")
   .should("be.visible");
   ```

4. The second assertion is a little more complex – this time, we check to make sure that:

   ```
       cy.get("div.demo-banner-container")
         .should("have.text", mockText);
       });
   });
   ```

5. Save the file as demobanner.cy.js in the \cypress\components folder, and close the file. Switch back to the Cypress GUI, where we should see demobanner.cy.js appear as an entry. Click the name to run the test – if all is well, we should see something akin to the screenshot extract shown in Figure 9-10.

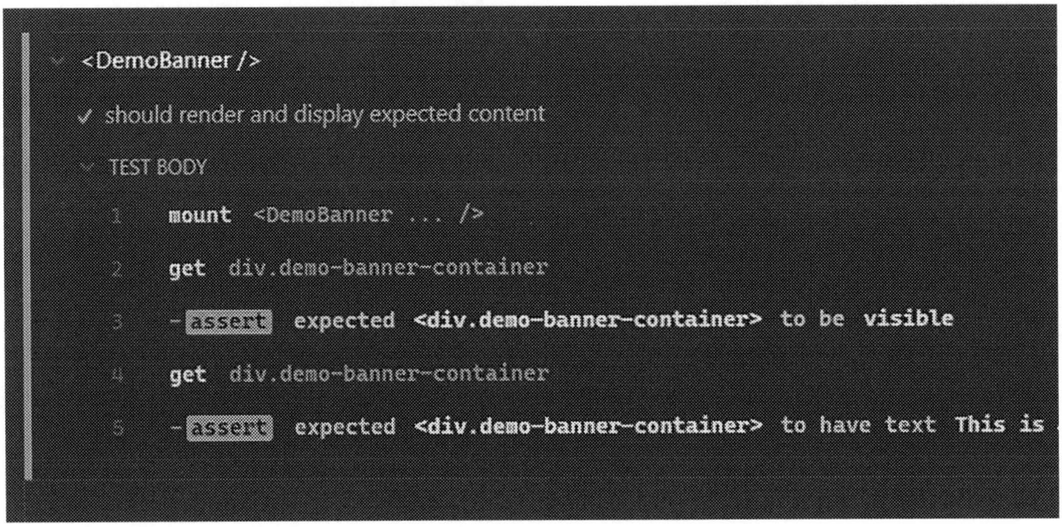

```
<DemoBanner />

✓ should render and display expected content

TEST BODY

  1    mount  <DemoBanner ... />

  2    get  div.demo-banner-container

  3    -assert  expected <div.demo-banner-container> to be visible

  4    get  div.demo-banner-container

  5    -assert  expected <div.demo-banner-container> to have text This is
```

Figure 9-10.   *The results of the DemoBanner test*

This next test is for the Info component – it's a little more complex, as we will be mocking out two pieces of data. Let's take a look at what's required in the next part of this demo.

6. Crack open a new file in your editor, then add this code – we'll start with adding an import and two constants:

```
import Info from "../../src/components/Info.jsx";

const mockTextFirstTab = "Description";
const mockTextSecondTab = "Additional Information";
```

7. Next, leave a line blank, then add the opening tags for our test, which includes mounting the component:

```
describe("<Info />", () => {
  it("should render and display expected content", () => {
    // Mount the Info component
    cy.mount(<Info />);
```

254

8. With the component mounted, we can now run our assertions – the first is to confirm that the tabs used in the component are visible on the page and that we have two displayed:

    ```
    cy.get("div.react-tabs").should("be.visible");

    cy.get("ul[role='tablist'] > li").should("have.length", 2);
    ```

9. Next up, we check to make sure that the first tab has a text element matching the contents of mockTextFirstTab and that the second tab matches mockTextSecondTab, in a similar way:

    ```
    cy.get("ul[role='tablist'] > li:nth-child(1)").should(
      "have.text",
      mockTextFirstTab
    );

    cy.get("ul[role='tablist'] > li:nth-child(2)").should(
      "have.text",
      mockTextSecondTab
    );
      });
    });
    ```

10. Save the file as info.cy.js in the \cypress\components folder, and close the file. Switch back to the Cypress GUI, where we should see info.cy.js appear as an entry. Click the name to run the test – if all is well, we should see something akin to the screenshot extract shown in Figure 9-11.

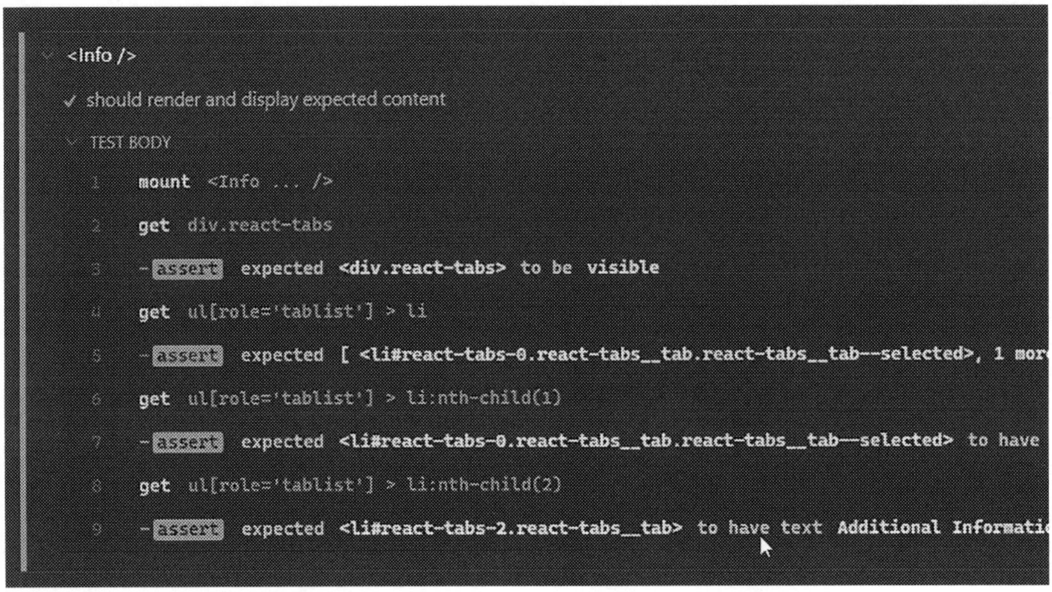

Figure 9-11. *The results of running the Info component test*

This final test is for the Product component – this steps things up again, as we're mocking a whole data object this time! Let's take a look at what's required in the next part of this demo.

11. Crack open a new file in your editor, then add this code – we'll start with adding an import and the mock data object:

```
import Product from "../../src/components/Product.jsx";

const mockProduct = {
  _type: "product",
  delivery:
    "We carefully package our macarons and use Royal Mail to post them
    to you under first class postage. We only deliver to the UK.",
  details:
    "Enjoy the taste of our indulgent Chocolate Orange Macarons.
    Bursting with 100% natural flavours, our perfectly proportioned
    treats are handcrafted in our kitchen and beautifully packaged for
    your enjoyment.",
  image: [
    {
      _key: "ba6786ee0e81",
```

```
    _type: "image",
    asset: {
      _ref: "image-812a8575cab31a81ea8352e913d173
      c9244151b7-456x456-jpg",
    },
  },
],
ingredients:
  "Ground Almonds (contains nuts) , Icing Sugar, Free Range Egg
  Whites (contains Eggs), Sugar, Milk Chocolate, (Sugar, Cocoa
  Butter, High Fat Milk Powder, Cocoa Mass, Whole Milk Powder,
  Skimmed Milk Powder, Lactose (Milk), Emulsifier: Lecithins (Soya);
  Vanilla Extract), Double Cream (contains Milk), Orange Extract,
  Colour E110 may have an adverse effect on activity and attention
  in children  Please note: product may contain allergens - if in
  doubt, please ask.",
name: "Chocolate Orange",
price: 18.5,
sku: "MACM001",
slug: {
  current: "chocolate-orange",
},
weight: "335g",
};
```

Don't worry – I'm not expecting you to copy the entire block! It will be in the code
download for you to copy and paste into your version.

12. Next, leave a line blank, then add the opening tags for our test, which includes
     mounting the component, as we've done before:

```
describe("<Product />", () => {
  it("should render and display expected content", () => {
    cy.mount(<Product product={mockProduct} />);
```

13. We then perform a quick check to make sure the main div container is present in the DOM:

```
cy.get("div").should("be.visible");
```

14. For the final check, we assert that the correct instance of the product name is present in our data (and therefore in the DOM):

```
cy.get("p.product-name:nth-child(2)").should("have.text",
mockProduct.name);
  });
});
```

15. Save the file as `product.cy.js` in the `\cypress\components` folder, and close the file. Switch back to the Cypress GUI, where we should see info. `cy.js` appear as an entry. Click the name to run the test – if all is well, we should see something akin to the screenshot extract shown in Figure 9-12.

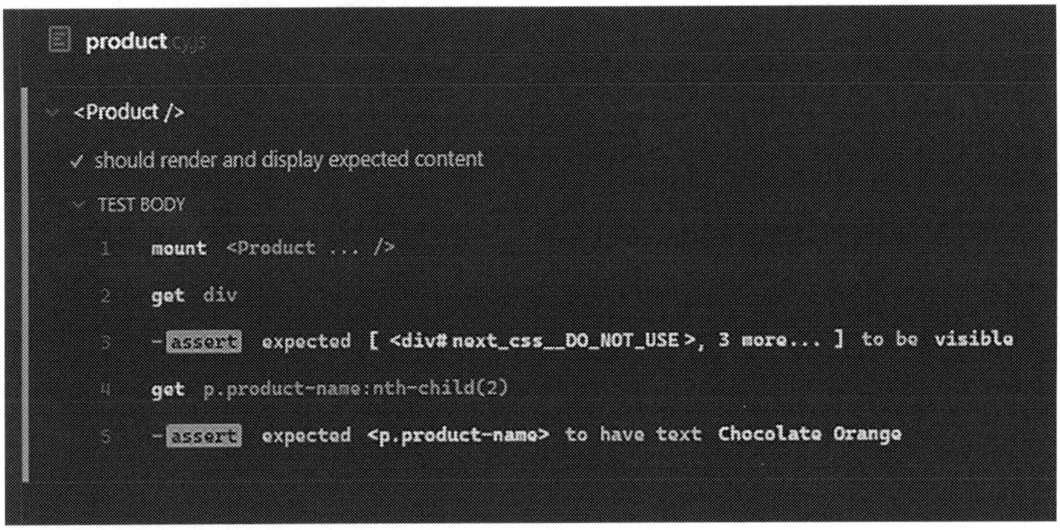

Figure 9-12. *The results of running the Product component test*

Excellent – we have three tests in place now: they may be relatively straightforward and nothing too complicated, but that doesn't matter. The important point here is that we can test them to ensure they perform as we expect on our site. We've covered a lot of code over the last few pages, so let's pause for a moment to review the changes we made in more detail.

Exploring the Changes Made

Cast your mind back to the end-to-end tests we created earlier in the chapter – although we tested different flows, most of them had one thing in common: using `cy.visit()` to go to a specific page before running the test.

In this latest set of tests, we had to take a different route to testing – instead of visiting pages, we used `cy.mount()` to mount the component so it was available to use in Cypress. We first imported the relevant component into the test in all three instances before using `cy.mount()` to initialize an instance of each component.

Our first assertion was to confirm that it was visible in the DOM (and therefore usable). We then ran a check on different aspects – for the Info component, we made sure it displayed two tabs and that the text for each matched that assigned to two constants within our test. We also did something similar for the Product component, but this time it was an object rather than a statement – we used a different format to reference the relevant value, but the effect is still the same.

In each instance, though, we ran the test in the Cypress GUI to confirm that it successfully executed each check and that we got the appropriate response on completing each test.

Things are not all as rosy as they may seem, though, as there are a couple of caveats to consider when it comes to using Cypress to test components created using Next.js. The issue stems from components that use methods that only run on the server – to understand what this means for us, let's dive in and take a closer look.

Understanding the Limits

When it came to choosing tests for this book, I had something of a dilemma – I discovered something that could affect how we test our site:

> A page component could have additional logic in its getServerSideProps or getStaticProps methods. These methods only run on the server, so they are not available to run inside a component test. Trying to test a page in a component test [will] result in the props being passed into the page to be undefined.

Taken from the Cypress main documentation at `https://docs.cypress.io/guides/component-testing/react/overview#Next-js`, it means that we won't be able to test some of the components on our site, at least not in the way we might want. For example, two components come to mind that would be affected – Footer and MiniCart. Both call in the Cart component, which runs server-side, owing to using the StateContext component.

What does it mean for us? Well, we could rework each to allow us to pass props in, but this won't cover the server-side methods. It's best, therefore, to concentrate on using E2E testing for Next.js pages and components – if we focus on testing the former, it will test the latter simultaneously. It just means we must pay particular attention to how we test each page!

Right – enough of that, let's crack on with the last task for this chapter: testing in a CI pipeline. Ordinarily, this might mean that we have to reconfigure lots of settings, but in our case, no – Cypress already had a headless version of its tool built in, so we need to adjust how we run our code. We'll explore this in more detail when we go to production in the next chapter, but for now, let's work through the steps required to ensure we're all ready to run the tests in our pipeline.

Preparing for CI Operation

So far, we've concentrated on creating tests offline, in our local environment – while this works very well (all things considered!), there will come a time when we will want to push our code into production.

As part of this, we will need to run the same tests in the pipeline to give us extra confidence that our production copy works as expected and doesn't cause any issues. We need to execute two different commands based on whether we want to execute the E2E tests or the component ones. Let's take a look at what we need to do to run these tests in our CI environment, ready for when we push our code up into production.

PREPARING FOR CI

The changes we're making mean that we're running Cypress in headless mode – to do this, follow these steps:

1. Crack open the package.json file at the root of our project folder, then look for the line `"cypress": "cypress open"` in the scripts block.

2. Immediately below and before the closing bracket, add these two lines:

   ```
   "cypress:headless": "cypress run --browser chrome
   --headless"
   "cypress:component": "cypress run --component"
   ```

3. Save and close the file. Fire up a Node.js terminal, then change the working folder to our project area.

4. At the prompt, enter `npm run cypress:headless` and press Enter. You'll see the same E2E tests run that we created earlier, but at the command line, not in the GUI.

5. Once complete, enter `npm run cypress:component` and press Enter – this will perform a similar operation, but this time with the component tests.

6. If all is well, we should see test results appear on the command line, similar to the extract shown in Figure 9-13. In this instance, we see the results for the `demobanner.cy.js` test, but they will look similar to any of the E2E tests we created earlier in the chapter.

```
(Run Starting)

┌─────────────────────────────────────────────────────────────────────────┐
│  Cypress:        12.8.1                                                    │
│  Browser:        Electron 106 (headless)                                   │
│  Node Version:   v16.18.0 (C:\Program Files\nodejs\node.exe)               │
│  Specs:          3 found (demobanner.cy.js, info.cy.js, product.cy.js)     │
│  Searched:       **/*.cy.{js,jsx,ts,tsx}                                   │
└─────────────────────────────────────────────────────────────────────────┘


  Running:   demobanner.cy.js                                       (1 of 3)


  <DemoBanner />
    ✓ should render and display expected content (261ms)


  1 passing (346ms)


(Results)

┌─────────────────────────────────────────────────────────────────────────┐
│  Tests:         1                                                          │
│  Passing:       1                                                          │
│  Failing:       0                                                          │
│  Pending:       0                                                          │
│  Skipped:       0                                                          │
│  Screenshots:   0                                                          │
│  Video:         true                                                       │
│  Duration:      0 seconds                                                  │
│  Spec Ran:      demobanner.cy.js                                           │
└─────────────────────────────────────────────────────────────────────────┘


(Video)

  -  Started processing:  Compressing to 32 CRF
  -  Finished processing: 0 seconds

  -  Video output: C:\macaronmagic\cypress\videos\demobanner.cy.js.mp4
```

Figure 9-13. *An extract of the test results run via the command line*

That was an easy change to make – particularly given that Cypress does most of the heavy lifting for us! The only change we made was adding two new commands into the script block of our package.json, then executing each in turn from the command line. Notice that we also get a video created of each test – you can see it listed in this example under the video entry toward the end of the test.

This success is all very good, but there is one catch – some of you may have noticed this warning appears when running the tests:

```
Couldn't find tsconfig.json. tsconfig-paths will be skipped
```

While it doesn't *seem* to be affecting the results, it is nevertheless a little weird – particularly given that we're not running TypeScript anywhere in our repo! You may or may not see this if you've elected to run this project using TypeScript – if you do, then there is a way to make this warning disappear. Add the following code to a new file at the root of your project, saving it as `tsconfig.json`:

```
{
  "compilerOptions": {
    "target": "es5",
    "lib": ["es5", "dom"],
    "types": ["cypress", "node"],
    "baseUrl": "./"
  },
  "include": ["**/*.ts", "**/*.js"]
}
```

You should now be able to run the tests from the command line, but without the warning message appearing in your command line. Why do we have it? It seems to stem (at least in part) from using `baseUrl`, and a missing `tsconfig.json` file. The latter is easy to add, even though we technically shouldn't need it given we're not using TypeScript, but the former is because Cypress and TypeScript have the `baseUrl` property, but they mean entirely different things! Adding the file seems to make the warnings go away, although I should point out from the outset that this isn't necessarily an official fix or workaround – it's based on comments I've seen in the Cypress repo on GitHub.

If you want to learn more, then feel free to read an ongoing ticket around this issue – `https://github.com/cypress-io/cypress/issues/22273`. It might have been resolved by the time this book comes into print, but given it's been ongoing since mid-2022 (at the time of writing), I'm not holding my hopes up for a speedy resolution!

Summary

Testing, testing, 123...

An essential part of designing any site is to test to ensure it works and performs to expectations – I know our site is only a proof of concept, but it doesn't diminish the need for creating and running suitable tests! We've covered a lot of changes in this chapter around using Cypress as our testing suite, so let's take a moment to review what we have learned in more detail.

We first began by setting expectations around the tool we would use to test our site and some of the tests we will create as our first pass into testing our site.

Next up, we installed Cypress and configured it for initial use – given we were going to create and run both end-to-end and component tests, we would focus first on end-to-end testing. As part of this, we worked our way through several tests, understanding how they worked and taking the opportunity to learn how to improve our tests in the spirit of Japanese kaizen.

Moving on, we then performed a similar process with component testing, although given some of the limitations around using Cypress with Next.js, we had to be more selective about which tests we could run, at least in the first pass! We then finished by exploring how to get the tests ready for use in a CI pipeline environment, so we can run them as part of committing and releasing code into production.

Ladies and gentlemen – the time has come... to deploy our site into production! Before you get all excited, we need to remember that our site is only a proof of concept, so we would have more to do before releasing our site into the wild. However, we still need to be familiar with the process – stay with me, and I will reveal all in the next chapter.

CHAPTER 10

Deployment into Production

Yikes – it's time for us to deploy our shop into production and let customers loose on it! This might seem scary, as we're about to show our efforts to customers, but don't worry: Next.js makes it easy to deploy sites into production use.

Throughout this chapter, we will work through the steps required to get our site ready for release before deploying it and making it available for others to see via the Web. At the same time, we'll also take a look at analyzing the code for performance (and in particular unused JavaScript!), as well as adding an extra touch in the form of a custom domain name for our site. We have to begin somewhere, so let's start with some key assumptions for our process.

Making Some Assumptions

To make our project work when it comes to releasing into production, there are a few assumptions I've had to make – some of this is necessary, while others are down to personal choice. Let's have a look at them:

- This is a proof-of-concept site, so hosting in GitHub is adequate for now – I recommend you choose a better host if only to protect your source code!

- I've based my choices in this chapter on my personal preferences – it does not mean you need to use them, but it is an option to consider if you don't already have a solution. The key here is to consider what you need to complete to publish your version of the site into production that suits your circumstances and the tools or processes needed to achieve this task.

© Alex Libby 2023
A. Libby, *Practical Next.js for E-Commerce*, https://doi.org/10.1007/978-1-4842-9612-7_10

- The release into production may incur a cost for hosting or registering a domain name. We must consider this and ensure we have registered anything we need beforehand, such as the domain name (if we choose to use one). Sites like Netlify (which we will use in this chapter) offer free allowances, but they may not be enough for your anticipated needs!

These are just a few of the things we need to bear in mind when we are ready to release our site into production – I'm sure there will be more, though, so it's good to keep this in mind.

Before we get to release, though, we should perform one crucial task: a final check of our site. You might say this is something that should be done earlier, such as during testing, but it can't harm to have one more final check, can it?

Working Through the Final Steps

We're fast approaching the point where we will want to upload our code to our hosting platform, so before we do so, it's worth doing a final check to make sure that everything is as we expect and that we don't have any loose ends, console logs, or errant code that shouldn't be in our repo.

The key is to remember that our site is a proof of concept, so it won't be perfect – that doesn't matter. It should, however, look tidy – no one likes to see console log entries in code, and there's no point in uploading files that are no longer needed, is there?

- Have a good look through the codebase – is there anything you see that looks untidy or not being used at all?

- How about running `npm run build` and seeing what comes out of the results at the end – does this throw any warnings? For example, I know there are some around the use of `<img>` tags; it would be better to use `<Image>`, but this isn't a breaking issue, so something we can revisit if we go into production.

- Look at images – are there any you want to replace, or optimize their size, perhaps?

- Now is also an excellent time to check for any spelling mistakes – even though this site is a proof of concept, seeing a spelling error can take the shine off your work!

- If you've commented out any code for now, then now's a good time to consider if you want to delete it or move it somewhere outside the repo for safekeeping.

This is one of those occasions where the tidy-up will be specific to your site – there is no right or wrong answer, but as I always say, "a tidy site is a tidy mind!" When you're ready to proceed, let's crack on with preparing our hosting site, ready to receive our code.

Preparing Our Host

Cast your mind back to the start of this book: remember how we talked about which provider we would use to host our site?

Well, it's time to put pen to proverbial paper and get our site out into the real world! The hosting provider we will be using is Netlify. We could use others (like GitHub Pages and GitLab), but I wanted to provide a little variety to what I've used before, and I also know that Netlify has some interesting features that are ideal for supporting Next.js!

Where do we start? The first task is to get our site into a GitHub repository – Netlify relies on sourcing content from a repository. I prefer to use GitHub, but we can use the likes of Bitbucket or GitLab instead. Hosting through GitHub means that we can make deployment out to Netlify an automatic process so that any time we upload, the website will be refreshed on Netlify within a few minutes.

For our site, we will push content to the root subdomain and hook it into Netlify; from there, we'll attach a custom domain. The latter isn't obligatory, but it will allow us to see what it will look like in front of customers! With that all in mind, let's take a look at the steps required first to get our GitHub repository set up and ready for use.

PREPARING THE HOST

Before we crack on with code, there are a couple of assumptions you need to bear in mind:

- For this exercise, I will assume we are using the username nextjsecommerce; you will need to consider a proper name and swap this in as appropriate.

- I'm also assuming you will create a new account and repository for this exercise; you can use an existing one, but it will complicate things!

Let's get started:

1. We'll start by creating a new repository – for this, browse to `https://github.com`, and click Sign Up in the top right.

2. Go ahead and follow the instructions provided on the screen, including adding an email account (it's worth it!) – make sure you take note of the details you use for your account. Once done, sign in with your new account, and get it validated.

3. Next, we need to create our repository – click the + sign in the top right, then New repository.

4. On the next screen, the Owner field will you're your account name; enter a repository name in the format <username>/<repository name>, where the username is your chosen username on GitHub and the repository name is the repository you will use.

5. If you want to fill in a description, then go ahead and do so – it is not compulsory for this exercise.

6. Next, choose Public as the repository type, and click the check box to initialize the repository with a readme file.

7. For the Add .gitignore option, choose Node, and set the Add a license to MIT.

8. Click Create repository – if all is working as expected, we should have an empty repository, similar to the screenshot shown in Figure 10-1.

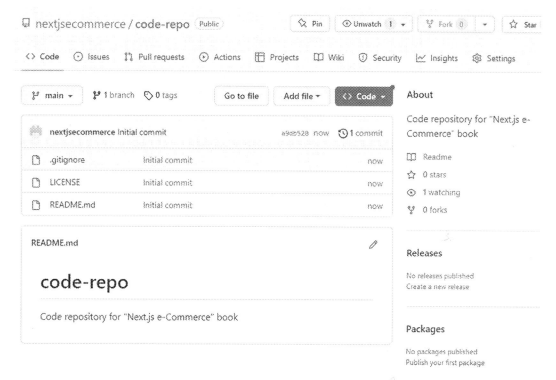

Figure 10-1. *Our new repository on GitHub*

If you've spent any time developing code, then the chances are that you will be familiar with Git and its GUI-based version GitHub. Many of the steps we covered in the last exercise are not unique to Next.js; we can use these tools to create sites using various frameworks.

In our case, we started by creating the basic repository; we entered the relevant details before initializing it with the readme and .gitignore files. This step gave us an empty storage facility ready to upload content, which we will cover shortly; first, there is a configuration change I want to make to help with one of the issues flagged when we configured our site for SEO back in Chapter 8.

Analyzing Code Usage

Cast your mind back (if you can – I know: it seemed a long time ago!) to Chapter 8, where we discussed setting up SEO. One of the things I said we should do is run an analysis of our code to make sure we're not including excess JavaScript that we should otherwise boot out of our codebase!

We could do this manually, but a better option – at least to highlight where we have excess code – is to use automation. Fortunately, we can use a third-party GitHub Action to help in this respect: it's made by HashiCorp, creators of the Terraform Infrastructure as a language framework, and is available from `https://github.com/hashicorp/nextjs-bundle-analysis`. It's a cinch to install, although we have to do it in two parts – let's look at the first part, which is installing it locally to create the configuration file.

It's worth noting that although the GitHub Action is a third-party package, it wraps the official bundle analyzer available from Vercel, for which you can see the codebase at `https://github.com/vercel/next.js/tree/canary/packages/next-bundle-analyzer`.

ADDING CODE ANALYSIS ACTION IN GITHUB

To set up the GitHub Action for Bundle Analyzer, follow these steps:

1. Fire up a Node.js terminal, then make sure to set the working folder to our project area.

2. At the prompt, enter this command and press Enter:

    `npx -p nextjs-bundle-analysis generate`

3. The package will ask a few questions, of which the first is whether to install the following packages – select Y or press Enter when prompted:

    `nextjs-bundle-analysis`

4. Let it install; it will serve a series of questions, one of which will be "Would you like to set up a performance budget?" – for this, select Y (for yes).

5. The next question is, "What would you like the maximum javascript on first load to be (in kb)?" – press Enter to accept the default value of 350.

6. The package will then prompt for this next question – "If you exceed this percentage of the budget or filesize, it will be highlighted in red." Press enter to select the default, which is 20.

7. For the last question, which is "If a page's size change is below the threshold (in bytes), it will be considered unchanged (0)." Press Enter again: this will set the value to the default, which is 0.

8. Node.js will return to the prompt – it will then create a `.github/workflows` directory in your project root and add a `next_bundle_analysis.yml` file to it. You can see this in the screenshot shown in Figure 10-2.

Figure 10-2. *YAML configuration file for Next.js Bundle Analyzer*

Perfect – this gives us a standard setup for the Bundle Analyzer action, which we can push up to GitHub when we upload our code later in this chapter. Before we do that, I want to cover some essential points arising from this exercise, so let's dive in quickly and take a look at the code in more detail and what we should do once we have run the report.

Reviewing the Changes Made

Analyzing bundle sizes should be a default part of any developer's workflow – it is essential to keep on top of sizes to ensure ours don't grow too large! Fortunately, the plug-in we used in the last demo made it easy to install and configure.

To do so, we first ran a command to both install the nextjs-bundle-analysis plug-in and for it to generate the configuration file in one step. At this point, it asked a series of questions, such as confirming if we wanted to set a performance budget, how to set the highlighting, and what the maximum size of the JavaScript bundle should be on first load.

Once answered, the plug-in generated a `next_bundle_analysis.yml` file in the `.github/workflows` directory; this was ready for us to upload at the next push-up to GitHub.

We can test it once we complete that step later in this chapter.

As an aside, it's worth noting that the plug-in has an API that allows us to use it programmatically – we could, for example, use it in the `next.config.js` file with environment variables. It's not something we need to do on our site (at least for now), but to give you an idea of how it would look, here's an example:

```
const withBundleAnalyzer = require('@next/bundle-analyzer')({
  enabled: process.env.ANALYZE === 'true',
})
module.exports = withBundleAnalyzer({})
```

Okay – let's crack on; with our repository up and running and the bundle analyzer ready to go, let's focus on the next task: upload code into our repository. We'll need to go through a few steps to "merge" it and our local project into one – all will become clear in the following demo, I promise!

Uploading to Our Host

Now that we have set up our repository area, it's time to upload the code for our site. We can do this using one of several ways – for example, we can drag and drop code via the GitHub website, use GitHub Desktop (or a different client), or even go old-school and use the command line.

For this next part, I will use the command line – purely out of personal preference; I used to be a fan of using tools such as GitHub Desktop, but those days have passed! I'll keep the steps relatively high-level, though, as I tend to use Visual Studio Code with Git Bash installed; I know that not everyone uses this tool.

If you want to try using VS Code and Git Bash together, Daniel Padua has a helpful blog post on integrating the latter with VS Code. You can see the article at `https://blog.danielpadua.dev/posts/git-bash-with-vscode/`. Alternatively, if you prefer to use an existing combination you already have, that is equally fine.

Okay – I will assume you have Git (and Git Bash) installed or a working alternative that allows you to push up code; let's crack on with the next exercise.

Note   I am assuming some prior knowledge at this point: you will likely need to be familiar with some of the finer points of `git push` and deal with merge conflicts. You may also want to take a copy of the site as a backup, just in case we run into any problems!

UPLOADING TO GITHUB

To upload our site to GitHub, follow these steps:

1. First, crack open a Node.js terminal, then make sure the working folder is set to our project area.

2. Next, we need to build a production version of our code, so at the prompt, enter `npm run build` and press Enter.

3. Assuming it doesn't flag errors, enter `npm run start` to confirm it starts the production server, allowing us to run the site in a browser.

This step isn't obligatory, but checking is helpful to ensure that our site runs without error. As long as no errors are reported, this will be OK – we can always work on warnings, but errors will stop a build from running.

4. We need to initialize our repository so that GitHub knows where to push content. To do this, stop the server with Ctrl+C (or Cmd+C, for Macs), and run this command, replacing `<username>` with your own, and `<repo>` with the name of your repository:

    `git remote add origin https://github.com/<username>/<repo>.git`

    At this point, we have a little extra work to do, as we need to merge what is effectively two projects into one. (Git sees the new repository and our local project as unrelated projects.) To do this, continue with these steps:

5. At the prompt, enter `git pull origin main --allow-unrelated-histories`. Running this command will likely throw two errors about merge conflicts for `.gitignore` and `README.md` – both files exist in the new repository but differ from our local versions. You will need to deal with these first before moving on to the next step.

If we do not include the `--allow-unrelated-histories` tag, we are likely to get this error appear: `fatal: refusing to merge unrelated histories`.

---

6. Once you have dealt with any merge conflicts, enter this command at the prompt and press Enter:

    `git push -u origin main`

7. We can now add the files together into a commit – for this, enter `git add .` at the prompt, and press Enter.

8. Git is now ready for us to push up our code – for this, enter this command at the prompt and press Enter to prepare our code for pushing:

    `git commit -m "Initial upload of site"`

9. Once done, enter this command to push the code up to GitHub:

    `git push -u origin main`

10. This step will take a couple of minutes to complete – once done, browse your GitHub repository to confirm all files are present – you should see something akin to that shown in Figure 10-3.

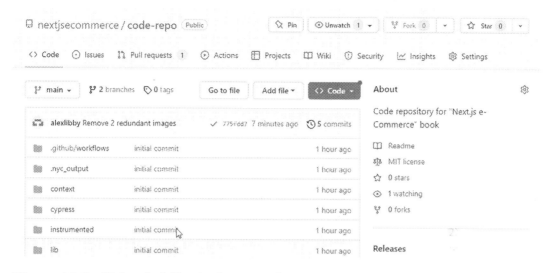

Figure 10-3. *Uploaded files in the GitHub repository*

Perfect – we now have our code in GitHub! This last demo may have only been a quick one, but it's the most critical to getting our code onto the hosting platform, ready for viewing the final site in a browser on the Web.

For many of you, the steps will be familiar – the typical commands of `git add`, `git commit`, and `git push` will be ones developers use multiple times a day when committing code to source. For those less familiar, let's go through the steps in more detail before we continue with the next stage of the process.

Understanding the Changes in Detail

Hands up – have you ever encountered any task where you think "This'll be easy to do, I'll have it done in no time..." when reality says otherwise?

Uploading our files was one of those tasks – the intention here was to create a local site first for development, then move to a repository online, and hook this up so we could commit code to a master source when required. Unfortunately, it didn't go according to plan: I think creating the repository first and checking it out would have been a better approach!

That said, we still managed to get our online GitHub repository created – to do so, we had already signed up for our account earlier in the chapter. We first created a test production build to ensure our site still runs as expected. It probably wasn't necessary, but just a little precaution to make sure our site will still build when we push it up to GitHub.

Next up, we told Git to add our remote repository as an origin before pulling down the contents of that repository into our local site. Notice that we used the `--allow-unrelated-histories` tag to get around an error that will otherwise appear. We effectively have to merge what Git treats as two different projects (our local site and the remote repository) so that we can commit code to source when needed. At the same time, we then dealt with any merge conflicts that appeared – in my case, I had two, around `.gitignore` and the `README.md` file.

With the site now connected and merge conflicts resolved, we then created a commit and pushed it up using standard Git commands before checking in GitHub that the files had successfully landed in our repository.

At this point, we now have our code in GitHub – if we peek at the Actions tab, we may find that the CI step for our next task is already running in the background!

This next item will be the code analysis step we set up locally in a previous exercise, ready for the upload; it's one of two extra tasks I want to complete before importing our site into Netlify. There is a reason for doing this which I will explain momentarily, so without further ado, let's dive into analyzing our codebase for unused code.

Running the Code Analysis

With the code now in GitHub, we would typically head over to Netlify and set it to import our site so it displays for anyone to view.

There is a minor issue with doing this, though – don't be alarmed, though: it's nothing major! It all has to do with the fact that Netlify only offers a limited number of build minutes as part of the free account we will create. It means we need to be mindful of what we do so we're not wasting that resource – one way we can do this is not to hook up the site until we're absolutely ready. There is one additional task I want to look at doing before hooking up the site: checking the code analysis for our site.

DEMO – RUNNING THE CODE ANALYSIS

To perform the code analysis, follow these steps:

1. First, head over to your repository in GitHub – log in with your user account if you have not already done so.

2. Next, click Actions, then New Workflow (in the left navigation).

3. Click Workflow Bundle Analysis, then Run workflow (for this, hit the button on the right, next to the `workflow_dispatch` trigger message).

4. A pop-up will appear, prompting us for the branch name to run the workflow from – make sure it shows `Branch: main`, then hit Run workflow.

5. Wait a moment – it will then show a job in the list, which will have a status of Queued initially, but change to In progress (Figure 10-4).

Figure 10-4. *The Next.js Bundle Analysis action in progress*

Keeping tabs on code sizes, particularly JavaScript bundles, is a thankless task – this is why we have plug-ins to do this work for us!

The nextjs-bundle-analysis does what it says on the tin – it just works: any time we make a change to code that involves JavaScript, it will flag up whether there are any changes in bundle size that we should be aware. We manually triggered the action in our demo to prove it works – don't worry, though, if you don't see any results!

The action has to compare code changes between a branch and the master version, so running it manually against the master won't show any differences. It only kicks in when you create a pull request from the `main` branch; you'll see a `github-actions` log appear in the PR, similar to that shown in Figure 10-5.

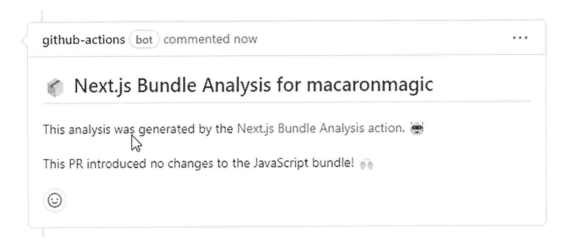

Figure 10-5. *The Github action for nextjs-bundle-analysis report*

In this example, I removed some redundant code files that I had added as a test but were no longer needed – removing them from the codebase will keep it tidy.

Okay – with our GitHub action now working and tested, let's move on: it's time to hook our site into Netlify, so we can ensure it renders for people to use on the Internet.

Linking to Netlify

It's with some trepidation, but I can now say this is pretty much the last big step to getting our site live.

So far, we've configured our repository and uploaded content – everything is in place for us to link to Netlify. This last step is one we should do when we're really happy with the state of the codebase; once we're happy, then we can complete this step. I'm working through it for this book now, but I recommend you not doing it until you've checked the code all works and that you're happy to release it into production.

Call me paranoid if you like, but a quick five to ten minutes now could save much pain later!

If we're 100% happy, let's crack on and see what's involved in releasing our code into production.

As a reminder: I'm using GitHub to host my version of this site – if you are using different Git hosts, such as GitLab, please alter accordingly.

LINKING GITHUB REPO TO NETLIFY

To link our site to Netlify, follow these steps:

1. First, head over to www.netlify.com, then click Log In, and choose the provider you have your Git account with (in my case, GitHub).

2. You will be prompted to authorize Netlify Auth to access your site in GitHub – click Authorize netlify and follow the prompts given on the screen.

3. Once done, Netlify will ask three questions, such as your planned use of Netlify – answer as you see fit.

4. Next, hit Continue to deploy – Netlify will show a "Deploy your first project" screen. Click Deploy with GitHub, then hit Authorize Netlify to adjust permissions (required to allow Netlify to host your site).

5. Click Install to set up Netlify – please enter your password for the repository if prompted.

6. On the screen marked "Let's deploy your project", click the name of your repository, then Deploy XXXXX to Netlify (where XXXXXX) is the name of your repository).

7. After a few moments, you will land on your dashboard screen for the project – give it a few minutes to deploy your site.

8. Netlify will flag a message to say "Deploy success!" when it has completed the build – hit Dismiss to close it.

9. You will see various boxes of information on the screen, but the one similar to that shown in Figure 10-6 will be your indicator that the site is now ready to view.

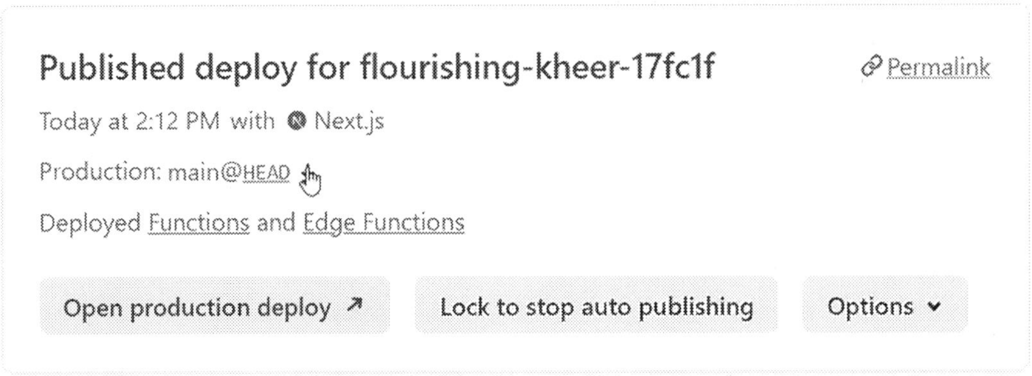

Figure 10-6. *Our site now published on Netlify*

If you head over to `https://app.netlify.com/sites/XXXXX/deploys`, you will see a list of all your site deploys – it will show Published for all that are successful or an error if the deploy failed.

We can now breathe a sigh of relief – our site is now available in the wild; hopefully, no one will think it's a real site and expect goods to be purchasable from it! We can't rest easy yet, though, as while the code is published, parts of the site that use values in the .env file won't work. We still have some work to do there; before we get to that, let's take a quick look at the steps we went through to publish the base site to Netlify in more detail.

Breaking Apart the Changes

One of the nice things about using Netlify is that everything we need to do to link the site is GUI-based; there is no need to execute anything via the command line.

We had to run through a few steps to authorize Netlify to access our Git account and install a few configuration settings, but Netlify took care of this for us automatically. It also automatically detected that we're running a Next.js site and allowed for this during the build process.

One downside is that our Sanity database and Stripe integration will likely fail at this point – don't worry, though, as it is to be expected. Do not forget that both use environment variables; we need to make one small change to import these into Netlify so that it can interact with both and restore access. Fortunately, this is a straightforward process – let's take a look at what we need to do as part of the next demo.

If you would like to look at my version of the site for this book, head over to `https://flourishing-kheer-17fc1f.netlify.app/`.

Using Environment Variables

One of the considerations when working in a serverless environment is using tokens – there will be occasions where we have to call out to third-party APIs, as we've done so with Sanity and Stripe. For those to work in our environment, we need to use environment variables – while we could do this locally using a .env file, this won't work in the same way once we publish our site. Without a change, both APIs will not function – not what we want when trying to publish our site!

To get around this, we need to create variables on Netlify to replace our `.env` file, so we can reference them similarly to how we did locally. This should mean that both Sanity and Stripe work as expected – let's dive in and look at how to do this as part of the next demo.

USING ENVIRONMENT VARIABLES

To add environment variables for our site, follow these steps:

1. First, log into the Netlify site, then go to Site settings ➤ Environment Variables. Click the Add a variable ➤ Import from a `.env` file.

2. Open the `.env` file from your local environment, then copy and paste the entire contents into the box under the Import environment variables title.

3. Once pasted, click Import variables.

4. If successful, you will see a list of variables appear, as shown in Figure 10-7.

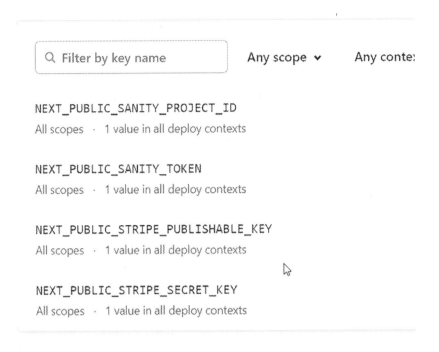

Figure 10-7. *The list of imported environment variables*

Perfect – assuming all went well, we should now have restored access to both Sanity and Stripe, so our site will function as expected on Netlify. It was a small but important change – we added four variables to the Environment Variables section of our Netlify account, so the two APIs we use can continue operating on our site.

Adding a Domain Name

Adding that last change for environment variables means we finally have a working site available online for anyone to browse, assuming they have the address. There is one thing, though – the URL they have to use isn't the most user-friendly, is it?

Of course, this is to be expected, as we're using a free service to host the site – there will be some limitations. At this point, we must decide whether we want a custom domain or to stay with the current URL that Netlify gives us?

Now – before you all get scared and run, it's not obligatory to register a domain name! It provides a nice touch to our site: the site will operate perfectly fine without it if we use the existing address provided by Netlify.

If we want to register one, then there are a few things to consider:

- The first point to consider is depending on your setup, then it's very likely you will have a cost associated with registering a domain. If you want to push the site into production, then you will need a better URL than the one offered by Netlify – indeed, we may need to consider alternative hosting, as GitHub is probably not ideal in this case.

- Duration – how long do you want to register the name for? Netlify work based on annual renewals, which is excellent for initial startups, but we might want to consider moving to a more extended registration in the future. It may require moving hosts, so something to bear in mind.

- Next, make sure you've chosen the name you want to use and that it's available! Even though I elected to register through Netlify, the original name of www.macaronmagic.com was already taken. It might have been available when I started researching for this book, but I foolishly didn't register it. It's not the end of the world, though, as I can change the name slightly to use macaron-magic.com instead. It's an important lesson, so make sure you have alternatives if your desired name is taken.

Assuming we want to register a domain and that annual renewal is satisfactory for now, we can do it one of several ways:

- Get Netlify to register a new domain, along with SSL support and configured name servers.

- If we already own a domain name, we can delegate the registration process to Netlify to complete.

- Register the domain ourselves and assign it manually – ideal if we want to use an existing domain or subdomain and be in complete control.

My personal preference is to get Netlify to register the domain and set up name servers automatically – this is for several reasons:

- I'm not a DNS expert by any means: setting up DNS can be tricky sometimes, so getting an expert to do it is easier!

- The domain name may cost a little more to register, but I can live with this – this is a small price to pay as Netlify will automatically register SSL, nameservers, and the like for me.

- This is a demo site, so if I needed to, I could either scrap the site at some point in the future or move it to more dedicated hosting if desired.

The critical point here is that what you do is **based on your circumstances**. I've elected to do several things here that suit my needs; this may not be the case for you, so it's essential to ensure you do what fits your requirements and works for you.

Okay – enough chat: let's crack on and get the name registered for use with our site!

ADDING A CUSTOM DOMAIN NAME

To register the domain name, follow these steps:

1. We first need to change the domain showing in our code – given in my case, it is only one character difference (the addition of a hyphen), I've chosen to complete that change directly on the GitHub site. I would recommend doing this as a PR, though, if you have to do this and your name is completely different!

2. First, log into your account on the Netlify site at `www.netlify.com`.

3. Next, go to your team's domains page, then select Add or register domain.

4. Enter the domain name you want to register, then hit Verify – if you've already checked it, it should return as available. Otherwise, you will need to select a new name to try.

5. Assuming the name is available, you will be shown the price to pay – this will be for one year, but the renewal for year two onward will likely be at a higher price. If you are OK with the cost, hit Register domain name to authorize payment and register your domain.

Note   If you do not have a payment record on file with Netlify, it will prompt you to add details before registering.

6.   On the next screen, it will prompt you to ask if Netlify should create DNS records for other services, such as email. For now, click Continue – we can always return and add these later if required. Hit Done when prompted.

7.   Netlify will register the domain name, create a DNS zone, and provision a wildcard HTTPS certificate for the site. We have one last step, which is to add it to our site in Netlify – for this, click Sites, then the name of your site.

8.   Next, click Site settings, then Domain settings.

9.   Click Add a domain in the Production domains box to add our newly registered domain.

10.   Go ahead and enter the domain without the www at the start. Hit Verify.

11.   Netlify should confirm it's already registered on its domain, so at this point, click Add domain.

12.   If all is well, we should see that Netlify has added it – it will require a DNS update on Netlify's site, which can take a little time. We can see the details displayed in Figure 10-8, where it is showing confirmation of that DNS update.

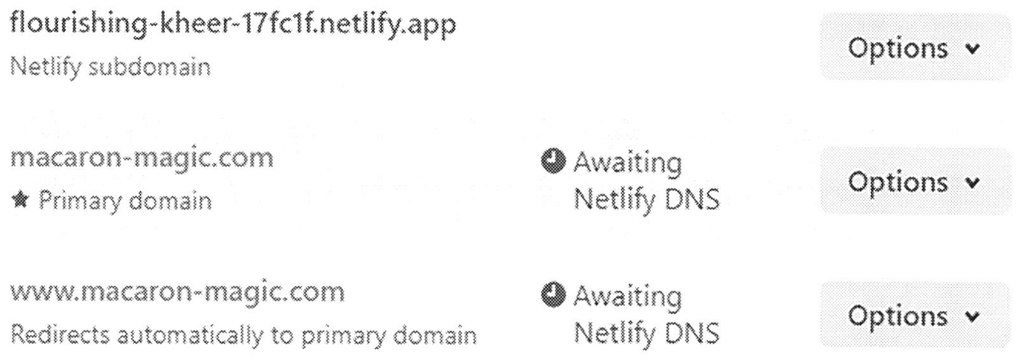

flourishing-kheer-17fc1f.netlify.app
Netlify subdomain   Options ∨

macaron-magic.com   ⬤ Awaiting   Options ∨
★ Primary domain   Netlify DNS

www.macaron-magic.com   ⬤ Awaiting   Options ∨
Redirects automatically to primary domain   Netlify DNS

Figure 10-8. *Confirmation that our site is now available via a custom domain*

At this point, we have to be patient – I could access the new domain with the site within about an hour of registering it, but it can take up to 24 hours to complete the update! When the domain is ready, the "Awaiting Netlify DNS" message will be replaced with a green tick.

And we can now relax...! Our site is up and running, even if it is only a proof of concept – we can access it via a custom domain of our choosing, and we've registered and applied a domain name for our use over the next year. We have plenty of time to update it if we want to or use it to push the site into production.

To get there, we may only have had to work through a handful of steps technically; the most important part is deciding what name we use and how we register the domain for our use. As we've used Netlify to register our domain, most of the process is hidden; this may suit us fine.

Netlify will set up the nameservers, create the appropriate domain records, and secure the site using an SSL certificate. We've only had to decide whether we can choose a suitable name, are happy with the cost involved, and get Netlify to add that domain to our site. I would love to say I could advise on the first two, but ultimately it will be down to you as my readers to make that final decision!

Testing the Site

Now that we have a site set up (and available via a custom domain if we've elected to add one), it's time for one final task – we need to test it!

I know we've completed testing back in Chapter 9, but it's still worth doing a final test – this will at least ensure that our site functions correctly, particularly if we've added a domain name. It's important to note that the site is still a proof of concept, so it won't be the final article – any testing we do will be more around ensuring we can complete a purchase with no issues.

To help with this, there is something we can do – we created tests using Cypress back in Chapter 9; these we had to run manually. Now that we have a working repository, we can go one step further and automate their running using a GitHub Action created by the Cypress developers. Let's take a look at how we can do this as part of the next demo.

For this change, you may need to commit this as a PR from a branch – I will assume you know how to do this or have suitable means in place to do so. We'll focus on the core of the change, which is the YAML file itself.

AUTOMATING TESTS IN CI PIPELINES

To add the GitHub action for running Cypress tests, follow these steps:

1. First, crack open a new file in your editor, then add the following code, saving it as cypress.yml in the \.github\workflows folder:

```
name: Cypress Tests

on: push

jobs:
  cypress-run:
    runs-on: ubuntu-22.04
    steps:
      - name: Checkout
        uses: actions/checkout@v3
      # Install NPM dependencies, cache them correctly
      # and run all Cypress tests
      - name: Cypress run
        uses: cypress-io/github-action@v5
        with:
          build: npm run build
          start: npm start
```

2. Next, go ahead and push this commit up, then create a PR for it – as part of this, you will see the tests kick in automatically, and a green tick will appear once they have been completed successfully (Figure 10-9).

Figure 10-9. *Confirmation that the GitHub action for Cypress was successful*

3.   At this point, go ahead and merge the change to close the branch.

As demos go, that was probably one of the shortest in the book! It's a great addition, though, as we don't need to worry about manually firing off tests when pushing up changes to this repository in the future. It gives us that extra confidence and means that if we want to add any future tests, they will automatically run at that time.

To implement the change, we created `cypress.yml`, which contains YAML commands to trigger and run our pipeline. We first give it a name, followed by a directive to only run on pushing code; this is followed by the platform we run on, which is `ubuntu-22.04`, or Ubuntu 22. This Action uses the `actions/checkout@v3` action to check out the code first before installing all dependencies and running the tests on the site's production build (npm run build). We, of course, have to start that site using npm start. Otherwise, the tests won't run.

To give you some idea of what happens – we can see a successful set of tests in the (partial) screenshot shown in Figure 10-10; any failures would be displayed at the same time.

	Spec		Tests	Passing	Failing	Pending	Skipped
358							
359							
360	✓ addingProducts.cy.js	00:02	1	1	-	-	-
361							
362	✓ app.cy.js	00:01	1	1	-	-	-
363							
364	✓ creditCardImages.cy.js	807ms	1	1	-	-	-
365							
366	✓ removingProducts.cy.js	00:03	1	1	-	-	-
367							
368	✓ starRating.cy.js	00:01	1	1	-	-	-
369							
370	✓ All specs passed!	00:09	5	5	-	-	-
371							

Figure 10-10. *A successful set of tests in our CI pipeline*

A small note of warning – you may find that the CI pipeline results for this action are somewhat lengthy; it's worth scrolling down if you want to view the details, particularly if they show a failure when the action is run.

Summary

It's been a long road, but we have our working site!

Throughout this chapter, we've worked through some critical steps. These act as a milestone to confirm that we've released our site, and any development work can now switch to maintenance and extending or developing new features for the site. We've learned a lot, and while some of the content we've covered may differ for your own Next. js e-commerce–driven projects, there are still some core themes in the release process. Let's take a quick look at what we learned in this chapter.

We started by setting some key assumptions around how we would publish our site – many were based on personal preference, so these could change based on your requirements. We then worked through preparing our GitHub repository before uploading the code and completing the initial code analysis.

Next up, we hooked our site to Netlify before testing that it displays our site as expected – we rounded off the chapter by adding a custom domain name to provide that nice extra touch to our project. As a last step, we then implemented a second GitHub action to automatically run the Cypress tests we created earlier in the book, which provides a little extra confidence that our site works as expected in the browser.

We've covered a lot, but it's all useful stuff! That's not the end, though – I have two more projects I want to work through, but they are ones we could apply once the site has been running for some time. The first of these is to give it an international flair – it's time for me to get my language dictionary out and figure out how to say "macaron" in a different language.

PART IV

Taking Things Further

CHAPTER 11

Project: Adding International Support

Our site has been up and running for a while and working as expected, with orders flowing in. To keep things fresh, what can we do next to develop it?

Sites are only good if we maintain and develop them. To help with this, I want to explore a couple of projects to improve and develop the customer experience.

The first project is adding support for different languages – in this day of global e-commerce, it's essential to have content in other languages – after all, we don't all speak English! Adding international support is great for giving customers a more personal experience and ensuring that we deal with cultural differences – particularly if a harmless word in English could give the wrong meaning.

This chapter will look at converting our store to accept multiple languages. We'll try adding a language, although I can't guarantee the translation will be perfect! As always, we need to start somewhere, so let's begin with setting the scene and answering a question: why should we localize content?

Setting the Scene

Cast your mind back to Chapter 8, where we explored how we could optimize our site for SEO purposes – remember how I mentioned that one of the ways to do this was to localize content into different languages? One of the reasons for doing this was to improve SEO, particularly if we're targeting an international audience; at the same time, we need to optimize that content for each market to help increase awareness and recognition and reduce bounce rates.

© Alex Libby 2023
A. Libby, *Practical Next.js for E-Commerce*, https://doi.org/10.1007/978-1-4842-9612-7_11

In days gone past, doing this could be tricky – we'd have to maintain two versions of the site, which brings its own issues around keeping the same content in both sites. However, Next.js makes it much easier – we can maintain the same codebase for all pages but use a plug-in (or two) to insert the appropriate content at the right time.

Making the transition to supporting multiple languages is one we can only really do once the site has been running for a while – we can do it from the outset, but to get the best effect, we need to know if people are visiting from other countries. After all, there is no point in adding language support if our target market is purely our home country!

Preparation Is Key

Assuming we want to target an international audience, we will need to make some changes to our site. These changes aren't a five-minute job – there are a few things we need to consider:

- Content structure: how we lay out our pages can influence the content structure in each domain and, ultimately, how customers access our site. There are several ways to do this, such as `www.example.com/fr` or `fr.example.com`. We're going to use the former of the two for our project.

- We've already touched on some upcoming changes to Next.js, specifically around using the app folder. As we've not implemented it in our project, we won't cover support for it regarding localization. It doesn't mean we should forget it; if we start using it in the future, we should adapt our site to allow these changes. I'll come back to this later in the chapter.

- I would 100% recommend working on a copy of the original site for this mini-project: we will have to make quite a few changes, so it's best to do this on a site where we can iron out any issues before putting them into production.

For this chapter, I'll use a copy of the project called `macaronmagic-lang` to implement the changes.

- I've chosen two languages to implement: English and Dutch. The former is my native tongue, so the changes are less around content and more around refactoring the codebase. The latter? I like a challenge and have been learning a little Dutch in my spare time! It doesn't matter which languages we use; we need at least one other for this to work. The process is the same, irrespective of which languages we use.

- We won't touch Stripe for now or content coming from Sanity – this will remain in English. This chapter focuses on localizing content using Next.js; the content coming from Sanity is just text, so we can add this anytime.

To implement the changes, we'll do it in two parts – the first is to reconfigure the site to support multiple locales and test that we can display different content depending on which version of the site we use. The second will be to add the translated text in JSON files; we'll then bring both together and test to ensure that content displays using the correct language on the appropriate site. We'll begin with setting up support for our chosen languages on our site.

Configuring Locale Support

For our first task, we need to tell Next.js that our site should support content for multiple locales. We'll do this using the i18n configuration property inside of `next.config.js`. At the same time, we'll add a test page to confirm it changes the site URL as expected and a drop-down option to switch between each locale.

ADDING LOCALE SUPPORT

To set up initial support for different countries, first stop the Next.js development server if it is running, then follow these steps:

1. First, go ahead and stop your development server if it is already running. We're making changes to the Next.js configuration, which require a restart of the server to take effect.

2.   Next, crack open a copy of next.config.js in your editor, then add the highlighted lines before the closing bracket, like so:

```
/** @type {import('next').NextConfig} */
const nextConfig = {
  ...
  i18n: {
    defaultLocale: "en",
    locales: ["en", "nl-NL"],
  },
};

module.exports = nextConfig;
```

3.   Next, take a copy of about.js and save it as test.js – we will use this to test that the country switching works. Crack open the test.js file in your editor, then add the import below to the top of the file:

```
import { useRouter } from "next/router";
```

4.   With the import in place, we now need to get the locale of the country we're using – add this line before the opening return (statement:

```
const About = () => {
  const { locale } = useRouter();

  return (
```

5.   Next, add this line after <p>About Macaron Magic<p>:

```
    <div className="about-us">
      <p>About Macaron Magic</p>

      <p>Hello world: {locale}</p>
```

6.   We need to make changes in one more file – crack open NavBar.jsx, then add the same useRouter import as we did before:

```
import { useStateContext } from "../../context/StateContext";
import { useRouter } from "next/router";
```

7. A few lines down (after the destructured entries for useStateContext()),
    add this definition and event handler:

```
const handleLocaleChange = (event) => {
  const value = event.target.value;

  router.push(router.route, router.asPath, {
    locale: value,
  });
};
```

8. To use both, we now need to amend the calls to <Link> – we'll do it for the
    first two, as this is enough to show the effect (but feel free to replicate it for the
    other two, if you wish). Change the first <Link…> line to this:

```
<Link href="/" className={router.asPath === "/" ? "active" : ""}>
  Home
</Link>
```

9. In the same way, change the second call to <Link...> to this:

```
<Link
  href="/about"
  className={router.asPath === "/about" ? "active" : ""}
>
  About
</Link>
```

10. For the last change, we need to add a drop-down box to change languages; add
    the highlighted lines as shown:

```
      {showCart && <Cart />}
    </div>
  </div>
  <select onChange={handleLocaleChange} value={router.locale}>
    <option value="en">English</option>
    <option value="nl-NL">Nederlands</option>
  </select>
  </div>
  );
};
```

11.   Save and close all files. Switch to a Node.js terminal, then at the prompt, change the working folder to our project area.

12.   Enter npm run dev and press Enter to fire up the Next.js development server. Wait for the server to fire up, then browse to http://localhost:3000/test. If all is well, we should see our site as before, but this time with two additions: notice the drop-down on the right in the header and the "Hello world:..." statement below the main title, as shown in Figure 11-1.

Mangez Macaron

Home   About   Shop   Contact

English

This is a demo store - no orders will be accepted or delivered

About Macaron Magic

Hello world: en

Lorem ipsum dolor sit amet, consectetur adipiscing elit. Mauris vulputate justo ac tellus egestas dictum. Aenean vestibulum diam eu risus cursus mollis. Nulla dapibus ante in

Figure 11-1. *Displaying the test page, with the addition of a new locale*

13.   Try clicking the language switcher to the right and changing it from English to Dutch. Notice how the "Hello world" statement changes from en to nl-NL (Figure 11-2).

Figure 11-2. *The same page, but this time with the Dutch locale chosen*

You can also see the same locale in the address bar: the two should match.

Excellent – we're one step closer to adding international support for our site! We still have plenty to do, but the changes in this last demo will at least allow Next.js to swap between different locales based on whether we want to see English or Dutch content. We've covered some crucial steps in this demo, so let's take a moment to explore them in more detail.

Exploring the Changes Made

Adding locale support to our site is critical to making localization work – it's all about telling Next.js to recognize which locale we're in, so we can alter what we display to each market.

To implement the changes, we first had to add the i18n object to the next.config.js file – this tells Next.js that our default locale is en, but it should support either the en or nl-NL locales in this site. It will show a locale in the URL; instead of just seeing http://localhost:3000/ (which is for the en locale as the default if no locale is chosen), we'll also have http://localhost:3000/nl-NL/ for Dutch content.

To test this, we took a copy of `about.js` and renamed it test.js – this is probably overkill, but it is just a precaution! We imported the `useRouter` function from `next/router` to this page, then added a constant for a locale we get from `useRouter()`. We then use this to determine which locale we should display – either en or `nl-NL`.

It's a good start, but for it to be really effective, we need a way of changing the locale. We added a drop-down box and wired it to a `handleLocaleChange` event handler, which changes the locale displayed on the screen when we click the drop-down box. To round things off, we ran up the site using the development server and tried changing the drop-down; we saw that the locale displayed on the screen changed from en to `nl-NL`, when changing the drop-down value from English to Nederland in the browser.

As an aside – you will notice in this chapter that I mention the need to restart the server before viewing any changes. Although we don't need to make too many changes to `next.config.js`, translation changes will only kick in when the server builds the site for the first time. The easiest way to do this is to stop it before making changes and restart it once we have completed them.

Okay – let's move on; we have locale support in place, so let's move on to the next task: adding translated content! This is where we need to install two packages – Next doesn't support this part out of the box, so it needs additional help; let's work through the steps required for the next demo.

Adding Language Support

With locale support now enabled, it's time to move on and tweak our codebase to support the display of copy in different languages.

Next.js doesn't support displaying different languages using placeholders by default, so we need to install packages to help support this process. A few packages are available, but I've elected to use i18next. It uses the react-i18next and next-i18next packages under the hood, so we need to install these as well.

Once these are in place, we can adapt our code to add placeholders for translated text – let's dive in and look at how in more detail.

ADDING LANGUAGE SUPPORT

To add language support, make sure the development server is stopped, then follow
these steps:

1. We first need to install two plug-ins, next-i18next i18next – normally, we would
    use npm i, but they need to be installed as peer dependencies. Instead, add
    these four lines to the package.json, then save and close it:

    ```
    "peerDependencies": {
      "i18next": "^22.4.15",
      "react-i18next": "^12.2.0",
      "next-i18next": "^13.2.2"
    },
    ```

A heads up – newer versions of these files may be available by the time this book
goes into print. Please update as appropriate; it's important to note that for this
demo to work properly, we have to add these packages as peer dependencies, not
standard dependencies.

2. Fire up a Node.js terminal, then change the working folder to our new
    project area.

3. At the prompt, enter npm install and press Enter – this will install the new
    plug-ins to their latest versions.

4. Next, we need to make a series of changes to different files – the first is to
    create a new i18n configuration file for locale and language support. Fire up
    your editor, then add this block to a new file, saving it as next-i18next.
    config.js:

    ```
    module.exports = {
      i18n: {
        defaultLocale: "en",
        locales: ["en", "nl-NL"],
      },
      react: { useSuspense: false },
    };
    ```

5. For the second change, go ahead and open `next.config.js`, then add this
   import below the `@type` directive at the top of the file:

```
const { i18n } = require("./next-i18next.config");
```

6. Go to the end of the file, then change the last entry to show this:

```
reactStrictMode: true,
sassOptions: {
  includePaths: ["styles"],
},
i18n,
};
```

7. We now need to add some test language files – extract a copy of the `locales`
   folder from the code download, then copy it to the `\public` folder. Inside, you
   should see two folders – en and nl-NL – each containing two test files that we
   will use to prove that language support works.

8. We have changes in three more files; the next one is in _app.js. Crack that
   file open in your editor, then add these two import statements:

```
import { appWithTranslation } from "next-i18next";
import nextI18NextConfig from "../../next-i18next.config";
```

The second one is significant, as without it, you get a You will need to pass
in an i18next instance by using initReactI18next error/warning,
and translations fail to show.

---

9. We need then to wrap the exported MyApp and nextI18NextConfig objects
   with appWithTranslation – amend the export statement at the bottom
   to this:

```
export default appWithTranslation(MyApp, nextI18NextConfig);
```

10. For this next change, open index.js from the \src\pages folder. Add this
    import to the list of imports at the top of the file:

```
import { useTranslation } from "next-i18next";
import { serverSideTranslations } from "next-i18next/
serverSideTranslations";
```

11. Scroll down to the bottom of the file, then add this exported function just before
     the export default Home line:

```
export async function getServerSideProps({ locale }) {
  return {
    props: {
      ...(await serverSideTranslations(locale, ["common", "test"])),
    },
  };
}
```

12. We have one more file to amend, which is test.js – open this file, then add
     these two imports to the top of the file:

```
import { useTranslation } from "next-i18next";
import { serverSideTranslations } from "next-i18next/
serverSideTranslations";
```

13. Scroll down a bit, then add this constant declaration just after the opening line
     of our component:

```
const About = () => {
  const { t } = useTranslation("test");
```

14. Inside the return block, go ahead and add this line – it's a test, for now, to prove
     that the page can render different languages:

```
  return (
    <div className="about-us">
      <p>About Macaron Magic</p>

      <p>{t("about")}</p>
      <p>
        Lorem ipsum dolor sit amet, consectetur adipiscing
        elit. Mauris
        (...shortened for brevity)
      </p>
    </div>
  );
};
```

15.   At the bottom of the file, add this async function call to `getServerSideProps`, just before the closing export default About statement:

```
export async function getServerSideProps({ locale }) {
  return {
    props: {
      ...(await serverSideTranslations(locale, ["test"])),
      // Will be passed to the page component as props
    },
  };
}

export default About;
```

16.   Save and close all open files. Switch to a Node.js terminal, then make sure the working folder points to our new project area.

17.   At the prompt, enter npm run dev and press Enter. When prompted, browse to http://localhost:3000/test – if all is well, we should see the word About appear below the main title, as shown in Figure 11-3.

About Macaron Magic

About

Lorem ipsum dolor sit amet, consectetur adipiscin
Nulla danibus ante in felis vulputate mattis. Mauris

Figure 11-3. *Displaying the localized phrase for the English locale*

18.   Try changing the drop-down to show Nederland – we should now see the content change to Over, which is Dutch for "About" (Figure 11-4).

About Macaron Magic

Over

Lorem ipsum dolor sit amet, consectetur adipiscing ε
Nulla dapibus ante in felis vulputate mattis. Mauris sι

Figure 11-4. *Displaying the localized content in Dutch*

Don't forget – we should also see the URL change: it will display `nl-NL` in the
URL when on the Dutch site but nothing when showing English, as this is the
default site.

Phew – although Next.js has support for different languages built-in, we still have to
go through a few steps to set it up!

This is part of the reason for recommending we use a copy of the original project. It's
too easy to make a change that can break our site's language support and other features!
We've covered some critical elements in this last demo when it comes to implementing
language support; let's take a moment to explore these in more detail before we move on
to refactoring the site's copy.

Understanding the Changes Made

Adding language support is not a particularly difficult task for most pages. There might
be occasions where it trips us up, but in the main, it's a three-step process to reconfigure
the page or component to accept languages.

Before running through that process, we had a few things to do first – we started by
installing three packages to support adding languages. We then reconfigured the `next.config.js` file to move the locale support into its file (`next-i18next.config.js`) and
amended the original config file to import this new file.

With the packages installed, we then imported two functions – `appWithTranslation`,
a HOC that wraps around our site; we also import the `nextI18NextConfig` object, which
is a requirement for localization to work. At the same time, we amended the export at the
end of `_app.js`, so that our site now understands and can accept different languages.

Next up, we turned to the index.js page under \src\pages – here, we added two imports: one for calling `useTranslation()` from next-i18next and the other for getting the translated content server-side. We use the first import to apply the translated values to each placeholder – in our case, we had two instances: `t{("shop-now")}` and `{t("welcome.para...")}`. At the same time, we updated the original `test.js` file, too; this gives us an extra page to test without affecting the site.

Toward the end of the file, we added a call to the function `getServerSideProps()` in both files to call the relevant JSON files we created earlier, which contain the translated keys and values for our page. A quick test confirms that we get translated content for both locales, `en` and `nl-NL`, when viewing the site in the browser.

Although these changes may seem relatively straightforward, a few hazards can trip us up if we're not careful. Let's have a look at them:

- The `getServerSideProps()` call only works on pages; it doesn't work for components.

- We have to apply `getServerSideProps()` to all pages on our site; in most cases, the code will be similar, with the only difference being the calls to each JSON file we include.

- Components will only render translated text if their parent page is fully operational; if there is an issue, this can stop labels in components from rendering correctly.

Other hazards can trip us up – I'll come to these when we apply the translations to each page and component later in this chapter.

In the meantime, our site can now support multiple locales, and we can switch between either English or Dutch as desired.

It's only part of the story: we need to update all the labels and text we used, so that the content on our "site" (now almost two!) is less of a mix of English and Dutch! It's a thankless task, but someone has to do it; let's walk through the process of generating the translated content in more detail.

Reconfiguring English Language Support

There are times when one wishes certain jobs don't exist – unfortunately, this next one is one of those, and one we need to do!

We now need to collect all of the labels and texts we want to include in our site, which we won't otherwise source from the Sanity back end. There isn't really any shortcut to doing it as such – it's one of those tasks where someone has to get their head down and create that list.

Fortunately for you, my dear readers, I've already done this hard work for you: files for both the EN and NL translations are available in the code download accompanying this book. Let's quickly walk through the steps for both languages in the following walkthrough to see how I got there.

WALKTHROUGH – TWEAKING ENGLISH LANGUAGE SUPPORT

To update the translation file structure, follow these steps:

1. I created JSON files for each page and component, except for the PaymentIcons component – there isn't any text in this one, so a JSON file is redundant.

2. I added opening brackets in each file, which is standard for JSON files. I then created placeholder keys for each value that should be included – in this example (for the Perfect callout on the homepage), I added three:

```
{
  "perfect": {
    "for": "PERFECT FOR",
    "special": "SPECIAL OCCASIONS",
    "text": "Share the love and give every guest a little explosion
    of sweetness with our show stopping macaron towers. Perfect for
    weddings, anniversaries and parties. You could even add a touch of
    luxury to party bags and wedding favors with these perfect bite
    sized treats."
  }
}
```

3. As you can see from this example, I've nested the keys inside more brackets – not strictly necessary, as the component only uses this file. However, if we were to merge this into one larger file, we would need a way to separate the text for each component, hence using the nested approach.

4. I repeated step 3 for the other JSON files, ending up with 20 (including the original two, `common.json` and `test.json`).

5. As the last step, we must put all these files into the `\public\locale\en` folder, ready for use on our site.

These are ready for use in the next demo when we link the component to each translation locale file.

It's a thankless task, but if we'd had to work through these steps, we would at least have all the content files we need ready for our site.

There isn't anything really special about how we do this part; as long as you are familiar with structuring JSON files, you should not have any issues with creating these files. The key lies in how we build up content – I'll come back and explain what I mean later, but for now, let's turn our attention to creating the Dutch language files as part of the next walkthrough.

Translating Content into Dutch

When it comes to translating content into Dutch, we're already halfway there – all of the files we need are in the EN folder, and we just need to take copies and update the values to Dutch.

It's one of those tasks we ultimately have to get right, as properly optimized content can benefit SEO. Getting the content right takes time to complete, but we can at least make a start with creating the source files and storing them on our site, ready for use.

WALKTHROUGH – ADDING DUTCH LANGUAGE SUPPORT

To update the translation file structure, follow these steps:

1. I copied over the JSON files for each page and component directly from the en folder – the same applies to the PaymentIcons component, as this doesn't need a translation locale file.

2. As each file already has content (albeit in English), the task here was to replace the values with Dutch equivalents. For this, I used Google Translate – I make no apologies for the accuracy here: blame Google if it's wrong! The critical thing to note here is that it's not about the quality of the translations but more the mechanics of getting them into the site. The keys to the left of the colons remain the same; we need to translate the values to the right into Dutch.

These are ready for use in the next demo when we link the component to each translation locale file.

Perfect – we have our locale support in place and language source files set up: we can now bring the two together! Before we do so, I want to cover a couple of points regarding how we structure the JSON files. There is no right or wrong answer, but these points will hopefully help create language files for future projects.

Breaking Apart the Code Changes

In the last two walkthroughs, we explored the steps required to create the translation source files for our site. We had to create the original English ones first to get the format right, but we could easily copy these to the Dutch locale folder; the file names stay the same, but the content will contain the phrases translated into the appropriate language.

The thing about this is that while there is a predetermined structure for storing the JSON files, it's up to us how many files we create and in which file we store the labels for a particular feature or page. Initially, we started with the locale layout shown in Figure 11-5.

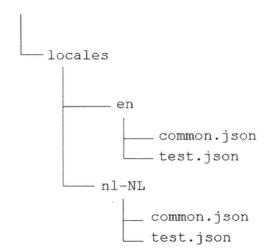

Figure 11-5. *The initial format of JSON locale files and folders*

However, we've since added 18 files each, making 40 files! While the site works, I think 20 JSON files would be a little excessive for a small site like ours, so if we took this site into production, it would be worth reconsidering the structure to see if we can slim it down, still achieving the same result. There is no right or wrong in terms of how we should structure the files – the important thing is to make sure that if we were to merge files, we get the right balance of loading content when needed on the site.

Applying the Translations

Ladies and gentlemen…it is time…

Indeed, it is time for us to bring everything together and apply our translations! We have already seen how to apply translations to a couple of pages, but only in a limited capacity. We have much more to update – including both pages and components!

Before we get to that in our next demo, there are a couple of things we should be aware of:

- Everything works on a key/value basis, as we saw earlier: when it comes to adding keys, there is no right or wrong way. Go with what works best for you – as long as you use the same key in both the JSON file and the codebase, it will display the text assigned to the hat key.

- We only need to use the useTranslation() function to call text in components – it makes life more straightforward when updating them! Any entries from JSON files will filter down to them via the getServerSideProps() call on the parent page.

We have a lot to cover, but most of them use exactly the same principles when adapting the code.

Instead of going through all 20 manually, I will work through examples of a page and component, so you can see how to do it. It will then be over to you for a bit of audience participation – you should be able to complete the remainder, but don't worry: I will give you lots of tips and help in doing so! With all that in mind, let's make a start – we'll use the homepage as the basis for our first exercise.

BRINGING IT ALL TOGETHER – PART 1: UPDATING A PAGE FILE

To apply the translations we've just added, follow these steps:

1. First, go ahead and stop the development server – we need to make changes which will require a restart at the end of the demo.

2. Next, extract copies of the translation JSON files from the code download, and put these in the \public\locales folder.

3. Switch to your editor, then crack open \src\Pages\index.js and add these two imports to the bottom of the list of imports at the top of the file:

```
import { useTranslation } from "next-i18next";
import { serverSideTranslations } from "next-i18next/
serverSideTranslations";
```

4. Next, we need to change the opening tag for the component and add the call to insert the correct text for the placeholder – change the first four lines of the component to look like this:

```
const Home = () => {
  const { t } = useTranslation("home");

  return (
```

Make sure to change the closing brackets at the end of the function!

---

5. In the getServerSideProps() function, look for the call to
    serverSideTranslations(…), and alter as shown:

```
...(await serverSideTranslations(locale, ["common", "test", "home"])),
```

6. With the configuration changes in place, we can now translate the text – look
    for the line starting with <span className="tagline"… and change it
    to this:

```
<span className="tagline">
  {t("luxury")}
</span>
```

7. Next, change the link for the Shop Now button to display this:

```
<Link className="shop-now" href="/shop">
  {t("shop-now")}
</Link>
```

8. We need to update the text displayed as the introduction – scroll down to
    the block starting with <div className="intro"… and change the three
    paragraphs to this:

```
<div className="intro">
  <p>{t("welcome.para1")}</p>
  <p>{t("welcome.para2")}</p>
  <p>{t("welcome.para3")}</p>
</div>
```

9. Save and close all open files. Switch to a Node.js terminal, then change the
    working folder to our new project area.

10. At the prompt, enter npm run dev to (re)start the development server, then
    browse to http://localhost:3000/. If all is well, we should not see any initial
    change, as text is still served from the JSON files and not hard-coded into the
    main codebase.

11. Try changing one of the entries in \public\locales\en\home.json to
    something else – it doesn't matter what, as long as you make it obvious it's a
    change! Restart the server, then browse to the page again. You should see it
    refreshed with your change.

Don't forget to reset your change so we don't have odd text on the site!

Phew – pages are done, check... what's next? Ah, yes, the components!

Now that we have updated the pages, it's time to focus on the components we call from our pages. We need to make changes using similar principles, although as we pass values down from the parent page as props, we do not need the getServerSideProps() call at the end of the file.

So – grab a drink and have a breather for a moment: when you're ready, let's continue with the second part of our exercise.

BRINGING IT ALL TOGETHER – PART 2:UPDATING A COMPONENT FILE

To update the demo banner component to take translations based on locale, follow these steps:

1. First, stop the development server by pressing Ctrl+C or Cmd+C. Keep the terminal session open, as we will need it shortly.

2. Crack open demobanner.jsx – add this import at the top of the file:

```
import { useTranslation } from "next-i18next";
```

3. Next, we need to add a constant that calls the useTranslation() function – go ahead and add this line just inside the DemoBanner component, like so:

```
const DemoBanner = () => {
  const { t } = useTranslation("demobanner");
```

4. We need to make one more change in this file – inside the <span>, change the text to show this:

```
<span>{t("demo")}</span>
```

5. Save and close that file. Next, crack open index.js – we need to add an entry to the getServerSideProps, so that locale text values filter down to child components. In the getServerSideProps function, add the entry as highlighted:

```
return {
  props: {
    ...(await serverSideTranslations(locale, [
      "home",
      "demobanner",
```

6. Save and close the file. Revert to your Node.js terminal session, then at the prompt, enter npm run dev and press Enter.

7. Browse to http://localhost:3000/ – if all is well, we should not see any visual change: this is to be expected. Try changing the locale drop-down from English to Nederland – this time around, we should see the URL change from http://localhost:3000/ to http://localhost:3000/nl-NL, and the text of the demo banner change from English to Dutch, as shown in Figure 11-6.

Mangez Macaron

Thuis   Over   Winkel   Contact

Dit is een demo-winkel - er worden geen bestellingen geaccepteerd of geleverd

Figure 11-6. *The demo banner text is now displayed in Dutch*

You will see the links below the site name are also in Dutch – I've already added similar changes to the NavBar.jsx component to display these in Dutch. I'll come back to this shortly.

Those last two demos might seem somewhat lengthy, particularly as we will have to do it multiple times for each component and page. However, most of the work is a one-off; if we want to support different languages in the future, our configuration changes should support that without any issues.

We covered a lot of changes in these two demos, so let's take a moment to explore the changes we made in more detail and understand how they fit into the bigger picture.

Understanding What Happened

Although the last two demos seem like a lot of work, it's essential to realize that most of this is a one-off task and that once done, we only need to focus on adding languages (and potentially tweaking content if required).

We had to make a series of changes to our files to get there. We could break these down into clear sections, starting with adding the relevant imports for `serverSideTranslations` and `useTranslation`. Next, we had to reconfigure each page and component to support a return block; this was critical, as we had to call the `useTranslation` function to get the relevant content from our JSON files.

Once these were in place, we could change the text to use placeholders – these placeholders match the terms specified in our JSON files. In our case, though, we had a full stop in the name – these signify nested names within the JSON, which is helpful to group values under a common tag. At the same time, we also had to make sure that the `serverSideProps` function had the correct calls to the JSON files we needed – in this case, we just needed to add home, but we will need to add more (see later in this chapter).

In terms of components, we followed largely the same process but with a few differences. For example, we only needed to import the `useTranslation` function, not both (as we did before). We still had to insert the relevant placeholders for each label, using the format `{t("....")}`.

We can't use `getServerSideProps()` in component files, as it affects how webpack chunks up the code when building the site – this is a general NextJS issue, not one specific to the `next-i18-next` plug-in.

The key point, though, was we had to add an additional call for `demobanner` into the `getServerSideProps` function on the `home` page – component labels won't render unless there is a call to the JSON file within the parent page or component. We rounded off both demos by running up the site using the development server to prove that when switching between languages, the site displayed the relevant content for each language.

Okay – let's move on: we have some audience participation coming up, but before we do so, I want to leave you with a thought.

From the two code demos, you've seen how I've set up the JSON files to organize the labels. The question I have is – does this look like a sensible format? The reason for asking is not because I can't create files but to show you that there is no right or wrong answer as to how we set up the content (or even group tags together). It will all depend on what labels you need to add and how often you need to call them – should they be in lowercase or camel case, for example? How about hyphenating any that uses more than one word?

It's just something to think about – I would recommend consistency throughout, though, as you might otherwise have problems if you can't find a label or need to change it!

Completing the Rest of the Files

Okay – it's time for some audience participation!

Don't worry – this sounds scarier than it is: we might have a few files to do, but most of the changes are very similar in each file, and we only need to do it once for each file.

The trick is to be systematic about how you make the changes; I mentioned at the start of the previous exercise that we can break down the changes into sections. We can then go through and update each file either with all changes required for that file or perhaps add the imports, then go back and refactor the component to have a return block, and so on. My best advice is to do whatever works for you!

Let's start with the remaining pages in the first of two guidance demos.

GUIDANCE – CONVERTING PAGES

To update the pages, here are the steps you need:

1. We need to add two imports to each page; they are

    ```
    import { useTranslation } from "next-i18next";
    import { serverSideTranslations } from "next-i18next/
    serverSideTranslations";
    ```

2. Next, we need to add a call to useTranslation, which we assign to the t constant
    and into which we pass the name of the locale JSON file. Here's the example
    from Home – replace "home" with the name of each JSON file from the locales
    folder in turn:

```
const { t } = useTranslation("home");
```

3. The most important change is to reconfigure the core of the component to have
    a return block – otherwise, the translations will not be applied. Reconfigure
    each page to use this format, replacing "home" with the name of the translation
    locale you want to use:

```
const Home = () => {
  const { t } = useTranslation("home");

  return (
    <>
...
    </>
  );
};
```

4. The last change is to add a call to getServerSideProps() at the end of
    each file, just before the closing export default… statement. Do this for all files,
    but **not** for [slug].js – the following code is an example taken from the
    Home component:

```
export async function getServerSideProps({ locale }) {
  return {
    props: {
      ...(await serverSideTranslations(locale, [
        "home",
        "demobanner",
        "navbar",
        "perfect",
        "newsletter",
        "footer",
        "minicart",
        "emptycart",
      ])),
```

```
        // Will be passed to the page component as props
    },
  };
}
```

I've added more here to allow for each component we call – the key is to make sure we add a reference for each component. For example, the newsletter sign-up component is here, referenced as `"newsletter"`.

5. You will see a list of JSON file names in the call to serverSideTranslations from the previous step. Replace them with the names of each component called from that page. So, for example, `index.js` (or Home component) calls the DemoBanner, NavBar, Perfect, Newsletter, Footer, and Minicart components – this page uses eight in total.

6. Make sure you add any component name you need in the call to `getServerSideTranslations`, and check how you spell it. The names are case-sensitive – if the names are missed or misspelled, they will throw a React hydration error, similar to this example:

```
Error: Text content does not match server-rendered HTML. Warning: Text
content did not match. Server: "Join" Client: "join" See more info
here: https://nextjs.org/docs/messages/react-hydration-error
```

In total, there are only nine pages we need to update (in addition to the index.js page we've already done). The pages are

- Success.js
- Terms.js
- About.js
- Canceled.js
- Contact.js
- Delivery.js
- Privacy.js
- Shop.js

I have, however, only listed eight – the exception is [slug].js, which requires a bit more work. Leave this one until the end: we'll go through it together toward the end of the chapter.

Well done for getting this far – adapting the pages is a little more complex than components! Go grab a drink and have a breather: when you're ready, let's proceed with the next part, which is converting the components.

GUIDANCE – CONVERTING COMPONENTS

The changes we need to make to the components are similar to those we've just done for the pages. We have seven in total that need converting – they are as follows:

- DemoBanner.jsx
- NavBar.jsx
- PerfectBanner.jsx
- Newsletter.jsx
- Footer.jsx
- Cart.jsx
- Info.jsx

Ignore the PaymentIcons component (as mentioned earlier) – this doesn't have any text within, so converting it is not required.

To do the conversions, here are the steps you need:

1. We need to add one import to each component; they are

   ```
   import { useTranslation } from "next-i18next";
   ```

2. Next, we need to call useTranslation(), which we assign to the t constant and into which we pass the name of the locale JSON file. Here's the example from Home – replace "demobanner" with the name of each component JSON file from the locales folder in turn:

   ```
   const { t } = useTranslation("demobanner");
   ```

3.   The most important change is to reconfigure the core of the component to have a return block – otherwise, the translations will not be applied. Reconfigure each page to use this format, replacing "home" with the name of the translation locale you want to use:

```
const Home = () => {
  const { t } = useTranslation("home");

  return (
    <>
...
    </>
  );
};
```

4.   In the MiniCart component, we have a conditional statement that displays the "s" in items. I would suggest adapting this to hard-code the word items, instead of item, for now – we can always come back and refine it once we get the remaining components working.

Phew – we're almost there! There is one more change we need to make, which is to the [slug].js page. If we try to apply the function getServerSideProps at the same time as getStaticProps or getStaticPaths (both of which we have in this component), then it throws an error.

Fortunately, we can get around this by merging the code into one function under getServerSideProps() – let's take a look at what we need to do as part of the next demo.

ADAPTING [SLUG].JS

If we try converting [slug].js to support languages in the same way as we've done previously for the other pages, then we will end up with this error:

```
You can not use getStaticProps or getStaticPaths with getServerSideProps. To
use SSG, please remove getServerSideProps
```

It's not one we want, but fixing it isn't tricky – let me walk through how:

1.   First, make sure you stop the development server – we're making configuration changes, so we will need to restart our server at the end of this demo.

2. Crack open [slug].js from the \src\pages\product\ folder, then add the same two imports as before:

```
import { useTranslation } from "next-i18next";
import { serverSideTranslations } from "next-i18next/
serverSideTranslations";
```

3. Next, we need to call useTranslation(), which we assign to the t constant and into which we pass the name of the locale JSON file. Here's the example from Home – replace "demobanner" with the name of each component JSON file from the locales folder in turn:

```
const { t } = useTranslation("demobanner");
```

4. The most important change is to reconfigure the core of the component to have a return block in the same way as other pages now have – otherwise, the translations will not be applied. Reconfigure the [slug] page to use this format, replacing "home" with slug:

```
const Home = () => {
  const { t } = useTranslation("home");

  return (
    <>
...
    </>
  );
};
```

Here's where things get interesting:

5. We can only have getServerSideProps(), or the other two, but not all three: first, go ahead and add a copy of the getServerSideProps() function from one of the other pages.

6. Next, inside serverSideTranslations(), you should have these calls:

```
        "demobanner",
        "navbar",
        "cart",
        "footer",
        "slug",
        "minicart",
```

```
"emptycart",
"shop",
"product",
"info",
```

7. Go ahead and copy the code from inside the getStaticPaths() function to after the opening line of the getServerSideProps() function.

8. Next, leave a line blank, then add a copy of the getStaticProps() function below the getStaticPaths() code.

9. If we run the code like it is now, it will error – indeed, your editor may already be flagging linting issues! To fix them, we need to rename a couple of variables:

   - Inside the code for getStaticPaths(), change products to productsPaths, like so:

   ```
   const productsPaths = await client.fetch(query);

   const paths = productsPaths.map((product) => ({
   ```

   - In the two original functions, we have values being returned. These need to move into the common return statement at the end of getServerSideProps(), like so:

   ```
   return {
     props: {
       paths,
       fallback: "blocking",
       products,
       product,
       ...(await serverSideTranslations(locale, [
         "demobanner",
         "navbar",
   ...rest as before...
   ```

At this point, we should not have any errors and be able to run the site in our browser; assuming this is the case, feel free to comment out the original getStaticPaths() and getStaticProps() functions!

Yikes – there was a lot to do there! I wouldn't be surprised if your head felt like a spinning top: making these changes requires work, and doing so is best done by taking a logical step-by-step approach. We've covered a lot over the last couple of walkthroughs, so let's relax for a moment and go through the changes we made in more detail.

Breaking Apart the Changes Made

Adding language support is necessary for any website that wants to sell in multiple markets – yes, we can keep using just one language, but having content in various languages will appeal to more customers. We can also tweak it to allow for nuances in different languages; we can start with translating, but ultimately content written by someone who speaks that tongue will give a much better experience.

To get there, we broke down the conversion process into two parts – first, we tackled the pages, followed by the components. In each case, we added the relevant imports – useTranslation does the actual translation, while serverSideTranslations deals with passing values from the JSON files down as props.

Next up, we reconfigured the component's main body to include a return block – this allows us to call useTranslation to get the correct translations for each label. Finally, and only where needed, we added the getServerSideProps() function to get the contents of each JSON file we need for a specific page.

To finish things off, we left the changes for s[slug].js until last – this uses similar changes, but given we already had getStaticProps() and getStaticPaths(), we couldn't use getServerSideProps (as it's incompatible with the other two functions). Instead, we had to merge the code from the other two functions into this one, so we ended up with a larger getServerSideProps() function that included code from all three functions.

Taking Things Further

Great – we finally have translated content showing on our site!

If you managed to get this far, then well done – tweaking the codebase to support internalization isn't a quick job, but it is well worth doing if people from more than one country visit your site.

With all the changes in place, the next task is easy – testing the site. It's vital to go through and test it thoroughly: I know our site is only a POC demo, but there is no reason why we shouldn't treat it as close to production as possible. After all, a POC aims to iron out any issues: there is every possibility you may get similar problems in production if you're not careful!

Assuming that everything we have tested works as expected, there are things we could do to develop the site even further when it comes to internationalization. Let's take a look at a few examples as a starting point:

- One area we could improve is the language switcher: it serves its purpose but doesn't look very good!

- Support for the app folder: we didn't need to use it on our site, but there will come a time when we will have to switch to using it on our site. We should bear this in mind – we may want to redesign the site to use it now or wait until support becomes more widely available.

- We should look at tidying up the JSON files we created for translations: while they work, we may want to realign where content is stored, rationalize the numbers, or remove any no longer needed (such as test.json!).

- One essential task we've not covered in this chapter is updating the hidden tags in our code. We should only have one language per site for SEO purposes; this includes any keywords or tags used, such as meta tags.

- Remember how we removed the conditional "s" for items? It's one area we should update so we can reinstate this change. We could also look at formatting prices – using US Dollars for this POC is fine, but it would be nicer if we could show prices in more than one currency!

These are just a few of the changes we could look at to help take the site forward – I'm sure there will be others, but much of this will depend on your requirements and the direction you decide to take your site.

Summary

Adding language support to any website can be a double-edged sword – the mechanics of adding the capability is relatively straightforward, but getting the right tone of content is another matter! In this chapter, we spent time working through how to add Dutch as a second language – we've covered some essential pointers, so let's take a moment to review what we have learned.

We started by setting the scene and working through a few key points as part of preparation before exploring how to set up locale support on our site. Once done, we then reconfigured the existing content to be sourced from JSON files once we brought everything together.

We then worked our way through how we would create the language files for our site – in this case, English and Dutch, but the same applies to any combination of languages. We then used those translations to our site by swapping out hard-coded text for placeholders and adding some extra functionality to render the correct text. To finish things off, we ran through a few ideas that we could do to help finesse and tweak the setup even further so that we have a fully developed capability for our customers.

Phew – we've covered a lot, but there is one more project left to do! For those sites starting out in life, it's likely that we will only offer a simple means of purchasing products, but with no means to review purchase history and the like. It's time to change that – we need to set up an authorization mechanism to secure details such as a customer's transaction history, preferences, and so on. Next.js supports various ways to achieve this – we'll explore this and more in the next chapter.

CHAPTER 12

Project: Authenticating Access

It might seem odd to cover authentication this late in the book, but there is a reason for doing so – authentication isn't just about recognizing who you are but ensuring you have valid access to a restricted part of our site. It can open doors to providing a more personal service; we need a site up and running first!

For the second of our two projects, I'll explore what we need to do to set up a starting point for authentication and explore some of the ideas we could implement with authentication installed. But first, we need to start somewhere, so let's begin by setting expectations around what we will achieve in this chapter.

Setting the Scene

Authentication is a vast topic and one we can only hope to scratch the surface on! There are many ways to authenticate access, from a simple username and password to certification via Google, Facebook, and more.

We may already have a suitable authentication system if we're running a larger corporate retail site. For a small site like ours, though, we won't have the manpower to manage user accounts, so we need to rely on third-party options to help reduce the burden.

With that in mind, we need to create something a little more realistic in size – for this chapter, we'll use the following as the basis for our solution:

- For this project, I'll use a copy of the site, which I will call macaronmagic-nextauth – this isn't strictly necessary, but given we're making changes, it's more of a precaution! It will be a copy of the site from the original project built up in Chapters 1-10, so it will contain all of the existing code.

© Alex Libby 2023
A. Libby, *Practical Next.js for E-Commerce*, https://doi.org/10.1007/978-1-4842-9612-7_12

- I'll use the next-auth package to provide authentication, available from `https://github.com/nextauthjs/next-auth`, and set it up with GitHub access. We're running a demo site, so this is adequate to prove it works; when we go into production, we would probably want to use different options, such as Facebook or Google.

- We won't deploy this change into production but treat it as a means to figure out what we would do if we had pushed it live. I will, however, go through some details on how we can deploy this change toward the end of the chapter.

- One thing we should absolutely consider when moving into production – if we are sourcing information from third-party providers like Stripe, can we do this in a way that doesn't conflict with the server-side rendering from Next.js?

I'll return to the final point at the end of the chapter – this raises a few crucial questions we need to consider when authenticating access.

Okay – with that out of the way, let's crack on! The first task is to register an application for OAuth access in GitHub, so we can use it to authenticate access.

Registering for a GitHub OAuth Account

OAuth is an authentication protocol that uses authentication tokens between consumers and service providers that allows us to prove our identity – without giving away our passwords! It is perfect for our needs: although we will use GitHub for now, we could use Facebook or Google as our service providers.

The first step is to register an OAuth application so that GitHub understands who we are – let's dive in and take a look at how to do this in more detail.

REGISTERING A GITHUB OAUTH APP

To register a GitHub OAuth app, follow these steps:

1. First, browse to `https://github.com/settings/developers`, then click New OAuth app to register a new application.

2. On the next page, add the following details:

Field	Value to enter
Application Name	Enter a name to identify it in your list – it's not critical what the name is.
Homepage URL	http://localhost:3000
Authorization callback URL	http://localhost:3000/api/auth/callback
Enable Device Flow	Leave unchanged.

3. Click Register application, then click Generate a new client secret on the next page.

4. You will be prompted to sign in – do so with your login for that repository.

5. Take a copy of both the client ID and secret and store them somewhere safely – we will need to add both in the next demo.

6. Finally, click Update application – GitHub will return you to the summary window, which looks similar to Figure 12-1.

7. Click Update application to save changes and return to your repository's main list of OAuth apps (Figure 12-1).

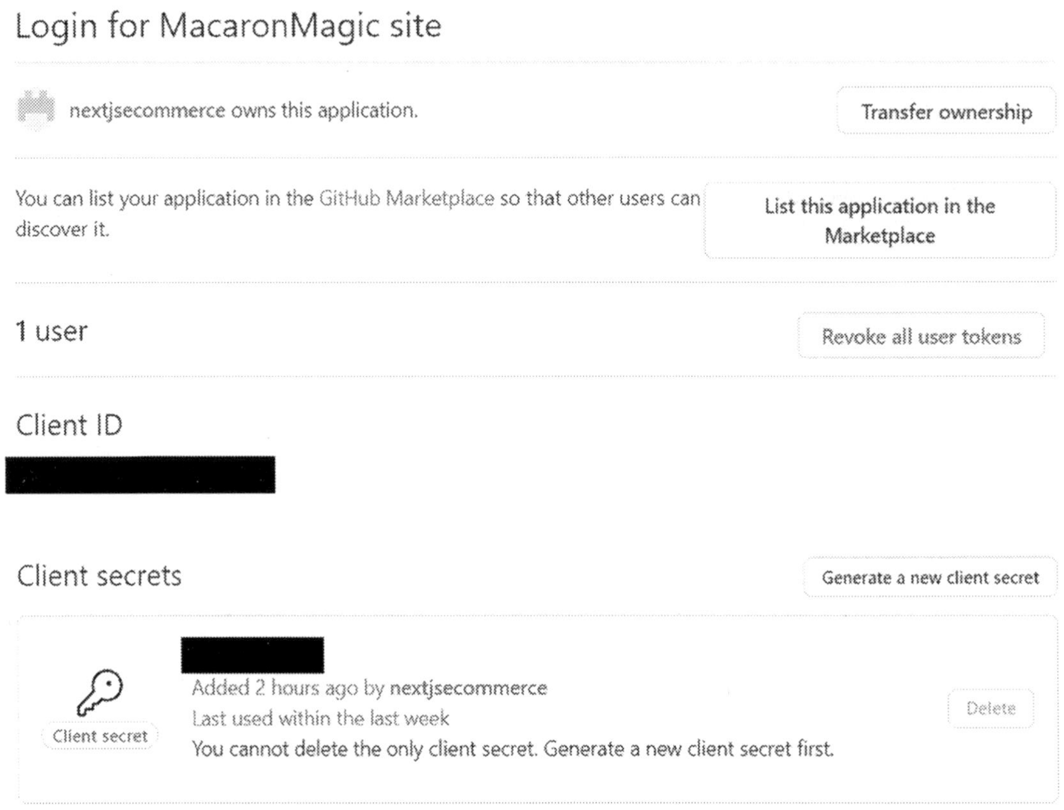

Login for MacaronMagic site

nextjsecommerce owns this application.   Transfer ownership

You can list your application in the GitHub Marketplace so that other users can discover it.

List this application in the Marketplace

1 user   Revoke all user tokens

Client ID

████████████████████

Client secrets   Generate a new client secret

████████████
Client secret   Added 2 hours ago by nextjsecommerce   Delete
                   Last used within the last week
                   You cannot delete the only client secret. Generate a new client secret first.

Figure 12-1. *Settings for GitHub OAuth app*

Perfect – that's the first job done; GitHub knows who we are now! Setting up the application was straightforward; we covered some important points in this demo, so let's take a closer look at the changes we made and how they fit into the bigger picture.

Exploring the Changes Made

This demo may have been short, but it plays a critical part in the authentication process – without it, we can't authorize any access using GitHub as our source provider.

It's a perfect way to access protected data without providing passwords, albeit in a limited capacity. The standard is also open source, which means we can add other providers later – I'll return to this at the end of the chapter.

For now, though, what did we achieve? We created an app in GitHub that contains details of our site's homepage and callback URL – the latter is the URL that GitHub will redirect users to once they have successfully logged in to our site. It's important to note that it will not exist as a physical URL but as a virtual one – we use the [...auth].js file as a placeholder to create that URL – in much the same way as we did for our products earlier in the book.

At the same time, we also had to generate a client secret – we use this and the client ID provided by GitHub to authenticate users when they try to log into the site.

Keeping a copy of that secret somewhere safe is essential – GitHub doesn't allow you to come back to see it, and you will have to re-create a new secret if you lose the original one!

Okay – let's crack on: with our OAuth app in place, it's time to move on to the next task: installing support for it on our site.

Installing and Configuring NextAuth

With our OAuth app in place, it's time to move on to the next task – we need to install next-auth and configure it for use on our site. It will require a few steps, so without further ado, let's get stuck in and see what we need to do as part of our next demo.

INSTALLING NEXTAUTH

To install and configure NextAuth, follow these steps:

1. First, crack open a Node.js terminal, then change the working folder to our new project area.

2. At the prompt, enter `npm i next-auth` and press Enter to install the next-auth package.

3. Once this is installed, switch to your text editor, then open a new file.

4. In the file, add the following code:

```
GITHUB_ID=<your GitHub ID, from the first exercise>
GITHUB_SECRET=<your GitHub secret from the first exercise>
NEXTAUTH_URL=http://localhost:3000
```

5. Save the file as .env.local, at the root of the folder.

6. Crack open _app.js, then add this line below the list of imports at the top of the file:

```
import { SessionProvider } from "next-auth/react";
```

7. Next, scroll down a bit, then amend the code within to add the SessionProvider tags like so:

```
<SessionProvider session={pageProps.session}>
    <StateContext>
      <Layout>
        <Toaster />
        <Component {...pageProps} />
      </Layout>
    </StateContext>
</SessionProvider>
```

8. In a new file, add the following code – save this as [...nextauth].js in the \src\pages\api\auth folder:

```
import NextAuth from "next-auth";
import GitHubProvider from "next-auth/providers/github";

const options = {
  providers: [
    GitHubProvider({
      clientId: process.env.GITHUB_ID,
      clientSecret: process.env.GITHUB_SECRET,
    }),
  ],
};

export default (req, res) => NextAuth(req, res, options);
```

9. Save and close all open files.

10. Revert to your Node.js terminal, then enter npm run dev and press Enter to restart the Next.js development server.

11. When ready, browse to http://localhost:3000/api/auth/signin and click Signin with GitHub.

12.   GitHub will prompt you to authorize access – follow the instructions shown on the screen.

13.   Once authorized, it will return you to the site's homepage – you are now logged in.

This is an important step forward – we now have the basics in place for authenticating ourselves, so that we can then implement a secured area in our site. To get here, we set up the next-auth package and made a few changes to our codebase: let's take a moment to review the changes we made in more detail.

Breaking Apart the Code Changes

We started by installing the next-auth package, using the typical npm package process; once we had installed it, we switched to adding a `.env.local` file that contains the `secret`, `ID`, and `URL` we created in the first exercise. We use this to authenticate our access to GitHub, so as long as we enter a valid username when signing in, it will recognize us and allow us in.

Next up, we had to make some changes to our site – the first was in `_app.js`, where we had to wrap our application with `SessionProvider` tags. This creates the session in our app, so we can identify who is logged in our out and control their access. At the same time, we also created a `[...nextuath].js` file, which authenticates with GitHub as our service provider, using details sourced from the `.local.env` file.

To finish things off, we ran up the site to test logging in. As part of the initial login, we ran through the process to authenticate ourselves with GitHub so that we could log in directly to our site on subsequent logins.

Okay – let's move on: did anyone notice a problem with the last demo? To put it another way – how can we tell if we're logged in or not?

Displaying Login Options

The simple answer to that last question is "we can't" – at least not now! We need to implement something that allows us to sign in and out via explicit links and show a welcome greeting if we're logged in. Fortunately, next-auth makes this a cinch to add using the `useSession` object – let's look at how as part of our next demo.

ALTERING THE UI

To amend the UI so we can see when we're logged in or out, follow these steps:

1. First, crack open DemoBanner.jsx – we have a few changes to make, so let's start with importing three functions from the next-auth/react package:

```
import React from "react";
import { useSession, signIn, signOut } from "next-auth/react";
```

2. Next, we need to destructure the values we need from useSession() – this we can use to tell who is logged in. Add this line immediately below the opening tag for our component, followed by two functions for signing in and out:

```
const DemoBanner = () => {
  const { data: session } = useSession();

  const handleSignin = (e) => {
    e.preventDefault();
    signIn();
  };
  const handleSignout = (e) => {
    e.preventDefault();
    signOut();
  };
```

3. Scroll down a little to just past the closing span for the banner text – go ahead and add this block, which adds a greeting and option to sign out for anyone signed in:

```
        <span>
          {session && (
            <>
              <img src={session.user.image} alt="" />
              <p> Welcome, {session.user.name ?? session.user.email}</p>
              <a href="#" onClick={handleSignout}
              className="btn-signin">
                Sign out
              </a>
            </>
          )}
```

4. Leave a line blank after the previous block, then add this code – this takes care of any instance where the user has not signed in to the site:

```
{!session && (
  <>
    <p>Welcome</p>
    <a href="#" onClick={handleSignin} className="btn-signin">
      Sign in
    </a>
  </>
)}
</span>
```

5. Open the `globals.css` file in the `\src\styles` folder, then add these styles:

```
/* CHANGES FOR AUTHENTICATION */
.demo-banner-container {
  display: flex;
  justify-content: space-evenly;
}

.demo-banner-container > span:nth-child(2) {
  display: flex;
}

.demo-banner-container > span:nth-child(2) > img {
  width: 20px;
  height: 20px;
  margin-right: 5px;
}

.demo-banner-container > span:nth-child(2) > p {
  margin-right: 15px;
}

.demo-banner-container > span:nth-child(2) > a {
  border-left: 2px solid #ffffff;
  padding-left: 15px;
}
```

6.   Save and close all open files. Revert to your Node.js terminal, then enter npm run dev and press Enter to restart the Next.js development server.

7.   Once running, you should see the screen shown in Figure 12-2, where we now have the option to log in to our site.

Figure 12-2.   *Updated site with login and welcome*

8.   Try clicking the Sign in link, then sign in – if all is well, we should now see our name appear in the banner, with an option to sign out (Figure 12-3).

Figure 12-3.   *Header displaying logged-in user and sign-out option*

Perfect – that looks better! We now have a proper option to sign in and out, which also recognizes us: we even have a picture to boot.

The code for this is relatively straightforward, although it looks a little complex – we work based on identifying a valid session and whether to display a username or a generic greeting. There are some valuable tips in this code we should take a closer look at, so let's dive in and review the changes in more detail.

Exploring the Changes Made

So far, we've set up support for OAuth on our site, so we can authorize access for customers to log into a secured part of the site. How can we show people they were logged in or out, though?

To fix that, we updated the DemoBanner component to add a login option and a welcome message for users who log into the site. We first imported three functions from the next-auth package before destructuring values from the useSession() function. To handle the login and logout processes, we also added two event handlers, which we call from within the return body of our component.

Next up, we added two blocks – the first takes care of adding a small logo and the name of the logged-in person; we source both from the session data collected by our application. At the same time, we added an anchor that we could click to trigger the handleSignout event handler, which we created at the top of the component.

We also have to cater to people who are not signed in – this we do with a second block, which displays a generic Welcome message and an anchor to click for signing into our site. We finished off by adding a handful of styles to make the feature a little more presentable – it is only a demo, but we still need to keep it looking nice! Once added, we ran up the site to confirm that the link now appears as expected and that if we logged in, we see it change to display the user's name and a sign-out option on the site.

If you would like to learn more about the inner workings of OAuth in NextAuth, then I would recommend taking a look at the configuration page on the NextAuth website at `https://next-auth.js.org/configuration/providers/oauth`, or the "Nuts and Bolts of OAuth 2.0" article by Aaron Parecki, at `https://aaronparecki.com/oauth-2-simplified/`. These are good starting points – there is plenty more available via Google!

Okay – let's move on to the next task: while we now have a working sign-in and sign-out option, it's only really effective if we have a secured area to work in! The next-auth plug-in makes this very easy to add: let's try adding something as part of the next demo.

Adding Account Page

Most e-commerce websites have a secured area where customers can view their account details, such as purchases, username, and contact delivery address. This secure area will, by default, be secured with SSL access but also require authentication – after all, we don't want people logging in and viewing details they should not be seeing!

There are several ways of setting up authenticated access – given the size of our site, we can use methods already included in the next-auth plug-in from the previous demo.

The files for this demo will all be available in the code download for this book.

Setting up secured access to a page will require a few changes across several components in our site – let's dive in and take a closer look at the steps needed to implement it in our site.

ADDING SECURED ACCESS

To add an area accessible by authorization, follow these steps:

1. First, crack open a new file, and save it as `DisplayProfile.jsx`, in the `\src\components` folder.

2. We need to add a good chunk of code into this component, so we'll do it in sections as before – starting with the imports:

   ```
   import React from "react";
   import { useSession, signIn } from "next-auth/react";
   ```

3. Next, miss a line, then add the opening tag for the component, along with two constants and an event handler:

   ```
   function DisplayProfile() {
     const { data: session } = useSession();

     const handleSignin = (e) => {
       e.preventDefault();
       signIn();
     };
   ```

4. Next, we come to the meat of the component – go ahead and add the following, which will take care of displaying the correct details if the customer is authenticated:

```
return (
  <>
    <div className="display-profile">
      {session && (
        <>
          <div>
            <div className="profile-image">
              <img src={session.user.image} alt="" />
            </div>
            <div className="profile-details">
              <h3>{session.user.name}</h3>
              <p> Email: {session.user.email}</p>
            </div>
          </div>
        </>
      )}
```

5. We also need to cater for instances when a customer is not authenticated – for this, add the following block of code, followed by the closing export:

```
      {!session && (
        <>
          <a href="#" onClick={handleSignin} className="btn-signin">
            Sorry - this page is restricted to members only. Please
            log in to
            view your details.
          </a>
        </>
      )}
    </div>
  </>
);
}

export default DisplayProfile;
```

6. To finish off this component, go ahead and add this line to \src\
components\index.js – this will make it easier to import into our pages:

```
export { default as DisplayProfile } from "./DisplayProfile";
```

7. We're now good to consume this component – go ahead and create a new file, called account.js, and save it in the \src\pages folder.

8. Inside this component, add the following lines – we have an import first, followed by the main part of the component, which will display some markup and call the DisplayProfile component:

```
import { DisplayProfile } from "src/components";

const Account = () => {
  return (
    <>
      <div className="your-account">
        <p>Your Account</p>
      </div>
      <DisplayProfile />
    </>
  );
};

export default Account;
```

9. A nice touch will be to make sure that the Account link is only visible in NavBar when logged in – for this, crack open NavBar.jsx, then add this import to the list at the top:

```
import { useSession } from "next-auth/react";
```

10. Next, add this line immediately after the opening tag for our component:

```
const { data: session } = useSession();
```

11. Scroll down a little, then add this line immediately after the last <Link...> tag in the list of links:

```
{session && <Link href="/account">Account</Link>}
```

12. We have one more big change to add, which is some styling – crack open
     globals.css, and add these rules:

```
.your-account {
  width: 70%;
  margin: 0 auto;
  text-align: center;
}

.your-account p {
  margin: 40px 0 0 0;
  font-family: "Oswald", sans-serif;
  font-size: 42px;
}

.display-profile {
  width: 60%;
  margin: 20px auto 50px auto;
  text-align: center;
}

.display-profile div:nth-child(1) { display: flex; }

.profile-image {
  margin-right: 20px;
}

.profile-image img {
  width: 100px;
  height: 100px;
}

.profile-details {
  text-align: left;
  border-left: 1px solid #dcdcdc;
  display: block;
  padding-left: 15px;
  min-height: 200px;
}
```

13. Save and close all open files. Next, revert to your Node.js terminal, then enter npm run dev and press Enter to restart the Next.js development server.

14. Once running, try logging in via the Sign in option (if you are not already logged in), then head over to http://localhost:3000/account. You should see the screen shown in Figure 12-4, where we are now calling some basic details about our logged-in session.

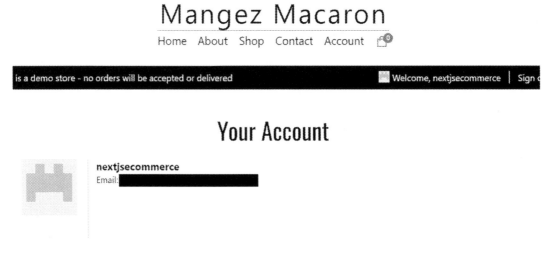

Figure 12-4. *The new Account page, showing basic details*

Excellent – we now have a secured area that is only accessible if we log in via our GitHub provider. Setting this up was straightforward, but it did expose a challenge; let's take a closer look at the changes we made before understanding the challenge in more detail.

Understanding What's Changed

Although I titled that last demo "Adding Secured Access," in reality, we were securing part of our site away from unauthorized access, then protecting it with SSL support! I can still remember the days when many websites were not secured under SSL by default... those were the days.

But I digress. In this demo, we implemented a new component called DisplayProfile – in this, we use the useSession and signIn functions from the React part of the next-auth plug-in to make content on the Account page inaccessible unless we logged in as valid users of the site. To handle that part, we also added a handleSignin event handler, to trigger the `signIn` function – allowing anyone who hadn't logged in but did have valid access to this page to log into the site.

Next up, we adapted the markup on the page to include two new sections – the first displayed the content if it could detect a valid `session` (i.e., someone had logged) in. We render the user's profile `image`, `name`, and `email` address on the screen. If no `session` was detected (the customer had not logged in), we render a message on the screen to say access was restricted and invite the customer to log into the site.

This component isn't of any use, though, unless we call it – with that in mind, we adapted account.js to call the component; this page contains minimal information, as most of it will be secured behind the authorized access in `DisplayProfile`. As a small extra, we also adapted the menu in `NavBar` to show or hide the link to `Account`, depending on the presence of a valid session. We finished the demo by running up the site in `localhost` to confirm that when logged in, the link was displayed correctly in `NavBar`, and that information was rendered or hidden based on the user's current `session` status on our site.

We covered a lot there, but it's all good stuff! We've now completed the development as far as we can take it in this chapter – there are a couple of important topics we should explore as a precursor to taking things forward. The first is probably the most important – what do we need to do when deploying our changes into production?

Deploying Changes

Throughout this chapter, we've created a basic authentication system using OAuth and the next-auth plug-in. While this works very well, it is just one way of authenticating users – it does open up a series of questions we should consider:

- Do we still want to use OAuth as our primary means of authenticating users, or is there a better solution that fits our needs?

- We used GitHub in our demo, but as most people don't own a GitHub account, do we use providers like Facebook, Google, or even a standard email address – assuming we still want to use OAuth?

- What would we include if we implemented an authentication method and secured access to our site? The obvious choice is a history of a customer's purchase, plus their account details – it falls a bit outside of the scope of this book, but it's still something to consider.

CHAPTER 12   PROJECT: AUTHENTICATING ACCESS

Assuming we still want to use OAuth (and next-auth as the plug-in), we need to consider a couple of things when deploying our site into production. They are as follows:

- We can run it anywhere where it supports Next.js (it's based on React, so a hosting provider that supports React will also support Next.js).

- We need to provide two NextAuth.js environment variables, which are `NEXTAUTH_SECRET` and `NEXTAUTH_URL`.

The former can be generated using one of two ways – `https://generate-secret.vercel.app/32`, or `openssl rand -base64 32` if using a Mac/Linux from the command line.

- We must also provide the NextAuth.js API Route and its configuration – this is the `[...nextauth].js` file in the `\src\pages\api\auth` folder.

As Next.js is JavaScript-based, to deploy a site using NextAuth.js we need to ensure that we set all environment variables correctly, the NextAuth.js API route is set up, and that configuration (such as callback URLs) is added to our chosen OAuth provider(s).

There are a few more things to consider if your hosting is provided by either Vercel or Netlify – details are available on the NextAuth site at `https://next-auth.js.org/deployment`.

Okay – let's crack on: we've spent a lot of time setting up a basic OAuth-based authentication system, but how can we develop it further? There are a few more things we can do – to complete our project, let's take a moment to explore what we could look at to help develop and refine the experience for our customers when implementing authentication.

Taking Things Further

Authentication is a vast topic – this is certainly no different for Next.js, where we've barely scratched the surface of what we could do! Throughout this chapter, we've implemented a basic setup that doesn't require any back-end database support, which reduces the risk for us and makes it easier to maintain.

It might not be enough for us, though, as we begin to develop the site even further – we may well want to consider creating a more customized solution that ties in with functionality we already use. This will, of course, raise some key questions – here are a few to start:

- A key question to ask – we've focused on using OAuth for our authentication, particularly as the plug-in we've used works very well with Next.js. Do we want to continue this approach or do something more customized to our needs?

- Next.js (from version 13) is changing where pages and components should be rendered by introducing the \app folder. It will impact how we implement authentication – for this reason, I had to reject using my first choice (Auth0 – `https://github.com/auth0/nextjs-auth0`), as it did yet support Next.js' app folder. It will change: we may want to consider switching to an alternative once the app folder gets more stable support.

- If we remain with OAuth, which providers would we want to use? We used GitHub to prove this demo – this works well, but probably not ideal as many people won't have GitHub accounts! A provider such as Facebook or Google would be better; ideally, we'd implement email authentication.

For more details on email authentication, have a look at `https://next-auth.js.org/configuration/providers/email` as a good starting point.

- We've already used Sanity as our CMS system – could (or should) we use this to store login details?

- When researching this chapter, one of the challenges I had was what information I wanted to display and how I would show it. Ideally, I would like to have displayed customer records from Stripe (displaying only that relevant to a customer account, of course!). However, the site's current setup is conflicting with Stripe because querying the API would typically be done client-side, whereas Next.js renders content server-side by default. We must consider it to ensure details render server-side and avoid caching any that we should not be caching!

That's just a few ideas to get us started – I am sure there are plenty more we should consider as part of developing our site. The critical thing to note is that we shouldn't feel obliged to have to implement authentication; it adds an overhead in managing it. If done correctly, it can help customers self-serve without submitting emails or requests for assistance!

With that in mind, we should only add authentication (and a secured area) if we have the resources to manage supporting it and for it to not get in the way of our primary role, which is selling products from our site.

Summary

All good things must come to an end sometime…

The great author Geoffrey Chaucer is credited with uttering those words as far back as 1300 – they first appeared in his poem Troilus and Criseyde.

Chaucer may have written those words in Middle English, but the meaning is the same no matter what language you speak – we have unfortunately come to the end of this book and our journey through creating Macaron Magic. We've covered a lot of valuable tips in this chapter, so let's take a moment to review what we have learned.

We began by setting the scene and our expectations around implementing authentication – it is such a large topic that we can only cover a certain amount on these pages! We then created an OAuth app as our first task before using it to install and configure NextAuth as our chosen plug-in to provide authentication.

Once done, we explored how to add a login option – we noted that while NextAuth will allow us to log in, it doesn't provide a means to show the logged-in/logged-out state, so we had to add this separately. At the same time, we also created a page to act as our secured area, which would be available when logged in as a valid user.

To round things off, we explored some of the points to consider around how we might deploy our changes and whether anything might affect this; we also looked at some of the areas to consider generally in terms of developing our offer over time.

Phew – we really have come to the end of our adventure in creating Macaron Magic! I've had a great time building and writing this book – it's had its ups and downs while highlighting that Next.js is a framework worthy of consideration when creating e-commerce sites. Sure, it has its own quirks and limitations, but hey, it's just a case of learning how to get around them to achieve your desired result. I hope you've enjoyed the content and found something helpful, as much as I have, and that you can put it to good use in your future projects.

Index

A, B

Animation effects
    cart button, 189–195
    product card, 197
Animation efforts
    flipping effect, 196–199
Application programming Interface
    (API), 125
Authentication system, 327
    GitHub OAuth account, 328–331
    globals.css file, 335
    header file, 336
    key questions, 345–347
    login options, 334–338
    NextAuth installation, 331–333
    OAuth/next-auth plug-in, 343, 344
    scene option, 327, 328
    secured access, 338–343
    updated site, 336
    useSession and signIn functions, 342
    useSession() function, 337

C

Cascading Style Sheets (CSS)
    approaches, 138
    big-bang approach, 138
    exploring options, 131–133
    footer component, 141
    globals.css, 30, 135, 137, 139, 144, 163,
        168, 172, 197
    homepage, 136

mobile devices, 172–175
mobile-first approach, 133
modules, 138–142
Next.js application, 135–137
Next.js site, 132
portable.css, 173
Sass configuration
    configuration steps, 143–146
    Next.js, 148
    source files, 146, 147
    variables, 147–149
tablet.css, 168
Tailwind, 150–152
theme process, 134
Checkout/payment process, 91
    button details
        handleBuyNow function, 96
        product page, 94–96
    cancel page, 186–189
    cart components
        basket view, 109
        code information, 110
        code references, 108–112
        product details, 109
        quantity indicator, 109
        steps, 104–108
    context components, 96–103
    minicart component
        decimal places, 113
        destructured constants, 112
        empty basket, 114
        partial image and quantity, 115

T, U, V, W, X, Y, Z

Printed in the United States
by Baker & Taylor Publisher Services